SIX SHORT PLAYS
OF EUGENE O'NEILL

Beverly Hills Publishing
P.O. Box ...
Beverly Hills, California 90210

SIX SHORT PLAYS

of

EUGENE

O'NEILL

VINTAGE BOOKS

A DIVISION OF RANDOM HOUSE

NEW YORK

CONTENTS

BEFORE BREAKFAST

A Play in One Act

1916-1917

BEFORE BREAKFAST

Scene. *A small room serving both as kitchen and dining room in a flat on Christopher Street, New York City. In the rear, to the right, a door leading to the outer hallway. On the left of the doorway, a sink, and a two-burner gas stove. Over the stove, and extending to the left wall, a wooden closet for dishes, etc. On the left, two windows looking out on a fire escape where several potted plants are dying of neglect. Before the windows, a table covered with oilcloth. Two cane-bottomed chairs are placed by the table. Another stands against the wall to the right of door in rear. In the right wall, rear, a doorway leading into a bedroom. Farther forward, different articles of a man's and a woman's clothing are hung on pegs. A clothes line is strung from the left corner, rear, to the right wall, forward.*

It is about eight-thirty in the morning of a fine, sunshiny day in the early fall.

Mrs. rowland *enters from the bedroom, yawning, her hands still busy putting the finishing touches on a slovenly toilet by sticking hairpins into her hair which is bunched up in a drab-colored mass on top of her round head. She is of medium height and inclined to a shapeless stoutness, accentuated by her formless blue dress, shabby and worn. Her face is characterless, with small regular features and eyes of a nondescript blue. There is a pinched expression about her eyes and nose and her weak, spiteful mouth. She is in her early twenties but looks much older.*

She comes to the middle of the room and yawns, stretching her arms to their full length. Her drowsy eyes stare about the room with the irritated look of one to whom a long sleep has not been a long rest. She goes wearily to the clothes hanging on the right and takes

3

an apron from a hook. She ties it about her waist, giving vent to an exasperated "damn" when the knot fails to obey her clumsy fingers. Finally gets it tied and goes slowly to the gas stove and lights one burner. She fills the coffee pot at the sink and sets it over the flame. Then slumps down into a chair by the table and puts a hand over her forehead as if she were suffering from headache. Suddenly her face brightens as though she had remembered something, and she casts a quick glance at the dish closet; then looks sharply at the bedroom door and listens intently for a moment or so.

MRS. ROWLAND. (*in a low voice*) Alfred! Alfred! (*There is no answer from the next room and she continues suspiciously in a louder tone*) You needn't pretend you're asleep. (*There is no reply to this from the bedroom, and, reassured, she gets up from her chair and tiptoes cautiously to the dish closet. She slowly opens one door, taking great care to make no noise, and slides out, from their hiding place behind the dishes, a bottle of Gordon gin and a glass. In doing so she disturbs the top dish, which rattles a little. At this sound she starts guiltily and looks with sulky defiance at the doorway to the next room.*)
(*Her voice trembling*) Alfred!

(*After a pause, during which she listens for any sound, she takes the glass and pours out a large drink and gulps it down; then hastily returns the bottle and glass to their hiding place. She closes the closet door with the same care as she had opened it, and, heaving a great sigh of relief, sinks down into her chair again. The large dose of alcohol she has taken has an almost immediate effect. Her features become more animated, she seems to gather energy, and she looks at the bedroom door with a hard, vindictive smile on her lips. Her eyes glance quickly about the room and are fixed on a man's coat and vest which hang from a hook at right. She moves stealthily over to the open doorway and stands there, out of sight of anyone inside, listening for any movement.*)
(*Calling in a half-whisper*) Alfred!

4

(*Again there is no reply. With a swift movement she takes the coat and vest from the hook and returns with them to her chair. She sits down and takes the various articles out of each pocket but quickly puts them back again. At last, in the inside pocket of the vest, she finds a letter.*)

(*Looking at the handwriting—slowly to herself*) Hmm! I knew it.

(*She opens the letter and reads it. At first her expression is one of hatred and rage, but as she goes on to the end it changes to one of triumphant malignity. She remains in deep thought for a moment, staring before her, the letter in her hands, a cruel smile on her lips. Then she puts the letter back in the pocket of the vest, and still careful not to awaken the sleeper, hangs the clothes up again on the same hook, and goes to the bedroom door and looks in.*)

(*In a loud, shrill voice*) Alfred! (*Still louder*) Alfred! (*There is a muffled, yawning groan from the next room*) Don't you think it's about time you got up? Do you want to stay in bed all day? (*Turning around and coming back to her chair*) Not that I've got any doubts about your being lazy enough to stay in bed forever. (*She sits down and looks out of the window, irritably*) Goodness knows what time it is. We haven't even got any way of telling the time since you pawned your watch like a fool. The last valuable thing we had, and you knew it. It's been nothing but pawn, pawn, pawn, with you—anything to put off getting a job, anything to get out of going to work like a man. (*She taps the floor with her foot nervously, biting her lips.*)

(*After a short pause*) Alfred! Get up, do you hear me? I want to make that bed before I go out. I'm sick of having this place in a continual muss on your account. (*With a certain vindictive satisfaction*) Not that we'll be here long unless you manage to get some money some place. Heaven knows I do my part—and more—going out to sew every day while you play the gentleman and loaf around barrooms with that good-for-nothing lot of artists from the Square.

(*A short pause during which she plays nervously with a cup and saucer on the table.*)

5

And where are you going to get money, I'd like to know? The rent's due this week and you know what the landlord is. He won't let us stay a minute over our time. You say you *can't* get a job. That's a lie and you know it. You never even look for one. All you do is moon around all day writing silly poetry and stories that no one will buy—and no wonder they won't. I notice I can always get a position, such as it is; and it's only that which keeps us from starving to death.

(*Gets up and goes over to the stove—looks into the coffee pot to see if the water is boiling; then comes back and sits down again.*)

You'll have to get money today some place. I can't do it all, and I won't do it all. You've got to come to your senses. You've got to beg, borrow, or steal it somewheres. (*With a contemptuous laugh*) But where, I'd like to know? You're too proud to beg, and you've borrowed the limit, and you haven't the nerve to steal.

(*After a pause—getting up angrily*) Aren't you up yet, for heaven's sake? It's just like you to go to sleep again, or pretend to. (*She goes to the bedroom door and looks in*) Oh, you are up. Well, it's about time. You needn't look at me like that. Your airs don't fool me a bit any more. I know you too well—better than you think I do—you and your goings-on. (*Turning away from the door—meaningly*) I know a lot of things, my dear. Never mind what I know, now. I'll tell you before I go, you needn't worry. (*She comes to the middle of the room and stands there, frowning.*)

(*Irritably*) Hmm! I suppose I might as well get breakfast ready —not that there's anything much to get. (*Questioningly*) Unless you have some money? (*She pauses for an answer from the next room which does not come*) Foolish question! (*She gives a short, hard laugh*) I ought to know you better than that by this time. When you left here in such a huff last night I knew what would happen. You can't be trusted for a second. A nice condition you came home in! The fight we had was only an excuse for you to make a beast of

6

yourself. What was the use pawning your watch if all you wanted
with the money was to waste it in buying drink?

(*Goes over to the dish closet and takes out plates, cups, etc., while
she is talking.*)

Hurry up! It don't take long to get breakfast these days, thanks
to you. All we got this morning is bread and butter and coffee; and
you wouldn't even have that if it wasn't for me sewing my fingers
off. (*She slams the loaf of bread on the table with a bang.*)

The bread's stale. I hope you'll like it. *You* don't deserve any
better, but I don't see why *I* should suffer.

(*Going over to the stove*) The coffee'll be ready in a minute, and
you needn't expect me to wait for you.

(*Suddenly with great anger*) What on earth are you doing all this
time? (*She goes over to the door and looks in*) Well, you're *almost*
dressed at any rate. I expected to find you back in bed. That'd be just
like you. How awful you look this morning! For heaven's sake,
shave! You're disgusting! You look like a tramp. No wonder no one
will give you a job. I don't blame them—when you don't even look
half-way decent. (*She goes to the stove*) There's plenty of hot water
right here. You've got no excuse. (*Gets a bowl and pours some of the
water from the coffee pot into it*) Here.

(*He reaches his hand into the room for it. It is a sensitive hand
with slender fingers. It trembles and some of the water spills on the
floor.*)

(*Tauntingly*) Look at your hand tremble! You'd better give up
drinking. You can't stand it. It's just your kind that get the D. T.'s.
That would be the last straw! (*Looking down at the floor*) Look at
the mess you've made of this floor—cigarette butts and ashes all over
the place. Why can't you put them on a plate? No, you wouldn't
be considerate enough to do that. You never think of me. You don't
have to sweep the room and that's all you care about.

(*Takes the broom and commences to sweep viciously, raising a*

7

cloud of dust. From the inner room comes the sound of a razor being stopped.)

(*Sweeping*) Hurry up! It must be nearly time for me to go. If I'm late I'm liable to lose my position, and then I couldn't support you any longer. (*As an afterthought she adds sarcastically*) And then you'd have to go to work or something dreadful like that. (*Sweeping under the table*) What I want to know is whether you're going to look for a job to-day or not. You know your family won't help us any more. They've had enough of you, too. (*After a moment's silent sweeping*) I'm about sick of all this life. I've a good notion to go home, if I wasn't too proud to let them know what a failure you've been—you, the millionaire Rowland's only son, the Harvard graduate, the poet, the catch of the town—Huh! (*With bitterness*) There wouldn't be many of them now envy my catch if they knew the truth. What has our marriage been, I'd like to know? Even before your *millionaire* father died owing everyone in the world money, you certainly never wasted any of your time on your wife. I suppose you thought I'd ought to be glad you were *honorable* enough to marry me—after getting me into trouble. You were ashamed of me with your fine friends because my father's only a grocer, that's what you were. At least he's honest, which is more than anyone could say about yours. (*She is sweeping steadily toward the door. Leans on her broom for a moment.*)

You hoped everyone'd think you'd been forced to marry me, and pity you, didn't you? You didn't hesitate much about telling me you loved me, and making me believe your lies, before it happened, did you? You made me think you didn't want your father to buy me off as he tried to do. I know better now. I haven't lived with you all this time for nothing. (*Somberly*) It's lucky the poor thing was born dead, after all. What a father you'd have been!

(*Is silent, brooding moodily for a moment—then she continues with a sort of savage joy.*)

But I'm not the only one who's got you to thank for being unhappy.

There's one other, at least, and *she* can't hope to marry you now. (*She puts her head into the next room*) How about Helen? (*She starts back from the doorway, half frightened.*)

Don't look at me that way! Yes, I read her letter. What about it? I got a right to. I'm your wife. And I know all there is to know, so don't lie. You needn't stare at me so. You can't bully me with your superior airs any longer. Only for me you'd be going without breakfast this very morning. (*She sets the broom back in the corner— whiningly*) You never did have any gratitude for what I've done. (*She comes to the stove and puts the coffee into the pot*) The coffee's ready. I'm not going to wait for you. (*She sits down in her chair again.*)

(*After a pause—puts her hand to her head—fretfully*) My head aches so this morning. It's a shame I've got to go to work in a stuffy room all day in my condition. And I wouldn't if you were half a man. By rights I ought to be lying on my back instead of you. You know how sick I've been this last year; and yet you object when I take a little something to keep up my spirits. You even didn't want me to take that tonic I got at the drug store. (*With a hard laugh*) I know you'd be glad to have me dead and out of your way; then you'd be free to run after all these silly girls that think you're such a wonderful, misunderstood person—this Helen and the others. (*There is a sharp exclamation of pain from the next room.*)

(*With satisfaction*) There! I knew you'd cut yourself. It'll be a lesson to you. You know you oughtn't to be running around nights drinking with your nerves in such an awful shape. (*She goes to the door and looks in.*)

What makes you so pale? What are you staring at yourself in the mirror that way for? For goodness sake, wipe that blood off your face! (*With a shudder*) It's horrible. (*In relieved tones*) There, that's better. I never could stand the sight of blood. (*She shrinks back from the door a little*) You better give up trying and go to a barber shop. Your hand shakes dreadfully. Why do you stare at me like that?

9

(*She turns away from the door*) Are you still mad at me about that letter? (*Defiantly*) Well, I had a right to read it. I'm your wife. (*She comes to the chair and sits down again. After a pause.*)

I knew all the time you were running around with someone. Your lame excuses about spending the time at the library didn't fool me. Who is this Helen, anyway? One of those artists? Or does she write poetry, too? Her letter sounds that way. I'll bet she told you your things were the best ever, and you believed her, like a fool. Is she young and pretty? I was young and pretty, too, when you fooled me with your fine, poetic talk; but life with you would soon wear anyone down. What I've been through!

(*Goes over and takes the coffee off the stove*) Breakfast is ready. (*With a contemptuous glance*) Breakfast! (*Pours out a cup of coffee for herself and puts the pot on the table.*) Your coffee'll be cold. What are you doing—still shaving, for heaven's sake? You'd better give it up. One of these mornings you'll give yourself a serious cut. (*She cuts off bread and butters it. During the following speeches she eats and sips her coffee.*)

I'll have to run as soon as I've finished eating. One of us has got to work. (*Angrily*) Are you going to look for a job today or aren't you? I should think some of your fine friends would help you, if they really think you're so much. But I guess they just like to hear you talk. (*Sits in silence for a moment.*)

I'm sorry for this Helen, whoever she is. Haven't you got any feelings for other people? What will her family say? I see she mentions them in her letter. What is she going to do—have the child—or go to one of those doctors? That's a nice thing, I must say. Where can she get the money? Is she rich? (*She waits for some answer to this volley of questions.*)

Hmm! You won't tell me anything about her, will you? Much I care. Come to think of it, I'm not so sorry for her after all. She knew what she was doing. She isn't any schoolgirl, like I was, from the looks of her letter. Does she know you're married? Of course, she must. All your friends know about your unhappy marriage. I know they pity you, but they don't know my side of it. They'd talk different if they did.

(*Too busy eating to go on for a second or so.*)

This Helen must be a fine one, if she knew you were married. What does she expect, then? That I'll divorce you and let her marry you? Does she think I'm crazy enough for that—after all you've made me go through? I guess not! And you can't get a divorce from me and you know it. No one can say *I've* ever done anything wrong. (*Drinks the last of her cup of coffee.*)

She deserves to suffer, that's all I can say. I'll tell you what I think; I think your Helen is no better than a common streetwalker, that's what I think. (*There is a stifled groan of pain from the next room.*)

Did you cut yourself again? Serves you right. (*Gets up and takes off her apron*) Well, I've got to run along. (*Peevishly*) This is a fine life for me to be leading! I won't stand for your loafing any longer. (*Something catches her ear and she pauses and listens intently*) There! You've overturned the water all over everything. Don't say you haven't. I can hear it dripping on the floor. (*A vague expression of fear comes over her face*) Alfred! Why don't you answer me?

(*She moves slowly toward the room. There is the noise of a chair being overturned and something crashes heavily to the floor. She stands, trembling with fright.*)

Alfred! Alfred! Answer me! What is it you knocked over? Are you still drunk? (*Unable to stand the tension a second longer she rushes to the door of the bedroom.*)

Alfred!

(*She stands in the doorway looking down at the floor of the inner room, transfixed with horror. Then she shrieks wildly and runs to the other door, unlocks it and frenziedly pulls it open, and runs shrieking madly into the outer hallway.*)

CURTAIN

THE DREAMY KID

A Play in One Act

1918

CHARACTERS

MAMMY SAUNDERS

ABE, *her grandson, "The Dreamy Kid"*

CEELY ANN

IRENE

THE DREAMY KID

SCENE. *Mammy Saunders' bedroom in a house just off Carmine Street, New York City. The left of the room, forward, is taken up by a heavy, old-fashioned wooden bedstead with a feather mattress. A gaudy red-and-yellow quilt covers the other bedclothes. In back of the bed, a chest of drawers placed against the left wall. On top of the chest, a small lamp. A rocking-chair stands beside the head of the bed on the right. In the rear wall, toward the right, a low window with ragged white curtains. In the right corner, a washstand with bowl and pitcher. Bottles of medicine, a spoon, a glass, etc., are also on the stand. Farther forward, a door opening on the hall and stairway.*

It is soon after nightfall of a day in early winter. The room is in shadowy half darkness, the only light being a pale glow that seeps through the window from the arc lamp on the nearby corner, and by which the objects in the room can be dimly discerned. The vague outlines of Mammy Saunders' figure lying in the bed can be seen, and her black face stands out in sharp contrast to the pillows that support her head.

MAMMY. (*weakly*) Ceely Ann! (*With faint querulousness*) Light de lamp, will you? Hit's mighty dark in yere. (*After a slight pause*) Ain't you dar, Ceely Ann? (*Receiving no reply she sighs deeply and her limbs move uneasily under the bedclothes. The door is opened and shut and the stooping form of another colored woman appears in the semi-darkness. She goes to the foot of the bed sobbing softly, and stands there evidently making an effort to control her emotion.*)

MAMMY. Dat you, Ceely Ann?

CEELY. (*huskily*) Hit ain't no yuther, Mammy.

MAMMY. Light de lamp, den. I can't see nowhars.

15

CEELY. Des one second till I finds a match. (*She wipes her eyes with her handkerchief—then goes to the chest of drawers and feels around on the top of it—pretending to grumble*) Hit beat all how dem pesky little sticks done hide umse'fs. Shoo! Yere dey is. (*She fumbles with the lamp.*)

MAMMY. (*suspiciously*) You ain't been cryin', is you?

CEELY. (*with feigned astonishment*) Cryin'? I clar' ter goodness you does git de mos' fool notions lyin' dar.

MAMMY. (*in a tone of relief*) I mos' thought I yeard you.

CEELY. (*lighting the lamp*) 'Deed you ain't. (*The two women are revealed by the light.* MAMMY SAUNDERS *is an old, white-haired Negress about ninety with a weazened face furrowed by wrinkles and withered by old age and sickness. Ceely is a stout woman of fifty or so with gray hair and a round fat face. She wears a loose-fitting gingham dress and a shawl thrown over her head.*)

CEELY. (*with attempted cheeriness*) Bless yo' soul, I ain't got nothin' to cry 'bout. Yere. Lemme fix you so you'll rest mo' easy. (*She lifts the old woman gently and fixes the pillows*) Dere. Now, ain't you feelin' better?

MAMMY. (*dully*) My strenk don' all went. I can't lift a hand.

CEELY. (*hurriedly*) Dat'll all come back ter you de doctor tole me des now when I goes down to de door with him. (*Glibly*) He say you is de mos' strongest 'oman fo' yo years ever he sees in de worl'; and he tell me you gwine ter be up and walkin' agin fo' de week's out. (*As she finds the old woman's eyes fixed on her she turns away confusedly and abruptly changes the subject*) Hit ain't too wa'm in dis room, dat's a fac'.

MAMMY. (*shaking her head—in a half whisper*) No, Ceely Ann. Hit ain't no use'n you tellin' me nothin' but de trufe. I feels mighty poo'ly. En I knows hit's on'y wid de blessin' er God I kin las' de night out.

CEELY. (*distractedly*) Ain't no sich a thing! Hush yo' noise, Mammy!

MAMMY. (*as if she hadn't heard—in a crooning sing-song*) I'se gwine soon fum dis wicked yearth—and may de Lawd have mercy on dis po' ole sinner. (*After a pause—anxiously*) All I'se prayin' fer is dat God don' take me befo' I sees Dreamy agin. Whar's Dreamy, Ceely Ann? Why ain't he come yere? Ain't you done sent him word I'se sick like I tole you?

CEELY. I tole dem boys ter tell him speshul, and dey swar dey would soon's dey find him. I s'pose dey ain't kotch him yit. Don' you pester yo'se'f worryin'. Dreamy 'ull come fo' ve'y long.

MAMMY. (*after a pause—weakly*) Dere's a feelin' in my haid like I was a-floatin' yander whar I can't see nothin', or 'member nothin', or know de sight er any pusson I knows; en I wants ter see Dreamy agin befo'—

CEELY. (*quickly*) Don' waste yo strenk talkin'. You git a wink er sleep en I wake you when he comes, you heah me?

MAMMY. (*faintly*) I does feel mighty drowsy. (*She closes her eyes. CEELY goes over to the window and pulling the curtains aside stands looking down into the street as if she were watching for someone coming. A moment later there is a noise of footfalls from the stairs in the hall, followed by a sharp rap on the door.*)

CEELY. (*turning quickly from the window*) Ssshh! Ssshh! (*She hurries to the door, glancing anxiously toward MAMMY. The old woman appears to have fallen asleep. CEELY cautiously opens the door a bare inch or so and peeks out. When she sees who it is she immediately tries to slam it shut again but a vigorous shove from the outside forces her back and IRENE pushes her way defiantly into the room. She is a young, good-looking Negress, highly rouged and powdered, dressed in gaudy, cheap finery.*)

IRENE. (*in a harsh voice—evidently worked up to a great state of nervous excitement*) No you don't, Ceely Ann! I said I was comin' here and it'll take mo'n you to stop me!

CEELY. (*almost speechless with horrified indignation—breathing heavily*) Yo' bad 'oman! Git back ter yo' bad-house whar yo' b'longs!

IRENE. (*raising her clenched hand—furiously*) Stop dat talkin' to me, nigger, or I'll split yo' fool head! (*As* CEELY *shrinks away* IRENE *lowers her hand and glances around the room*) Whar's Dreamy?

CEELY. (*scornfully*) Yo' ax me dat! Whar's Dreamy? Ax yo'se'f. Yo's de one ought ter know whar he is.

IRENE. Den he ain't come here?

CEELY. I ain't tellin' de likes er you wedder he is or not.

IRENE. (*pleadingly*) Tell me, Ceely Ann, ain't he been here? He'd be sure to come here 'count of Mammy dyin', dey said.

CEELY. (*pointing to* MAMMY—*apprehensively*) Ssshh! (*Then lowering her voice to a whisper—suspiciously*) Dey said? Who said?

IRENE. (*equally suspicious*) None o' your business who said. (*Then pleading again*) Ceely Ann, I jest got ter see him dis minute, dis secon'! He's in bad, Dreamy is, and I knows somep'n I gotter tell him, somep'n I jest heard—

CEELY. (*uncomprehendingly*) In bad? What you jest heah?

IRENE. I ain't tellin' no one but him. (*Desperately*) For Gawd's sake, tell me whar he is, Ceely!

CEELY. I don' know no mo'n you.

IRENE. (*fiercely*) You's lyin', Ceely! You's lyin' jest 'cause I'se bad.

CEELY. De good Lawd bar witness I'se tellin' you de trufe!

IRENE. (*hopelessly*) Den I gotter go find him, high and low, somewheres. (*Proudly*) You ain't got de right not ter trust me, Ceely, where de Dreamy's mixed in it. I'd go ter hell for Dreamy!

CEELY. (*indignantly*) Hush yo' wicked cussin'! (*Then anxiously*) Is Dreamy in trouble?

IRENE. (*with a scornful laugh*) Trouble? Good Lawd, it's worser'n dat! (*Then in surprise*) Ain't you heerd what de Dreamy done last night, Ceely?

CEELY. (*apprehensively*) What de Dreamy do? Tell me, gal. Somep'n bad?

IRENE. (*with the same scornful laugh*) Bad? Worser'n bad, what he done!

CEELY. (*lamenting querulously*) Oh good Lawd, I knowed it! I knowed with all his carryin's-on wid dat passel er tough young niggers—him so uppity 'cause he's de boss er de gang—sleepin' all de day 'stead er workin' an' Lawd knows what he does in de nights —fightin' wid white folks, an' totin' a pistol in his pocket—(*With a glance of angry resentment at* IRENE)—an' as fo' de udder company he's been keepin'—

IRENE. (*fiercely*) Shut your mouth, Ceely! Dat ain't your business.

CEELY. Oh, I knowed Dreamy'd be gittin' in trouble fo' long! De lowflung young trash! An' here's his ole Mammy don' know no dif'frunt but he's de mos' innercent young lamb in de worl'. (*In a strained whisper*) What he do? Is he been stealin' somep'n?

IRENE. (*angrily*) You go ter hell, Ceely Ann! You ain't no fren' of de Dreamy's, you talk dat way, and I ain't got no time ter waste argyin' wid your fool notions. (*She goes to the door*) Dreamy'll go ter his death sho's yo' born, if I don't find him an' tell him quick!

CEELY. (*terrified*) Oh Lawd!

IRENE. (*anxiously*) He'll sho'ly try ter come here and see his ole Mammy befo' she dies, don't you think, Ceely?

CEELY. Fo' Gawd I hopes so! She's been a-prayin' all de day—

IRENE. (*opening the door*) You hopes so, you fool nigger! I tells you it's good-by to de Dreamy, he come here! I knows! I gotter find an' stop him. If he come here, Ceely, you tell him git out quick and hide, he don't wanter git pinched. You hear? You tell him dat, Ceely, for Gawd's sake! I'se got ter go—find him—high an' low. (*She goes out leaving* CEELY *staring at her in speechless indignation.*)

CEELY. (*drawing a deep breath*) Yo' street gal! I don' b'lieve one word you says—stuffin' me wid yo' bad lies so's you kin keep de Dreamy frum leavin' you! (MAMMY SAUNDERS *awakes and groans faintly.* CEELY *hurries to her bedside*) Is de pain hurtin' agin, Mammy?

MAMMY. (*vaguely*) Dat you, Dreamy?

CEELY. No, Mammy, dis is Ceely. Dreamy's comin' soon. Is you restin' easy?

19

MAMMY. (*as if she hadn't heard*) Dat you, Dreamy?

CEELY. (*sitting down in the rocker by the bed and taking one of the old woman's hands in hers*) No. Dreamy's comin'.

MAMMY. (*after a pause—suddenly*) Does you 'member yo' dead Mammy, chile?

CEELY. (*mystified*) My dead Mammy?

MAMMY. Didn' I heah yo' talkin' jest now, Dreamy?

CEELY. (*very worried*) I clar ter goodness, she don' know me ary bit. Dis is Ceely Ann talkin' ter yo', Mammy.

MAMMY. Who was yo' talkin' wid, Dreamy?

CEELY. (*shaking her head—in a trembling voice*) Hit can't be long befo' de en'. (*In a louder tone*) Hit was me talkin' wid a pusson fum ovah de way. She say tell you Dreamy comin' heah ter see yo' right away. You heah dat, Mammy? (*The old woman sighs but does not answer. There is a pause.*)

MAMMY. (*suddenly*) Does yo' 'member yo' dead Mammy, chile? (*Then with a burst of religious exaltation*) De Lawd have mercy!

CEELY. (*like an echo*) Bless de Lawd! (*Then in a frightened half-whisper to herself*) Po' thing! Her min's done leavin' her jest like de doctor said. (*She looks down at the old woman helplessly. The door on the right is opened stealthily and the* DREAMY KID *slinks in.*)

CEELY. (*hearing a board creak, turns quickly toward the door and gives a frightened start*) Dreamy!

DREAMY. (*puts his fingers to his lips—commandingly*) Ssshh! (*He bends down to a crouching position and holding the door about an inch open, peers out into the hallway in an attitude of tense waiting, one hand evidently clutching some weapon in the side pocket of his coat. After a moment he is satisfied of not being followed, and, after closing the door carefully and locking it, he stands up and walks to the center of the room casting a look of awed curiosity at the figure in the bed. He is a well-built, good-looking young Negro, light in color. His eyes are shifty and hard, their expression one of tough, scornful defiance. His mouth is cruel and perpetually drawn back at the corners into a snarl. He is dressed in well-fitting clothes of a flashy pattern. A light cap is pulled down on the side of his head.*)

CEELY. (*coming from the bed to meet him*) Bless de Lawd, here you is at las'!

DREAMY. (*with a warning gesture*) Nix on de loud talk! Talk low, can't yuh! (*He glances back at the door furtively—then continues with a sneer*) Yuh're a fine nut, Ceely Ann! What for you sendin' out all ober de town for me like you was crazy! D'yuh want ter git me in de cooler? Don' you know dey're after me for what I done last night?

CEELY. (*fearfully*) I heerd somep'n—but—what you done, Dreamy?

DREAMY. (*with an attempt at a careless bravado*) I croaked a guy, dat's what! A white man.

CEELY. (*in a frightened whisper*) What you mean—croaked?

DREAMY. (*boastfully*) I shot him dead, dat's what! (*As* CEELY *shrinks away from him in horror—resentfully*) Aw say, don' gimme none o' dem looks o' yourn. 'Twarn't my doin' nohow. He was de one lookin' for trouble. I wasn't seekin' for no mess wid him dat I could help. But he told folks he was gwine ter git me for a fac', and dat fo'ced my hand. I had ter git him ter pertect my own life. (*With cruel satisfaction*) And I got him right, you b'lieve me!

CEELY. (*putting her hands over her face with a low moan of terror*) May de good Lawd pardon yo' wickedness! Oh Lawd! What yo' po' ole Mammy gwine say if she hear tell—an' she never knowin' how bad you's got.

DREAMY. (*fiercely*) Hell! You ain't tole her, is you?

CEELY. Think I want ter kill her on de instant? An' I didn' know myse'f—what you done—till you tells me. (*Frightenedly*) Oh, Dreamy, what you gwine do now? How you gwine git away? (*Almost wailing*) Good Lawd, de perlice do' kotch you shuah!

DREAMY. (*savagely*) Shut yo' loud mouth, damn yo'! (*He stands tensely listening for some sound from the hall. After a moment he points to the bed*) Is Mammy sleepin'?

CEELY. (*tiptoes to the bed*) Seems like she is. (*She comes back to him*) Dat's de way wid her—sleep fo' a few minutes, den she wake, den sleep again.

DREAMY. (*scornfully*) Aw, dere ain't nothin' wrong wid her 'ceptin' she's ole. What yuh wanter send de word tellin' me she's croakin', and git me comin' here at de risk o' my life, and den find her sleepin'. (*Clenching his fist threateningly*) I gotter mind ter smash yo' face for playin' de damn fool and makin' me de goat. (*He turns toward the door*) Ain't no us'en me stayin' here when dey'll likely come lookin' for me. I'm gwine out where I gotta chance ter make my git-away. De boys is all fixin' it up for me. (*His hand on the door-knob*) When Mammy wakes, you tell her I couldn't wait, you hear?

CEELY. (*hurrying to him and grabbing his arm—pleadingly*) Don' yo' go now, Dreamy—not jest yit. Fo' de good Lawd's sake, don' you go befo' you speaks wid her! If yo' knew how she's been a-callin' an' a-prayin' for yo' all de day—

DREAMY. (*scornfully but a bit uncertainly*) Aw, she don' need none o' me. What good kin I do watchin' her do a kip? It'd be dif'frunt if she was croakin' on de level.

CEELY. (*in an anguished whisper*) She's gwine wake up in a secon' an' den she call: "Dreamy. Whar's Dreamy?"—an' what I gwine tell her den? An' yo' Mammy is dyin', Dreamy, sho's fate! Her min' been wanderin' an' she don' even recernize me no mo', an' de doctor say when dat come it ain't but a sho't time befo' de en'. Yo' gotter stay wid yo' Mammy long 'nuff ter speak wid her, Dreamy. Yo' jest gotter stay wid her in her las' secon's on dis yearth when she's callin' ter yo'. (*With conviction as he hesitates*) Listen heah, yo' Dreamy! Yo' don' never git no bit er luck in dis worril ary agin, yo' leaves her now. Der perlice gon' kotch yo' shuah.

DREAMY. (*with superstitious fear*) Ssshh! Can dat bull, Ceely! (*Then boastfully*) I wasn't pinin' to beat it up here, git me? De boys was all persuadin' me not ter take de chance. It's takin' my life in my hands, dat's what. But when I heerd it was ole Mammy croakin' and axin' ter see me, I says ter myse'f: "Dreamy, you gotter make good wid old Mammy no matter what come—or you don' never git a bit of luck in yo' life no mo'." And I was game and come, wasn't I? Nary body in dis worril kin say de Dreamy ain't game ter de core, n'matter what. (*With sudden decision walks to the foot of the bed and stands looking down at* MAMMY. *A note of fear creeps into his voice*) Gawd, she's quiet 'nuff. Maybe she done passed away in her sleep like de ole ones does. You go see, Ceely; an' if she's on'y sleepin', you wake her up. I wanter speak wid her quick—an' den I'll make a break outa here. You make it fast, Ceely Ann, I tells yo'.

CEELY. (*bends down beside the bed*) Mammy! Here's de Dreamy.

MAMMY. (*opens her eyes—drowsily and vaguely, in a weak voice*) Dreamy?

DREAMY. (*shuffling his feet and moving around the bed*). Here I is, Mammy.

MAMMY. (*fastening her eyes on him with fascinated joy*) Dreamy! Hit's yo'! (*Then uncertainly*) I ain't dreamin' nor seein' ha'nts, is I?

DREAMY. (*coming forward and taking her hand*) 'Deed I ain't no ghost. Here I is, sho' 'nuff.

MAMMY. (*clutching his hand tight and pulling it down on her breast—in an ecstasy of happiness*) Didn' I know you'd come! Didn' I say: "Dreamy ain't gwine let his ole Mammy die all lone by he'se'f an' him not dere wid her." I knows yo'd come. (*She starts to laugh joyously, but coughs and sinks back weakly.*)

DREAMY. (*shudders in spite of himself as he realizes for the first time how far gone the old woman is—forcing a tone of joking reassurance*) What's dat foolishness I hears you talkin', Mammy? Wha' d'yuh mean pullin' dat bull 'bout croakin' on me? Shoo! Tryin' ter kid me, ain't yo'? Shoo! You live ter plant de flowers on my grave, see if you don'.

MAMMY. (*sadly and very weakly*) I knows! I knows! Hit ain't long

23

now. (*Bursting into a sudden weak hysteria*) Yo' stay heah, Dreamy! Yo' stay heah by me, yo' stay heah—till de good Lawd takes me home. Yo' promise me dat! Yo' do dat fo' po' ole Mammy, won't yo'?

DREAMY. (*uneasily*) 'Deed I will, Mammy, 'deed I will.

MAMMY. (*closing her eyes with a sigh of relief—calmly*) Bless de Lawd for dat. Den I ain't skeered no mo'. (*She settles herself comfortably in the bed as if preparing for sleep.*)

CEELY. (*in a low voice*) I gotter go home fo' a minute, Dreamy. I ain't been dere all de day and Lawd knows what happen. I'll be back yere befo' ve'y long.

DREAMY. (*his eyes fixed on* MAMMY) Aw right, beat it if yuh wanter. (*Turning to her—in a fierce whisper*) On'y don' be long. I can't stay here an' take dis risk, you hear?

CEELY. (*frightenedly*) I knows, chile. I come back, I swar! (*She goes out quietly.* DREAMY *goes quickly to the window and cautiously searches the street below with his eyes.*)

MAMMY. (*uneasily*) Dreamy. (*He hurries back and takes her hand again*) I got de mos' 'culiar feelin' in my head. Seems like de years done all roll away an' I'm back down home in de ole place whar yo' was bo'n. (*A short pause*) Does yo' 'member yo' own mammy, chile?

DREAMY. No.

MAMMY. Yo' was too young, I s'pec'. Yo' was on'y a baby w'en she tuck 'n' die. My Sal was a mighty fine 'oman, if I does say hit m'se'f.

DREAMY. (*fidgeting nervously*) Don' you talk, Mammy. Better you'd close yo' eyes an' rest.

MAMMY. (*with a trembling smile—weakly*) Shoo! W'at is I done come ter wid my own gran'chile bossin' me 'bout? I wants ter talk. You knows you ain't give me much chance ter talk wid yo' dese las' years.

DREAMY. (*sullenly*) I ain't had de time, Mammy; but you knows I was always game ter give you anything I got. (*A note of appeal in his voice*) You knows dat, don' you, Mammy?

MAMMY. Sho'ly I does. Yo' been a good boy, Dreamy; an' if dere's one thing more'n 'nother makes me feel like I mighter done good in de sight er de Lawd, hit's dat I raised yo' fum a baby.

DREAMY. (*clearing his throat gruffly*) Don' talk so much, Mammy.

MAMMY. (*querulously*) I gotter talk, chile. Come times—w'en I git thinkin' yere in de bed—w'at's gwine ter come ter me a'mos' b'fore I knows hit—like de thief in de night—en den I gits skeered. But w'en I talks wid yo' I ain't skeered a bit.

DREAMY. (*defiantly*) You ain't got nothin' to be skeered of—not when de Dreamy's here.

MAMMY. (*after a slight pause, faintly*) Dere's a singin' in my ears all de time. (*Seized by a sudden religious ecstasy*) Maybe hit's de singin' hymns o' de blessed angels I done heah fum above. (*Wildly*) Bless Gawd! Bless Gawd! Pity dis po' ole sinner.

DREAMY. (*with an uneasy glance at the door*) Ssshh, Mammy! Don' shout so loud.

MAMMY. De pictures keep a whizzin' fo' my eyes like de thread in a sewing machine. Seem 's if all my life done fly back ter me all ter once. (*With a flickering smile—weakly*) Does you know how yo' come by dat nickname dey alls call yo'—de Dreamy? Is I ever tole yo' dat?

DREAMY. (*evidently lying*) No, Mammy.

MAMMY. Hit was one mawnin' b'fo' we come No'th. Me an' yo' mammy—yo' was des a baby in arms den—

DREAMY. (*hears a noise from the hall*) Ssshh, Mammy! For God's sake, don't speak for a minute. I hears somep'n. (*He stares at the door, his face hardening savagely, and listens intently.*)

MAMMY. (*in a frightened tone*) W'at's de matter, chile?

DREAMY. Ssshh! Somebody comin'. (*A noise of footsteps comes from the hall stairway.* DREAMY *springs to his feet*) Leggo my hand, Mammy—jest for a secon'. I come right back to you. (*He pulls his hand from the old woman's grip. She falls back on the pillows moaning.* DREAMY *pulls a large automatic revolver from his coat pocket and tiptoes quickly to the door. As he does so there is a sharp rap. He stands listening at the crack for a moment, then noiselessly turns the key, unlocking the door. Then he crouches low down by the wall so that the door, when opened, will hide him from the sight of anyone entering. There is another and louder rap on the door.*)

MAMMY. (*groaning*) W'at's dat, Dreamy? Whar is yo'?

DREAMY. Ssshh! (*Then muffling his voice he calls*) Come in. (*He raises the revolver in his hand. The door is pushed open and Irene enters, her eyes peering wildly about the room. Her bosom is heaving as if she had been running and she is trembling with terrified excitement.*)

IRENE. (*not seeing him calls out questioningly*) Dreamy?

DREAMY. (*lowering his revolver and rising to his feet roughly*) Close dat door!

IRENE. (*whirling about with a startled cry*) Dreamy!

DREAMY. (*shutting the door and locking it—aggressively*) Shut yo' big mouth, gal, or I'll bang it shut for you! You wanter let de whole block know where I is?

IRENE. (*hysterical with joy—trying to put her arms around him*) Bless God, I foun' you at last!

DREAMY. (*pushing her away roughly*) Leggo o' me! Why you come here follerin' me? Ain't yo' got 'nuff sense in yo' fool head ter know de bulls is liable ter shadow you when dey knows you's my gal? Is you pinin' ter git me kotched an' sent to de chair?

IRENE. (*terrified*) No, no!

DREAMY. (*savagely*) I gotter mind ter hand you one you won't ferget! (*He draws back his fist.*)

IRENE. (*shrinking away*) Don' you hit me, Dreamy! Don' you beat me up now! Jest lemme 'xplain, dat's all.

MAMMY. (*in a frightened whimper*) Dreamy! Come yere to me. Whar is yo'? I'se skeered!

DREAMY. (*in a fierce whisper to Irene*) Can dat bull or I'll fix you. (*He hurries to the old woman and pats her hand*) Here I is, Mammy.

MAMMY. Who dat yo's a-talkin' wid?

DREAMY. On'y a fren' o' Ceely Ann's, askin' where she is. I gotter talk wid her some mo' yit. You sleep, Mammy? (*He goes to Irene.*)

MAMMY. (*feebly*) Don' yo' leave me, Dreamy.

DREAMY. I'se right here wid you. (*Fiercely, to Irene*) You git the hell outa here, you Reeny, you heah—quick! Dis ain't no place for de likes o' you wid ole Mammy dyin'.

IRENE. (*with a horrified glance at the bed*) Is she dyin'—honest?

DREAMY. Ssshh! She's croakin', I tells yo'—an' I gotter stay wid her fo' a while—an' I ain't got no time ter be pesterin' wid you. Beat it, now! Beat it outa here befo' I knocks yo' cold, git me?

IRENE. Jest wait a secon' for de love o' Gawd. I got somep'n ter tell you—

DREAMY. I don' wanter hear yo' fool talk. (*He gives her a push toward the door*) Git outa dis, you hear me?

IRENE. I'll go. I'm going soon—soon's ever I've had my say. Lissen, Dreamy! It's about de coppers I come ter tell you.

DREAMY. (*quickly*) Why don' you say dat befo'? What you know?

IRENE. Just befo' I come here to find you de first time, de Madam sends me out to Murphy's ter git her a bottle o' gin. I goes in de side door but I ain't rung de bell yet. I hear yo' name spoken an' I stops ter lissen. Dey was three or four men in de back room. Dey don't hear me open de outside door, an' dey can't see me, 'course. It was Big Sullivan from de Central Office talkin'. He was talkin' 'bout de killin' you done last night and he tells dem odders he's heerd 'bout de ole woman gittin' so sick, and dat if dey don't fin' you none of de udder places dey's lookin', dey's goin' wait for you here. Dey s'pecs you come here say good-by to Mammy befo' you make yo' git-away.

DREAMY. It's aw right den. Dey ain't come yit. Twister Smith done tole me de coast was clear befo' I come here.

IRENE. Dat was den. It ain't now.

DREAMY. (*excitedly*) What you mean, gal?

IRENE. I was comin' in by de front way when I sees some pusson hidin' in de doorway 'cross de street. I gits a good peek at him and when I does—it's a copper. Dreamy, shuah's yo' born, in his plain clo'se, and he's a watchin' de door o' dis house like a cat.

DREAMY. (*goes to the window and stealthily crouching by the dark side peeks out. One glance is enough. He comes quickly back to Irene*) You got de right dope, gal. It's dat Mickey. I knows him even in de dark. Dey're waitin'—so dey ain't wise I'm here yit, dat's suah.

IRENE. But dey'll git wise befo' long.

DREAMY. He don' pipe you comin' in here?

IRENE. I skulked roun' and sneaked in by de back way froo de yard. Dey ain't none o' dem dar yit. (*Raising her voice—excitedly*) But dere will be soon. Dey're boun' to git wise to dat back door. You ain't got no time to lose, Dreamy. Come on wid me now. Git back where yo' safe. It's de cooler for you certain if you stays here. Dey'll git you like a rat in de trap. (*As Dreamy hesitates*) For de love of Gawd, Dreamy, wake up to youse'f!

DREAMY. (*uncertainly*) I can't beat it—wid Mammy here alone. My luck done turn bad all my life, if I does.

IRENE. (*fiercely*) What good's you gittin' pinched and sent to de chair gwine do her? Is you crazy mad? Come wid me, I tells you!

DREAMY. (*half-persuaded—hesitatingly*) I gotter speak wid her. You wait a secon'.

IRENE. (*wringing hands*) Dis ain't no time for fussin' wid her.

DREAMY. (*gruffly*) Shut up! (*He makes a motion for her to remain where she is and goes over to the bed—in a low voice*) Mammy.

MAMMY. (*hazily*) Dat you, Dreamy? (*She tries to reach out her hand and touch him.*)

DREAMY. I'm gwine leave you—jest for a moment, Mammy. I'll send de word for Ceely Ann—

MAMMY. (*wide awake in an instant—with intense alarm*) Don' yo' do dat! Don' yo' move one step out er yere or yo'll be sorry, Dreamy.

DREAMY. (*apprehensively*) I gotter go, I tells you. I'll come back.

MAMMY. (*with wild grief*) O good Lawd! W'en I's drawin' de

las' bre'fs in dis po' ole body—(*Frenziedly*) De Lawd have mercy! Good Lawd have mercy!

DREAMY. (*fearfully*) Stop dat racket, Mammy! You bring all o' dem down on my head! (*He rushes over and crouches by the window to peer out—in relieved tones*) He ain't heerd nothin'. He's dar yit.

IRENE. (*imploringly*) Come on, Dreamy! (*Mammy groans with pain.*)

DREAMY. (*hurrying to the bed*) What's de matter, Mammy?

IRENE. (*stamping her foot*) Dreamy! Fo' Gawd's sake!

MAMMY. Lawd have mercy! (*She groans*) Gimme yo' han', chile Yo' ain't gwine leave me now, Dreamy? Yo' ain't, is yo'? Yo' ole Mammy won't bodder yo' long. Yo' know w'at yo' promise me, Dreamy! Yo' promise yo' sacred word yo' stay wid me till de en'. (*With an air of somber prophecy—slowly*) If yo' leave me now, yo' ain't gwine git no bit er luck s'long's yo' lives, I tells yo' dat!

DREAMY. (*frightened—pleadingly*) Don' you say dat, Mammy!

IRENE. Come on, Dreamy!

DREAMY. (*slowly*) I can't. (*In awed tones*) Don' you hear de curse she puts on me if I does?

MAMMY. (*her voice trembling with weak tears*) Don' go, chile!

DREAMY. (*hastily*) I won't leave dis room, I swar ter you! (*Relieved by the finality in his tones, the old woman sighs and closes her eyes. DREAMY frees his hand from hers and goes to IRENE. With a strange calm*) De game's up, gal. You better beat it while de goin's good.

IRENE (*aghast*) You gwine stay?

DREAMY. I gotter, gal. I ain't gwine agin her dyin' curse. No, suh!

IRENE. (*pitifully*) But dey'll git you shuah!

DREAMY. (*slapping the gun in his pocket significantly*) Dey'll have some gittin'. I git some o' dem fust. (*With gloomy determination*) Dey don't git dis chicken alive! Lawd Jesus, no suh. Not de Dreamy!

IRENE (*helplessly*) Oh, Lawdy, Lawdy! (*She goes to the window—with a short cry*) He's talkin' wid someone. Dere's two o' dem. (*Dreamy hurries to her side.*)

DREAMY. I knows him—de udder. It's Big Sullivan. (*Pulling her away roughly*) Come out o' dat! Dey'll see you. (*He pushes her toward the door*) Dey won't wait down dere much longer. Dey'll be comin' up here soon. (*Prayerfully, with a glance at the bed*) I hopes she's croaked by den, 'fo' Christ I does!

IRENE. (*as if she couldn't believe it*) Den you ain't gwine save youse'f while dere's time? (*Pleadingly*) Oh, Dreamy, you can make it yit!

DREAMY. De game's up, I tole you. (*With gloomy fatalism*) I s'pect it hatter be. Yes, suh. Dey'd git me in de long run anyway—and wid her curse de luck'd be agin me. (*With sudden anger*) Git outa here, you Reeny! You ain't aimin' ter get shot up too, is you? Ain't no sense in dat.

IRENE. (*fiercely*) I'se stayin' too, here wid you!

DREAMY. No you isn't! None o' dat bull! You ain't got no mix in dis jam.

IRENE. Yes, I is! Ain't you my man?

DREAMY. Don't make no dif. I don't wanter git you in Dutch more'n you is. It's bad 'nuff fo' me. (*He pushes her toward the door*) Blow while you kin, I tells you!

IRENE. (*resisting him*) No, Dreamy! What I care if dey kills me? I'se gwine stick wid you.

DREAMY. (*gives her another push*) No, you isn't, gal. (*Unlocking the door—relentlessly*) Out wid you!

IRENE. (*hysterically*) You can't gimme no bum's rush. I stays.

DREAMY. (*gloomily*) On'y one thing fo' me ter do den. (*He hits her on the side of the face with all his might knocking her back against the wall where she sways as if about to fall. Then he opens the door and grabs her two arms from behind*) Out wid you, gal!

IRENE. (*moaning*) Dreamy! Dreamy! Lemme stay wid you! (*He pushes her into the hallway and holds her there at arm's length*) Fo' Gawd's sake, Dreamy!

MAMMY. (*whimperingly*) Dreamy! I'se skeered!

IRENE. (*from the hall*) I'se gwine stay right here at de door. You might s'well lemme in.

DREAMY. (*frowning*) Don' do dat, Reeny. (*Then with a sudden idea*) You run roun' and tell de gang what's up. Maybe dey git me outa dis, you hear?

IRENE. (*with eager hope*) You think dey kin?

DREAMY. Never kin tell. You hurry—through de back yard, 'member —an' don' git pinched, now.

IRENE. (*eagerly*) I'm gwine! I'll bring dem back!

DREAMY. (*stands listening to her retreating footsteps—then shuts and locks the door—gloomily to himself*) Ain't no good. Dey dassent do nothin'—but I hatter git her outa dis somehow.

MAMMY. (*groaning*) Dreamy!

DREAMY. Here I is. Jest a secon'. (*He goes to the window.*)

MAMMY. (*weakly*) I feels—like—de en's comin'. Oh, Lawd, Lawd!

DREAMY. (*absent-mindedly*) Yes, Mammy. (*Aloud to himself*) Dey're sneakin' cross de street. Dere's anudder of 'em. Dat's tree. (*He glances around the room quickly—then hurries over and takes hold of the chest of drawers. As he does so the old woman commences to croon shrilly to herself.*)

DREAMY. Stop dat noise, Mammy! Stop dat noise!

MAMMY. (*wanderingly*) Dat's how come yo' got dat—dat nickname —Dreamy.

DREAMY. Yes, Mammy. (*He puts the lamp on the floor to the rear of the door, turning it down low. Then he carries the chest of drawers over and places it against the door as a barricade.*)

MAMMY. (*rambling as he does this—very feebly*) Does yo' know— I gives you dat name—w'en yo's des a baby—lyin' in my arms—

DREAMY. Yes, Mammy.

MAMMY. Down by de crik—under de ole willow—whar I uster take yo'—wid yo' big eyes a-chasin'—de sun flitterin' froo de grass—an' out on de water—

31

DREAMY. (*takes the revolver from his pocket and puts it on top of the chest of drawers*) Dey don't git de Dreamy alive—not for de chair! Lawd Jesus, no suh!

MAMMY. An' yo' was always—a-lookin'—an' a-thinkin' ter yo'se'f —an' yo' big eyes jest a-dreamin' an' a-dreamin'—an' dat's w'en I gives yo' dat nickname—Dreamy—Dreamy—

DREAMY. Yes, Mammy. (*He listens at the crack of the door—in a tense whisper*) I don' hear dem—but dey're comin' sneakin' up de stairs, I knows it.

MAMMY. (*faintly*) Whar is yo', Dreamy? I can't—ha'dly—breathe —no mo'. Oh, Lawd have mercy!

DREAMY. (*goes over to the bed*) Here I is, Mammy.

MAMMY. (*speaking with difficulty*) Yo'—kneel down—chile—say a pray'r—Oh, Lawd!

DREAMY. Jest a secon', Mammy. (*He goes over and gets his revolver and comes back.*)

MAMMY. Gimme—yo' hand—chile. (*Dreamy gives her his left hand. The revolver is in his right. He stares nervously at the door*) An' yo' kneel down—pray fo' me. (*Dreamy gets on one knee beside the bed. There is a sound from the hallway as if someone had made a misstep on the stairs—then silence. Dreamy starts and half aims his gun in the direction of the door. Mammy groans weakly*) I'm dyin', chile. Hit's de en'. You pray for me—out loud—so's I can heah. Oh, Lawd! (*She gasps to catch her breath.*)

DREAMY. (*abstractedly, not having heard a word she has said*) Yes, Mammy. (*Aloud to himself with an air of grim determination as if he were making a pledge*) Dey don't git de Dreamy! Not while he's 'live! Lawd Jesus, no suh!

MAMMY. (*falteringly*) Dat's right—yo' pray—Lawd Jesus—Lawd Jesus—(*There is another slight sound of movement from the hallway.*)

CURTAIN

THE STRAW

A Play in Three Acts

1918-1919

CHARACTERS

BILL CARMODY

MARY
NORA
TOM } his children
BILLY

DOCTOR GAYNOR

FRED NICHOLLS

EILEEN CARMODY, *Bill's eldest child*

STEPHEN MURRAY

MISS HOWARD, *a nurse in training*

MISS GILPIN, *superintendent of the Infirmary*

DOCTOR STANTON, *of the Hill Farm Sanatorium*

DOCTOR SIMMS, *his assistant*

MR. SLOAN

PETERS, *a patient*

MRS. TURNER, *matron of the Sanatorium*

MISS BAILEY
MRS. ABNER } *Patients*
FLYNN

OTHER PATIENTS OF THE SANATORIUM

MRS. BRENNAN

SCENES

ACT ONE

Scene I: The Kitchen of the Carmody Home—Evening.

Scene II: The Reception Room of the Infirmary, Hill Farm Sanatorium—An Evening a Week Later.

ACT TWO

Scene I: Assembly Room of the Main Building at the Sanatorium—A Morning Four Months Later.

Scene II: A Crossroads Near the Sanatorium—Midnight of the Same Day.

ACT THREE

An Isolation Room and Porch at the Sanatorium—An Afternoon Four Months Later.

THE STRAW

ACT ONE—SCENE ONE

THE *kitchen of the Carmody home on the outskirts of a manufactur-ing town in Connecticut. On the left, forward, the sink. Farther back, two windows looking out on the yard. In the left corner, rear, the icebox. Immediately to the right of it, in the rear wall, a window opening on the side porch. To the right of this, a dish closet, and a door leading into the hall where the main front entrance to the house and the stairs to the floor above are situated. On the right, to the rear, a door opening on the dining room. Farther forward, the kitchen range with scuttle, wood box, etc. In the center of the room, a table with a red and white cover. Four cane-bottomed chairs are pushed under the table. In front of the stove, two battered, wicker rocking chairs. The floor is partly covered by linoleum strips. The walls are papered a light cheerful color. Several old framed picture-supplement prints hang from nails. Everything has a clean, neatly-kept appearance. The supper dishes are piled in the sink ready for wash-ing. A dish pan of water simmers on the stove.*

It is about eight o'clock in the evening of a bitter cold day in late February.

As the curtain rises, BILL CARMODY *is discovered sitting in a rocker by the stove, reading a newspaper and smoking a blackened clay pipe. He is a man of fifty, heavy-set and round-shouldered, with long muscular arms and swollen-veined, hairy hands. His face is bony and ponderous; his nose, short and squat; his mouth large, thick-lipped and harsh; his complexion mottled—red, purple-streaked, and freckled: his hair, short and stubby with a bald spot on the crown.*

37

The expression of his small, blue eyes is one of selfish cunning. His voice is loud and hoarse. He wears a flannel shirt, open at the neck, criss-crossed by red suspenders; black, baggy trousers gray with dust; muddy brogans.

His youngest daughter, MARY, *is sitting on a chair by the table, front, turning over the pages of a picture book. She is a delicate, dark-haired, blue-eyed, quiet little girl about eight years old.*

CARMODY. (*after watching the child's preoccupation for a moment, in a tone of half-exasperated amusement*) Well, but you're the quiet one, surely! It's the dead spit and image of your sister, Eileen, you are, with your nose always in a book; and you're like your mother, too, God rest her soul. (*He crosses himself with pious unction and* MARY *also does so*) It's Nora and Tom has the high spirits in them like their father; and Billy, too,—if he is a lazy shiftless divil—has the fightin' Carmody blood like me. You're a Cullen like your mother's people. They always was dreamin' their lives out. (*He lights his pipe and shakes his head with ponderous gravity*) It's out rompin' and playin' you ought to be at your age, not carin' a fig for books. (*With a glance at the clock*) Is that auld fool of a doctor stayin' the night? Run out in the hall, Mary, and see if you hear him.

MARY. (*goes out into the hall, rear, and comes back*) He's upstairs. I heard him talking to Eileen.

CARMODY. Close the door, ye little divil! There's a freezin' draught comin' in. (*She does so and comes back to her chair.* CARMODY *continues with a sneer*) I've no use for their drugs at all. They only keep you sick to pay more visits. I'd not have sent for this bucko if Eileen didn't scare me by faintin'.

MARY. (*anxiously*) Is Eileen very sick, Papa?

CARMODY. (*spitting—roughly*) If she is, it's her own fault entirely— weakenin' her health by readin' here in the house. (*Irritably*) Put down that book on the table and leave it be. I'll have no more readin' or I'll take the strap to you!

38

MARY. (*laying the book on the table*) It's only pictures.

CARMODY. No back talk! Pictures or not, it's all the same mopin' and lazin' in it. (*After a pause—morosely*) Who's to do the work and look after Nora and Tom and yourself, if Eileen is bad took and has to stay in her bed? All that I've saved from slavin' and sweatin' in the sun with a gang of lazy Dagoes'll be up the spout in no time. (*Bitterly*) What a fool a man is to be raisin' a raft of children and him not a millionaire! (*With lugubrious self-pity*) Mary, dear, it's a black curse God put on me when he took your mother just when I needed her most. (MARY *commences to sob.* CARMODY *starts and looks at her angrily*) What are you snifflin' at?

MARY. (*tearfully*) I was thinking—of Mama.

CARMODY. (*scornfully*) It's late you are with your tears, and her cold in her grave for a year. Stop it, I'm tellin' you! (MARY *gulps back her sobs.*)

(*There is a noise of childish laughter and screams from the street in front. The outside door is opened and slammed, footsteps pound along the hall. The door in the rear is shoved open, and* NORA *and* TOM *rush in breathlessly.* NORA *is a bright, vivacious, red-haired girl of eleven—pretty after an elfish, mischievous fashion—light-hearted and robust.*)

(TOM *resembles* NORA *in disposition and appearance. A healthy, good-humored youngster with a shock of sandy hair. He is a year younger than* NORA. *They are followed into the room, a moment later, by their brother,* BILLY, *who is evidently loftily disgusted with their antics.* BILLY *is a fourteen-year-old replica of his father, whom he imitates even to the hoarse, domineering tone of voice.*)

CARMODY. (*grumpily*) Ah, here you are, the lot of you. Shut that door after you! What's the use in me spendin' money for coal if all you do is to let the cold night in the room itself?

NORA. (*hopping over to him—teasingly*) Me and Tom had a race, Papa. I beat him. (*She sticks her tongue out at her younger brother*) Slow poke!

TOM. You didn't beat me, neither!

NORA. I did, too!

TOM. You tripped me comin' up the steps. Brick-top! Cheater!

NORA. (*flaring up*) You're a liar! I beat you fair. Didn't I, Papa?

CARMODY. (*with a grin*) You did, darlin'. (TOM *slinks back to the chair in the rear of the table, sulking.* CARMODY *pats* NORA's *red hair with delighted pride*) Sure it's you can beat the divil himself!

NORA. (*sticks out her tongue again at* TOM) See? Liar! (*She goes and perches on the table near* MARY *who is staring sadly in front of her.*)

CARMODY. (*to* BILLY—*irritably*) Did you get the plug I told you?

BILLY. Sure. (*He takes a plug of tobacco from his pocket and hands it to his father.* NORA *slides down off her perch and disappears, unnoticed, under the table.*)

CARMODY. It's a great wonder you didn't forget it—and me without a chew. (*He bites off a piece and tucks it into his cheek.*)

TOM. (*suddenly clutching at his leg with a yell*) Ouch! Darn you! (*He kicks frantically at something under the table, but* NORA *scrambles out at the other end, grinning.*)

CARMODY. (*angrily*) Shut your big mouth!

TOM. (*indignantly*) She pinched me—hard as she could, too—and look at her laughin'!

NORA. (*hopping on the table again*) Cry-baby!

TOM. I'll tell Eileen, wait 'n' see!

NORA. Tattle-tale! Eileen's sick.

TOM. That's why you dast do it. You dasn't if she was up.

CARMODY. (*exasperated*) Go up to bed, the two of you, and no more talk, and you go with them, Mary.

NORA. (*giving a quick tug at* MARY's *hair*) Come on, Mary.

MARY. Ow! (*She begins to cry.*)

CARMODY. (*raising his voice furiously*) Hush your noise! It's nothin' but blubberin' you do be doin' all the time. (*He stands up threaten-*

40

ingly) I'll have a moment's peace, I will! Go on, now! (*They scurry out of the rear door.*)

NORA. (*sticks her head back in the door*) Can I say good-night to Eileen, papa?

CARMODY. No. The doctor's with her yet. (*Then he adds hastily*) Yes, go in to her, Nora. It'll drive himself out of the house maybe, bad cess to him, and him stayin' half the night. (NORA *waits to hear no more but darts back, shutting the door behind her.* BILLY *takes the chair in front of the table.* CARMODY *sits down again with a groan*) The rheumatics are in my leg again. (*Shakes his head*) If Eileen's in bed long those brats'll have the house down. Arra, well, it's God's will, I suppose, but where the money'll come from, I dunno. (*With a disparaging glance at his son*) They'll not be raisin' your wages soon, I'll be bound.

BILLY. (*surlily*) Naw.

CARMODY. (*still scanning him with contempt*) A divil of a lot of good it was for me to go against Eileen's wish and let you leave off your schoolin' this year thinkin' the money you'd earn would help with the house.

BILLY. Aw, goin' to school didn't do me no good. The teachers was all down on me. I couldn't learn nothin' there.

CARMODY. (*disgustedly*) Nor any other place, I'm thinkin', you're that thick. (*There is a noise from the stairs in the hall*) Wisht! It's the doctor comin' down from Eileen. (*The door in the rear is opened and Doctor Gaynor enters. He is a stout, bald, middle-aged man, forceful of speech, who in the case of patients of the* CARMODYS' *class dictates rather than advises.* CARMODY *adopts a whining tone*) Aw, Doctor, and how's Eileen now?

GAYNOR. (*does not answer this but comes forward into the room holding out two slips of paper—dictatorially*) Here are two prescriptions that'll have to be filled immediately.

CARMODY. (*frowning*) You take them, Billy, and run round to the drug store. (GAYNOR *hands them to* BILLY.)

41

BILLY. Give me the money, then.

CARMODY. (*reaches down into his pants pocket with a sigh*) How much will they come to, Doctor?

GAYNOR. About a dollar, I guess.

CARMODY. (*protestingly*) A dollar! Sure it's expensive medicines you're givin' her for a bit of a cold. (*He meets the doctor's cold glance of contempt and he wilts—grumblingly, as he peels a dollar bill off a small roll and gives it to* BILLY) Bring back the change—if there is any. And none of your tricks!

BILLY. Aw, what do you think I am? (*He takes the money and goes out.*)

CARMODY. (*grudgingly*) Take a chair, Doctor, and tell me what's wrong with Eileen.

GAYNOR. (*seating himself by the table—gravely*) Your daughter is very seriously ill.

CARMODY. (*irritably*) Aw, Doctor, didn't I know you'd be sayin' that, anyway!

GAYNOR. (*ignoring this remark—coldly*) She has tuberculosis of the lungs.

CARMODY. (*with puzzled awe*) Too-ber-c'losis?

GAYNOR. Consumption, if that makes it plainer to you.

CARMODY. (*with dazed terror—after a pause*) Consumption? Eileen? (*With sudden anger*) What lie is it you're tellin' me?

GAYNOR. (*icily*) Look here, Carmody!

CARMODY. (*bewilderedly*) Don't be angry, now. Sure I'm out of my wits entirely. Ah, Doctor, sure you must be mistaken!

GAYNOR. There's no chance for a mistake, I'm sorry to say. Her right lung is badly affected.

CARMODY. (*desperately*) It's a cold only, maybe.

GAYNOR. (*curtly*) Don't talk nonsense. (CARMODY *groans*. GAYNOR *continues authoritatively*) She'll have to go to a sanatorium at once. She ought to have been sent to one months ago. (*Casts a look of indignant scorn at* CARMODY *who is sitting staring at the floor with an expression of angry stupor on his face*) It's a wonder to me you didn't see the condition she was in and force her to take care of herself.

CARMODY. (*with vague fury*) God blast it!

GAYNOR. She kept on doing her work, I suppose—taking care of her brothers and sisters, washing, cooking, sweeping, looking after your comfort—worn out—when she should have been in bed—and— (*He gets to his feet with a harsh laugh*) But what's the use of talking? The damage is done. We've got to set to work to repair it at once. I'll write tonight to Dr. Stanton of the Hill Farm Sanatorium and find out if he has a vacancy.

CARMODY. (*his face growing red with rage*) Is it sendin' Eileen away to a hospital you'd be? (*Exploding*) Then you'll not! You'll get that notion out of your head damn quick. It's all nonsense you're stuffin' me with, and lies, makin' things out to be the worst in the world. She'll not move a step out of here, and I say so, and I'm her father!

GAYNOR. (*who has been staring at him with contempt—coldly angry*) You refuse to let her go to a sanatorium?

CARMODY. I do.

GAYNOR. (*threateningly*) Then I'll have to report her case to the Society for the Prevention of Tuberculosis of this county and tell them of your refusal to help her.

CARMODY. (*wavering a bit*) Report all you like, and be damned to you!

GAYNOR. (*ignoring the interruption—impressively*) A majority of the most influential men of this city are back of the Society. (*Grimly*) We'll find a way to move you, Carmody, if you try to be stubborn.

CARMODY. (*thoroughly frightened but still protesting*) Arra, Doctor, you don't see the way of it at all. If Eileen goes to the hospital, who's to be takin' care of the others, and mindin' the house when I'm off to work?

GAYNOR. You can easily hire some woman.

43

CARMODY. (*at once furious again*) Hire? D'you think I'm a million-aire itself?

GAYNOR. (*contemptuously*) That's where the shoe pinches, eh? (*In a rage*) I'm not going to waste any more words on you, Carmody, but I'm damn well going to see this thing through! You might as well give in first as last.

CARMODY. (*wailing*) But where's the money comin' from?

GAYNOR. The weekly fee at the Hill Farm is only seven dollars. You can easily afford that—the price of a few rounds of drinks.

CARMODY. Seven dollars! And I'll have to pay a woman to come in—and the four of the children eatin' their heads off! Glory be to God, I'll not have a penny saved for me old age—and then it's the poor house!

GAYNOR. Well, perhaps I can get the Society to pay half for your daughter—if you're really as hard up as you pretend.

CARMODY. (*brightening*) Ah, Doctor, thank you.

GAYNOR. (*abruptly*) Then it's all settled?

CARMODY. (*grudgingly—trying to make the best of it*) I'll do my best for Eileen, if it's needful—and you'll not be tellin' them people about it at all, Doctor?

GAYNOR. Not unless you force me to.

CARMODY. And they'll pay the half, surely?

GAYNOR. I'll see what I can do.

CARMODY. God bless you, Doctor! (*Grumblingly*) It's the whole of it they ought to be payin', I'm thinkin', and them with sloos of money. 'Tis them builds the hospitals and why should they be wantin' the poor like me to support them?

GAYNOR. (*disgustedly*) Bah! (*Abruptly*) I'll telephone to Doctor Stanton tomorrow morning. Then I'll know something definite when I come to see your daughter in the afternoon.

CARMODY. (*darkly*) You'll be comin' again tomorrow? (*Half to himself*) Leave it to the likes of you to be drainin' a man dry. (GAYNOR *has gone out to the hall in rear and does not hear this last remark.*

*There is a loud knock from the outside door. The Doctor comes back
into the room carrying his hat and overcoat.)*

GAYNOR. There's someone knocking.

CARMODY. Who'll it be? Ah, it's Fred Nicholls, maybe. (*In a low
voice to* GAYNOR *who has started to put on his overcoat*) Eileen's
young man, Doctor, that she's engaged to marry, as you might say.

GAYNOR. (*thoughtfully*) Hmm—yes—she spoke of him. (*As another knock sounds* CARMODY *hurries to the rear.* GAYNOR, *after a
moment's indecision, takes off his overcoat again and sits down. A
moment later* CARMODY *re-enters followed by* FRED NICHOLLS, *who has
left his overcoat and hat in the hallway.* NICHOLLS *is a young fellow
of twenty-three, stockily built, fair-haired, handsome in a commonplace, conventional mold. His manner is obviously an attempt at
suave gentility; he has an easy, taking smile and a ready laugh, but
there is a petty, calculating expression in his small, observing, blue
eyes. His well-fitting, readymade clothes are carefully pressed. His
whole get-up suggests an attitude of man-about-small-town com-
placency.*)

CARMODY. (*as they enter*) I had a mind to phone to your house but
I wasn't wishful to disturb you, knowin' you'd be comin' to call
tonight.

NICHOLLS. (*with disappointed concern*) It's nothing serious, I hope.

CARMODY. (*grumblingly*) Ah, who knows? Here's the doctor.
You've not met him?

NICHOLLS. (*politely, looking at* GAYNOR *who inclines his head stiffly*)
I haven't had the pleasure. Of course I've heard—

CARMODY. It's Doctor Gaynor. This is Fred Nicholls, Doctor. (*The
two men shake hands with conventional pleased-to-meet yous*) Sit
down, Fred, that's a good lad, and be talkin' to the Doctor a moment
while I go upstairs and see how is Eileen.

NICHOLLS. Certainly, Mr. Carmody—and tell her how sorry I am
to learn she's under the weather.

CARMODY. I will so. (*He goes out.*)

GAYNOR. (*after a pause in which he is studying* NICHOLLS) Do you happen to be any relative to Albert Nicholls over at the Downs Manufacturing Company?

NICHOLLS. (*smiling*) He's sort of a near relative—my father.

GAYNOR. Ah, yes?

NICHOLLS. (*with satisfaction*) I work for the Downs Company myself—bookkeeper.

GAYNOR. Miss Carmody had a position there also, didn't she, before her mother died?

NICHOLLS. Yes. She had a job as stenographer for a time. When she graduated from the business college—I was already working at the Downs—and through my father's influence—you understand. (GAYNOR *nods curtly*) She was getting on finely, too, and liked the work. It's too bad—her mother's death, I mean—forcing her to give it up and come home to take care of those kids.

GAYNOR. It's a damn shame. That's the main cause of her breakdown.

NICHOLLS. (*frowning*) I've noticed she's been looking badly lately. Well, it's all her father's fault—and her own, too, because whenever I raised a kick about his making a slave of her, she always defended him. (*With a quick glance at the Doctor—in a confidential tone*) Between us, Carmody's as selfish as they make 'em, if you want my opinion.

GAYNOR. (*with a growl*) He's a hog on two legs.

NICHOLLS. (*with a gratified smile*) You bet! (*With a patronizing air*) I hope to get Eileen away from all this as soon as—things pick up a little. (*Making haste to explain his connection with the dubious household*) Eileen and I have gone around together for years—went to Grammar and High School together—in different classes, of course. She's really a corker—very different from the rest of the family you've seen—like her mother. My folks like her awfully well. Of course, they'd never stand for him.

GAYNOR. You'll excuse my curiosity, but you and Miss Carmody are engaged, aren't you? Carmody said you were.

NICHOLLS. (*embarrassed*) Why, yes, in a way—but nothing definite—no official announcement or anything of that kind. (*With a sentimental smile*) It's always been sort of understood between us. (*He laughs awkwardly.*)

GAYNOR. (*gravely*) Then I can be frank with you. I'd like to be because I may need your help. Besides, you're bound to know anyway. She'd tell you.

NICHOLLS. (*a look of apprehension coming over his face*) Is it—about her sickness?

GAYNOR. Yes.

NICHOLLS. Then—it's serious?

GAYNOR. It's pulmonary tuberculosis—consumption.

NICHOLLS. (*stunned*) Consumption? Good heavens! (*After a dazed pause—lamely*) Are you sure, Doctor?

GAYNOR. Positive. (NICHOLLS *stares at him with vaguely frightened eyes*) It's had a good start—thanks to her father's blind selfishness—but let's hope that can be overcome. The important thing is to ship her off to a sanatorium immediately. That's where you can be of help. It's up to you to help me convince Carmody that it's imperative she be sent away at once—for the safety of those around her as well as her own.

NICHOLLS. (*confusedly*) I'll do my best, Doctor. (*As if he couldn't yet believe his ears—shuddering*) Good heavens! She never said a word about—being so ill. She's had a cold. But Doctor,—do you think this sanatorium will—?

GAYNOR. (*with hearty hopefulness*) She has every chance. The Hill Farm has a really surprising record of arrested cases. Of course, she'll never be able to live as carelessly as before, even after the most favorable results. (*Apologetically*) I'm telling you all this as being the one most intimately concerned. You're the one who'll have to assume responsibility when she returns to everyday life.

NICHOLLS. (*answering as if he were merely talking to screen the thoughts in his mind*) Yes—certainly—. Where is this sanatorium, Doctor?

GAYNOR. Half an hour by train to the town. The sanatorium is two miles out on the hills. You'll be able to see her whenever you've a day off.

NICHOLLS. (*a look of horrified realization has been creeping into his eyes*) You said—Eileen ought to be sent away—for the sake of those around her—?

GAYNOR. T. B. is extremely contagious, you must know that. Yet I'll bet she's been fondling and kissing those brothers and sisters of hers regardless. (NICHOLLS *fidgets uneasily on his chair.*)

NICHOLLS. (*his eyes shiftily avoiding the doctor's face*) Then the kids might have gotten it—by kissing Eileen?

GAYNOR. It stands to reason that's a common means of communication.

NICHOLLS. (*very much shaken*) Yes. I suppose it must be. But that's terrible, isn't it? (*With sudden volubility, evidently extremely anxious to wind up this conversation and conceal his thoughts from* GAYNOR) I'll promise you, Doctor, I'll tell Carmody straight what's what. He'll pay attention to me or I'll know the reason why.

GAYNOR. (*getting to his feet and picking up his overcoat*) Good boy! Tell him I'll be back tomorrow with definite information about the sanatorium.

NICHOLLS. (*helping him on with his overcoat, anxious to have him go*) All right, Doctor.

GAYNOR. (*puts on his hat*) And do your best to cheer the patient up. Give her confidence in her ability to get well. That's half the battle.

NICHOLLS. (*hastily*) I'll do all I can.

GAYNOR. (*turns to the door and shakes* NICHOLLS' *hand sympathetically*) And don't take it to heart too much yourself. In six months she'll come back to you her old self again.

NICHOLLS. (*nervously*) It's hard on a fellow—so suddenly, but I'll remember—and—(*Abruptly*) Good-night, Doctor.

GAYNOR. Good-night. (*He goes out. The outer door is heard shutting behind him.* NICHOLLS *closes the door, rear, and comes back and sits in the chair in front of table. He rests his chin on his hands and stares before him, a look of desperate, frightened calculation coming into his eyes.* CARMODY *is heard clumping heavily down the stairs. A moment later he enters. His expression is glum and irritated.*)

CARMODY. (*coming forward to his chair by the stove*) Has he gone away?

NICHOLLS. (*turning on him with a look of repulsion*) Yes. He said to tell you he'd be back tomorrow with definite information—about the sanatorium business.

CARMODY. (*darkly*) Oho, he did, did he? Maybe I'll surprise him. I'm thinkin' it's lyin' he is about Eileen's sickness, and her lookin' as fresh as a daisy with the high color in her cheeks when I saw her now.

NICHOLLS. (*impatiently*) Gaynor knows his business. (*After a moment's hesitation*) He told me all about Eileen's sickness.

CARMODY. (*resentfully*) Small thanks to him to be tellin' our secrets to the town.

NICHOLLS. (*exasperated*) He only told me because you'd said I and Eileen were engaged. You're the one who was telling—secrets.

CARMODY. (*irritated*) Arra, don't be talkin'! That's no secret at all with the whole town watchin' Eileen and you spoonin' together from the time you was kids.

NICHOLLS. (*vindictively*) Well, the whole town is liable to find out— (*He checks himself.*)

CARMODY. (*too absorbed in his own troubles to notice this threat*) So he told you he'd send Eileen away to the hospital? I've half a mind not to let him—and let him try to make me! (*With a frown*) But Eileen herself says she's wantin' to go, now. (*Angrily*) It's all that divil's notion he put in her head that the children'd be catchin' her sickness that makes her willin' to go.

49

NICHOLLS. (*with a superior air*) From what he told me, I should say it's the only thing for Eileen to do if she wants to get well quickly. (*Spitefully*) And I'd certainly not go against Gaynor, if I was you.

CARMODY. (*worriedly*) But what can he do—him and his Sasiety? I'm her father.

NICHOLLS. (*seeing* CARMODY's *uneasiness with revengeful satisfaction*) You'll make a mistake if you think he's bluffing. It'd probably get in all the papers about you refusing. Everyone would be down on you. (*As a last jab—spitefully*) You might even lose your job over it, people would be so sore.

CARMODY. (*jumping to his feet*) Ah, divil take him! Let him send her where he wants, then.

NICHOLLS. (*as an afterthought*) And, honestly, Mr. Carmody, I don't see how you can object for a second. (*Seeing* CARMODY's *shaken condition, he finishes boldly*) You've some feeling for your own daughter, haven't you?

CARMODY. (*apprehensively*) Whisht! She might hear you. Let her do what she's wishful.

NICHOLLS. (*complacently—feeling his duty in the matter well done*) That's the right spirit. And you and I'll do all we can to help her. (*He gets to his feet*) Well, I guess I'll have to go. Tell Eileen—

CARMODY. You're not goin'? Sure, Eileen is puttin' on her clothes to come down and have a look at you.

NICHOLLS. (*suddenly panic-stricken by the prospect of facing her*) No—no—I can't stay—I only came for a moment—I've got an appointment—honestly. Besides, it isn't right for her to be up. You should have told her. (*The door in the rear is opened and* EILEEN *enters. She is just over eighteen. Her wavy mass of dark hair is parted in the middle and combed low on her forehead, covering her ears, to a knot at the back of her head. The oval of her face is spoiled by a long, rather heavy, Irish jaw contrasting with the delicacy of her other features. Her eyes are large and blue, confident in their compelling candor and sweetness; her lips, full and red, half-open, over strong even teeth, droop at the corners into an expression of wistful sadness; her clear complexion is unnaturally striking in its contrasting colors, rose and white; her figure is slight and undeveloped. She wears a plain black dress with a bit of white at the neck and wrists. She stands looking appealingly at* NICHOLLS *who avoids her glance. Her eyes have a startled, stunned expression as if the doctor's verdict were still in her ears.*)

EILEEN. (*faintly—forcing a smile*) Good evening, Fred. (*Her eyes search his face anxiously.*)

NICHOLLS. (*confusedly*) Hello, Eileen. I'm so sorry to—. (*Clumsily trying to cover up his confusion, he goes over and leads her to a chair*) You sit down. You've got to take care of yourself. You never ought to have gotten up tonight.

EILEEN. (*sits down*) I wanted to talk to you. (*She raises her face with a pitiful smile.* NICHOLLS *hurriedly moves back to his own chair.*)

NICHOLLS. (*almost brusquely*) I could have talked to you from the hall. You're silly to take chances just now. (EILEEN's *eyes show her hurt at his tone.*)

CARMODY. (*seeing his chance—hastily*) You'll be stayin' a while now, Fred? I'll take a walk down the road. I'm needin' a drink to clear my wits. (*He goes to the door in rear.*)

EILEEN. (*reproachfully*) You won't be long, Father? And please don't—you know.

CARMODY. (*exasperated*) Sure who wouldn't get drunk with all the sorrows of the world piled on him? (*He stamps out. A moment later the outside door bangs behind him.* EILEEN *sighs.* NICHOLLS *walks up and down with his eyes on the floor.*)

NICHOLLS. (*furious at* CARMODY *for having left him in this situation*) Honestly, Eileen, your father is the limit. I don't see how you stand for him. He's the most selfish—

EILEEN. (*gently*) Sssh! You mustn't, Fred. He just doesn't understand. (NICHOLLS *snorts disdainfully*) Don't! Let's not talk about him now. We won't have many more evenings together for a long, long time. Did Father or the doctor tell you— (*She falters.*)

NICHOLLS. (*not looking at her—glumly*) Everything there was to tell, I guess.

EILEEN. (*hastening to comfort him*) You mustn't worry, Fred. Please don't! It'd make it so much worse for me if I thought you did. I'll be all right. I'll do exactly what they tell me, and in a few months I'll be back so fat and healthy you won't know me.

NICHOLLS. (*lamely*) Oh, there's no doubt of that. No one's worrying about your not getting well quick.

EILEEN. It won't be long. We can write often, and it isn't far away. You can come out and see me every Sunday—if you want to.

NICHOLLS. (*hastily*) Of course I will!

EILEEN. (*looking at his face searchingly*) Why do you act so funny? Why don't you sit down—here, by me? Don't you want to?

NICHOLLS. (*drawing up a chair by hers—flushing guiltily*) I—I'm all bawled up, Eileen. I don't know what I'm doing.

EILEEN. (*putting her hand on his knee*) Poor Fred! I'm so sorry I have to go. I didn't want to at first. I knew how hard it would be on Father and the kids—especially little Mary. (*Her voice trembles a bit*) And then the doctor said if I stayed I'd be putting them all in danger. He even ordered me not to kiss them any more. (*She bites her lips to restrain a sob—then coughs, a soft, husky cough.* NICHOLLS *shrinks away from her to the edge of his chair, his eyes shifting nervously with fright.* EILEEN *continues gently*) So I've got to go and get well, don't you see?

NICHOLLS. (*wetting his dry lips*) Yes—it's better.

EILEEN. (*sadly*) I'll miss the kids so much. Taking care of them has meant so much to me since Mother died. (*With a half-sob she suddenly throws her arms about his neck and hides her face on his shoulder. He shudders and fights against an impulse to push her away*) But I'll miss you most of all, Fred. (*She lifts her lips towards his, expecting a kiss. He seems about to kiss her—then averts his face with a shrinking movement, pretending he hasn't seen.* EILEEN's *eyes grow wide with horror. She throws herself back into her own chair, staring accusingly at* NICHOLLS. *She speaks chokingly*) Fred! Why—why didn't you kiss—what is it? Are you—afraid? (*With a moaning sound*) Oooh!

NICHOLLS. (*goaded by this accusation into a display of manhood, seizes her fiercely by the arms*) No! What—what d'you mean? (*He tries to kiss her but she hides her face.*)

EILEEN. (*in a muffled voice of hysterical self-accusation, pushing his head away*) No, no, you mustn't! The doctor told you not to, didn't he? Please don't, Fred! It would be awful if anything happened to you—through me. (NICHOLLS *gives up his attempts, recalled to caution by her words. She raises her face and tries to force a smile through her tears*) But you can kiss me on the forehead, Fred. That can't do any harm. (*His face crimson, he does so. She laughs hysterically*) It seems so silly—being kissed that way—by you. (*She gulps back a sob and continues to attempt to joke*) I'll have to get used to it, won't I?

CURTAIN

ACT ONE—SCENE TWO

THE *reception room of the Infirmary, a large, high-ceilinged room painted white, with oiled, hardwood floor. In the left wall, forward, a row of four windows. Farther back, the main entrance from the driveway, and another window. In the rear wall left, a glass partition looking out on the sleeping porch. A row of white beds, with the faces of patients barely peeping out from under piles of heavy bedclothes, can be seen. To the right of this partition, a bookcase, and a door leading to the hall past the patients' rooms. Farther right, another*

53

door opening on the examining room. In the right wall, rear, a door
to the office. Farther forward, a row of windows. In front of the windows, a long dining table with chairs. On the left of the table, toward
the center of the room, a chimney with two open fireplaces, facing left
and right. Several wicker armchairs are placed around the fireplace
on the left in which a cheerful wood fire is crackling. To the left of
center, a round reading and writing table with a green-shaded electric
lamp. Other electric lights are in brackets around the walls. Easy
chairs stand near the table which is stacked with magazines. Rocking
chairs are placed here and there about the room, near the windows,
etc. A Victrola stands near the left wall, forward.

It is nearing eight o'clock of a cold evening about a week later.

At the rise of the curtain STEPHEN MURRAY is discovered sitting in a
chair in front of the fireplace, left. MURRAY is thirty years old—a tall,
slender, rather unusual-looking fellow with a pale face, sunken under
high cheek bones, lined about the eyes and mouth, jaded and worn
for one still so young. His intelligent, large hazel eyes have a tired,
dispirited expression in repose, but can quicken instantly with a concealment mechanism of mocking, careless humor whenever his inner
privacy is threatened. His large mouth aids this process of protection
by a quick change from its set apathy to a cheerful grin of cynical good
nature. He gives off the impression of being somehow dissatisfied with
himself but not yet embittered enough by it to take it out on others.
His manner, as revealed by his speech—nervous, inquisitive, alert—
seems more an acquired quality than any part of his real nature. He
stoops a trifle, giving him a slightly round-shouldered appearance. He
is dressed in a shabby dark suit, baggy at the knees. He is staring into
the fire, dreaming, an open book lying unheeded on the arm of his
chair. The Victrola is whining out the last strains of Dvorak's Humor-
esque. In the doorway to the office, MISS GILPIN stands talking to MISS
HOWARD. The former is a slight, middle-aged woman with black hair,
and a strong, intelligent face, its expression of resolute efficiency
softened and made kindly by her warm, sympathetic gray eyes. MISS

HOWARD *is tall, slender and blonde—decidedly pretty and provokingly conscious of it, yet with a certain air of seriousness underlying her apparent frivolity. She is twenty years old. The elder woman is dressed in the all white of a full-fledged nurse.* MISS HOWARD *wears the gray-blue uniform of one still in training. The record peters out.* MURRAY *sighs with relief but makes no move to get up and stop the grinding needle.* MISS HOWARD *hurries across to the machine.* MISS GILPIN *goes back into the office.*

MISS HOWARD. (*takes off the record, glancing at* MURRAY *with amused vexation*) It's a wonder you wouldn't stop this machine grinding itself to bits, Mr. Murray.

MURRAY. (*with a smile*) I was hoping the darn thing would bust. (MISS HOWARD *sniffs.* MURRAY *grins at her teasingly*) It keeps you from talking to me. That's the real music.

MISS HOWARD. (*comes over to his chair laughing*) I think you're a natural born kidder. All newspaper reporters are like that, I've heard.

MURRAY. You wrong me terribly. (*Then frowning*) And it isn't charitable to remind me of my job.

MISS HOWARD. (*surprised*) I think it's great to be able to write. You ought to be proud of it.

MURRAY. (*glumly*) I'm not. You can't call it writing—not what I did—small town stuff. (*Changing the subject*) Do you know when I'm to be moved to the shacks?

MISS HOWARD. In a few days, I guess. (MURRAY *grunts and moves nervously on his chair*) What's the matter? Don't you like us here at the Infirmary?

MURRAY. (*smiling*) Oh—you—yes! (*Then seriously*) I don't care for the atmosphere, though. (*He waves his hand toward the partition looking out on the porch*) All those people in bed out there on the porch seem so sick. It's depressing.

MISS HOWARD. All the patients have to come here first until Doctor

Stanton finds out whether they're well enough to be sent out to the shacks and cottages. And remember you're a patient.

MURRAY. I know it. But I don't feel as if I were—really sick like them.

MISS HOWARD. (*wisely*) None of them do, either.

MURRAY. (*after a moment's reflection—cynically*) Yes, I suppose it's that pipe dream keeps us all going, eh?

MISS HOWARD. Well, you ought to be thankful. (*Lowering her voice*) Shall I tell you a secret? I've seen your chart and *you've* no cause to worry. Doctor Stanton joked about it. He said you were too uninteresting—there was so little the matter with you.

MURRAY. (*pleased but pretending indifference*) Humph! He's original in that opinion.

MISS HOWARD. I know it's hard your being the only one up the week you've been here; but there's another patient due today. Maybe she'll be well enough to be around with you. (*With a quick glance at her wrist watch*) She can't be coming unless she got in on the last train.

MURRAY. (*interestedly*) It's a she, eh?

MISS HOWARD. Yes.

MURRAY. (*grinning provokingly*) Young?

MISS HOWARD. Eighteen, I believe. (*Seeing his grin—with feigned pique*) I suppose you'll be asking if she's pretty next! Her name is Carmody, that's the only other thing I know. So there!

MISS GILPIN. (*appearing in the office doorway*) Miss Howard.

MISS HOWARD. Yes, Miss Gilpin. (*In an aside to* MURRAY *as she leaves him*) It's time for those horrid diets. (*She hurries back into the office.* MURRAY *stares into the fire.* MISS HOWARD *reappears from the office and goes out by the door to the hall, rear. Carriage wheels are heard from the driveway in front of the house on the left. They stop. After a pause there is a sharp rap on the door and a bell rings insistently. Men's muffled voices are heard in argument.* MURRAY *turns curiously in his chair.* MISS GILPIN *comes from the office and walks quickly to the door, unlocking and opening it.* EILEEN *enters, followed by* NICHOLLS, *who is carrying her suitcase, and by her father.*)

EILEEN. I'm Miss Carmody. I believe Doctor Gaynor wrote—

MISS GILPIN. (*taking her hand—with kind affability*) We've been expecting you all day. How do you do? I'm Miss Gilpin. You came on the last train, didn't you?

EILEEN. (*heartened by the other woman's kindness*) Yes. This is my father, Miss Gilpin—and Mr. Nicholls. (MISS GILPIN *shakes hands cordially with the two men who are staring about the room in embarrassment.* CARMODY *has very evidently been drinking. His voice is thick and his face puffed and stupid.* NICHOLLS' *manner is that of one who is accomplishing a necessary but disagreeable duty with the best grace possible, but is frightfully eager to get it over and done with.* CARMODY's *condition embarrasses him acutely and when he glances at him it is with hatred and angry disgust.*)

MISS GILPIN. (*indicating the chairs in front of the windows on the left, forward*) Won't you gentlemen sit down? (CARMODY *grunts sullenly and plumps himself into the one nearest the door.* NICHOLLS *hesitates, glancing down at the suitcase he carries.* MISS GILPIN *turns to* EILEEN) And now we'll get you settled immediately. Your room is all ready for you. If you'll follow me— (*She turns toward the door in rear, center.*)

EILEEN. Let me take the suitcase now, Fred.

MISS GILPIN. (*as he is about to hand it to her—decisively*) No, my dear, you mustn't. Put the case right down there, Mr. Nicholls. I'll have it taken to Miss Carmody's room in a moment. (*She shakes her finger at* EILEEN *with kindly admonition*) That's the first rule you'll have to learn. Never exert yourself or tax your strength. You'll find laziness is a virtue instead of a vice with us.

EILEEN. (*confused*) I— I didn't know—

MISS GILPIN. (*smiling*) Of course you didn't. And now if you'll come with me I'll show you your room We'll have a little chat there and I can explain all the other important rules in a second. The gentlemen can make themselves comfortable in the meantime. We won't be gone more than a moment.

NICHOLLS. (*feeling called upon to say something*) Yes—we'll wait— certainly, we're all right. (CARMODY *remains silent, glowering at the fire.* NICHOLLS *sits down beside him.* MISS GILPIN *and* EILEEN *go out.* MURRAY *switches his chair so he can observe the two men out of the corner of his eye while pretending to be absorbed in his book.*)

CARMODY. (*looking about shiftily and reaching for the inside pocket of his overcoat*) I'll be havin' a nip now we're alone, and that cacklin' hen gone. (*He pulls out a pint flask, half full.*)

NICHOLLS. (*excitedly*) Put that bottle away! (*In a whisper*) Don't you see that fellow in the chair there?

CARMODY. (*taking a big drink*) Ah, I'm not mindin' a man at all. Sure I'll bet it's himself would be likin' a taste of the same. (*He appears about to get up and invite* MURRAY *to join him but* NICHOLLS *grabs his arm.*)

NICHOLLS. (*with a frightened look at* MURRAY *who appears buried in his book*) Stop it, you— Don't you know he's probably a patient and they don't allow them—

CARMODY. (*scornfully*) It's queer they'd be allowin' the sick ones to read books when I'll bet it's the same lazy readin' in the house brought the half of them down with the consumption itself. (*Raising his voice*) I'm thinkin' this whole shebang is a big, thievin' fake—and I've always thought so.

NICHOLLS. (*furiously*) Put that bottle away, damn it! And don't shout. You're not in a barrel-house.

CARMODY. (*with provoking calm*) I'll put it back when I'm ready, not before, and no lip from you!

NICHOLLS. (*with fierce disgust*) You're drunk now.

CARMODY. (*raging*) Drunk, am I? Is it the like of a young jackass like you that's still wet behind the ears to be tellin' me I'm drunk?

NICHOLLS. (*half-rising from his chair—pleadingly*) For heaven's sake, Mr. Carmody, remember where we are and don't raise any rumpus. What'll Eileen say?

CARMODY. (*puts the bottle away hastily, mumbling to himself—then glowers about the room scornfully with blinking eyes*) It's a grand hotel this is, I'm thinkin', for the rich to be takin' their ease, and not a hospital for the poor, but the poor has to pay for it.

NICHOLLS. (*fearful of another outbreak*) Sshh!

CARMODY. Don't be shshin' at me? I'd make Eileen come back out of this tonight if that divil of a doctor didn't have me by the throat.

NICHOLLS. (*glancing at him nervously*) I wonder how soon she'll be back? We'll have to hurry to make that last train.

CARMODY. (*angrily*) Is it anxious to get out of her sight you are, and you engaged to marry her? (NICHOLLS *flushes guiltily.* MURRAY *pricks up his ears and stares over at* NICHOLLS. *The latter meets his glance, scowls, and hurriedly averts his eyes.* CARMODY *goes on accusingly*) Sure, it's no heart at all you have—and her your sweetheart for years —and her sick with the consumption—and you wild to run away and leave her alone.

NICHOLLS. (*springing to his feet—furiously*) That's a—! (*He controls himself with an effort. His voice trembles*) You're not responsible for the idiotic things you're saying or I'd— (*He turns away, seeking some escape from the old man's tongue*) I'll see if the man is still there with the rig. (*He goes to the door on left and goes out.*)

CARMODY. (*following him with his eyes*) Go to hell, for all I'm preventin'. You've got no guts of a man in you. (*He addresses* MURRAY *with the good nature inspired by the flight of* NICHOLLS) Is it true you're one of the consumptives, young fellow?

MURRAY. (*delighted by this speech—with a grin*) Yes, I'm one of them.

CARMODY. My name's Carmody. What's yours, then?

MURRAY. Murray.

CARMODY. (*slapping his thigh*) Irish as Paddy's pig! (MURRAY *nods.*

CARMODY *brightens and grows confidential*) I'm glad to be knowin' you're one of us. You can keep an eye on Eileen.

MURRAY. I'll be glad to do all I can.

CARMODY. Thanks to you—though it's a grand life she'll be havin' here from the fine look of the place. (*With whining self-pity*) It's me it's hard on, God help me, with four small children and me widowed, and havin' to hire a woman to come in and look after them and the house now that Eileen's sick; and payin' for her curin' in this place, and me with only a bit of money in the bank for my old age. That's hard, now, on a man, and who'll say it isn't?

MURRAY. (*made uncomfortable by this confidence*) Hard luck always comes in bunches. (*To head off* CARMODY *who is about to give vent to more woe—quickly, with a glance toward the door from the hall*) If I'm not mistaken, here comes your daughter now.

CARMODY. (*as* EILEEN *comes into the room*) I'll make you acquainted. Eileen! (*She comes over to them, embarrassed to find her father in his condition so chummy with a stranger.* MURRAY *rises to his feet*) This is Mr. Murray, Eileen. He's Irish and he'll put you on to the ropes of the place. He's got the consumption, too, God pity him.

EILEEN. (*distressed*) Oh, Father, how can you— (*With a look at* MURRAY *which pleads for her father*) I'm glad to meet you, Mr. Murray.

MURRAY. (*with a straight glance at her which is so frankly admiring that she flushes and drops her eyes*) I'm glad to meet you. (*The front door is opened and* NICHOLLS *re-appears, shivering with the cold. He stares over at the others with ill-concealed irritation.*)

CARMODY. (*noticing him—with malicious satisfaction*) Oho, here you are again. (NICHOLLS *scowls and turns away.* CARMODY *addresses his daughter with a sly wink at* MURRAY) I thought Fred was slidin' down hill to the train, and him so desperate hurried to get away from here. Look at the knees on him clappin' together with the great fear he'll be catchin' a sickness in this place! (NICHOLLS, *his guilty conscience stabbed to the quick, turns pale with impotent rage.*)

EILEEN. (*remonstrating pitifully*) Father! Please! (*She hurries over to* NICHOLLS) Oh, please don't mind him, Fred! You know what he is when he's drinking.

NICHOLLS. (*thickly*) That's all right—for you to say. But I won't forget—I'm sick and tired standing for—I'm not used to—such people.

EILEEN. (*shrinking from him*) Fred!

NICHOLLS. (*with a furious glance at* MURRAY) Before that cheap slob, too.

EILEEN. (*faintly*) He seems—very nice.

NICHOLLS. You've got your eyes set on him already, have you?

EILEEN. Fred!

NICHOLLS. Well, go ahead if you want to. I don't care. I'll— (*Startled by the look of anguish which comes over her face, he hastily swallows his words. He takes out watch—fiercely*) We'll miss that train, damn it!

EILEEN. (*in a stricken tone*) Oh, Fred! (*Then forcing back her tears she calls to* CARMODY *in a strained voice*) Father! You'll have to go now.

CARMODY. (*shaking hands with* MURRAY) Keep your eye on her. I'll be out soon to see her and you and me'll have another chin.

MURRAY. Glad to. Good-by for the present. (*He walks to windows on the far right, turning his back considerately on their leave-taking.*)

EILEEN. (*comes to* CARMODY *and hangs on his arm as they proceed to the door*) Be sure and kiss them all for me—and bring them out to see me as soon as you can, Father, please! And don't forget to tell Mrs. Brennan all the directions I gave you coming out on the train. I told her but she mightn't remember—about Mary's bath—and to give Tom his—

CARMODY. (*impatiently*) Hasn't she brought up brats of her own, and doesn't she know the way of it?

EILEEN. (*helplessly*) Never mind telling her, then. I'll write to her.

CARMODY. You'd better not. She'll not wish you mixin' in with her work and tellin' her how to do it.

EILEEN. (*aghast*) Her work! (*She seems at the end of her tether—*

wrung too dry for any further emotion. She kisses her father at the door with indifference and speaks calmly) Good-by, Father.

CARMODY. *(in a whining tone of injury)* A cold kiss! Is your heart a stone? *(Drunken tears well from his eyes and he blubbers)* And your own father going back to a lone house with a stranger in it!

EILEEN. *(wearily in a dead voice)* You'll miss your train, Father.

CARMODY. *(raging in a second)* I'm off, then! Come on, Fred. It's no welcome we have with her here in this place—and a great curse on this day I brought her to it! *(He stamps out.)*

EILEEN. *(in the same dead tone)* Good-by, Fred.

NICHOLLS. *(repenting his words of a moment ago—confusedly)* I'm sorry, Eileen—for what I said. I didn't mean—you know what your father is—excuse me, won't you?

EILEEN. *(without feeling)* Yes.

NICHOLLS. And I'll be out soon—in a week if I can make it. Well then,—good-by for the present. *(He bends down as if to kiss her but she shrinks back out of his reach.)*

EILEEN. *(a faint trace of mockery in her weary voice)* No, Fred. Remember you mustn't now.

NICHOLLS. *(in an instant huff)* Oh, if that's the way you feel about — (*He strides out and slams the door viciously behind him.* EILEEN *walks slowly back toward the fireplace, her face fixed in the dead calm of despair. As she sinks into one of the armchairs, the strain becomes too much. She breaks down, hiding her face in her hands, her frail shoulders heaving with the violence of her sobs. At this sound,* MURRAY *turns from the windows and comes over near her chair.)*

MURRAY. *(after watching her for a moment—in an embarrassed tone of sympathy)* Come on, Miss Carmody, that'll never do. I know it's hard at first—but— It isn't so bad up here—really—once you get used to it! *(The shame she feels at giving way in the presence of a stranger only adds to her loss of control and she sobs heartbrokenly.* MURRAY *walks up and down nervously, visibly nonplussed and upset.*

Finally he hits upon something) One of the nurses will be in any minute. You don't want them to see you like this.

EILEEN. (*chokes back her sobs and finally raises her face and attempts a smile*) I'm sorry—to make such a sight of myself.

MURRAY. (*jocularly*) Well, they say a cry does you a lot of good.

EILEEN. (*forcing a smile*) I do feel—better.

MURRAY. (*staring at her with a quizzical smile—cynically*) You shouldn't take those lovers' squabbles so seriously. Tomorrow he'll be sorry. He'll write begging forgiveness. Result—all serene again.

EILEEN. (*a shadow of pain on her face—with dignity*) Don't—please.

MURRAY. (*angry at himself—hanging his head contritely*) Pardon me. I'm rude sometimes—before I know it. (*He shakes off his confusion with a renewed attempt at a joking tone*) You can blame your father for any breaks I make. He told me to see that you behaved.

EILEEN. (*with a genuine smile*) Oh, Father! (*Flushing*) You mustn't mind anything he said tonight.

MURRAY. (*thoughtlessly*) Yes, he was well lit up. I envied him. (EILEEN *looks very shamefaced.* MURRAY *sees it and exclaims in exasperation at himself*) Darn! There I go again putting my foot in it! (*With an irrepressible grin*) I ought to have my tongue operated on —that's what's the matter with me. (*He laughs and throws himself in a chair.*)

EILEEN. (*forced in spite of herself to smile with him*) You're candid, at any rate, Mr. Murray.

MURRAY. I said I envied him his jag and that's the truth. The same candor compels me to confess that I was pickled to the gills myself when I arrived here. Fact! I made love to all the nurses and generally disgraced myself—and had a wonderful time.

EILEEN. I suppose it does make you forget your troubles.

MURRAY. (*waving this aside*) I didn't want to forget—not for a second. I wasn't drowning my sorrow. I was hilariously celebrating.

EILEEN. (*astonished—by this time quite interested in this queer fel-*

low to the momentary forgetfulness of her own grief) Celebrating—coming here? But—aren't you sick?

MURRAY. Yes, of course. (*Confidentially*) But it's only a matter of time when I'll be all right again. I hope it won't be too soon.

EILEEN. (*with wide eyes*) I wonder if you really mean—

MURRAY. I sure do—every word of it!

EILEEN. (*puzzled*) I can't understand how anyone could— (*With a worried glance over her shoulder*) I think I'd better look for Miss Gilpin, hadn't I? She may wonder— (*She half rises from her chair.*)

MURRAY. (*quickly*) No. Please don't go yet. (*She glances at him irresolutely, then resumes her chair*) I'll see to it that you don't fracture any rules. (*Hitching his chair nearer hers,—impulsively*) In all charity to me you've got to stick awhile. I haven't had a chance to really talk to a soul for a week. You found what I said a while ago hard to believe, didn't you?

EILEEN. (*with a smile*) You said you hoped you wouldn't get well too soon!

MURRAY. And I meant it! This place is honestly like heaven to me —a lonely heaven till your arrival. (EILEEN *looks embarrassed*) And why wouldn't it be? Just let me tell you what I was getting away from — (*With a sudden laugh full of weary bitterness*) Do you know what it means to work from seven at night till three in the morning on a morning newspaper in a town of twenty thousand people—for *ten years?* No. You don't. You can't. But what it did to me—it made me happy—yes, happy!—to get out here!

EILEEN. (*looking at him curiously*) But I always thought being a reporter was so interesting.

MURRAY. (*with a cynical laugh*) On a small town rag? A month of it, perhaps, when you're new to the game. But ten years! With only a raise of a couple of dollars every blue moon or so, and a weekly spree on Saturday night to vary the monotony. (*He laughs again*) Interesting, eh? Getting the dope on the Social of the Queen Esther Circle in the basement of the Methodist Episcopal Church, unable to sleep through a meeting of the Common Council on account of the noisy oratory caused by John Smith's application for a permit to build a house; making a note that a tugboat towed two barges loaded with coal up the river, that Mrs. Perkins spent a week-end with relatives in Hickville, that John Jones— Oh help! Why go on? I'm a broken man. God, how I used to pray that our Congressman would commit suicide, or the Mayor murder his wife—just to be able to write a real story!

EILEEN. (*with a smile*) Is it as bad as that? But weren't there other things that were interesting?

MURRAY. (*decidedly*) Nope. Never anything new—and I knew everyone and everything in town by heart years ago. (*With sudden bitterness*) Oh, it was my own fault. Why didn't I get out of it? Well, I was always going to—tomorrow—and tomorrow never came. I got in a rut—and stayed put. People seem to get that way, somehow—in that town. It took T. B. to blast me loose.

EILEEN. (*wonderingly*) But—your family—

MURRAY. I haven't much of a family left. My mother died when I was a kid. My father—he was a lawyer—died when I was nineteen, just about to go to college. He left nothing, so I went to work instead. I've two sisters, respectably married and living in another part of the state. We don't get along—but they're paying for me here, so I suppose I've no kick. (*Cynically*) A family wouldn't have changed things. From what I've seen that blood-thicker-than-water dope is all wrong. It's thinner than table-d'hôte soup. You may have seen a bit of that truth in your own case already.

EILEEN. (*shocked*) How can you say that? You don't know—

MURRAY. Don't I, though? Wait till you've been here three months or four. You'll see then!

EILEEN. (*angrily, her lips trembling*) You must be crazy to say such things! (*Fighting back her tears*) Oh, I think it's hateful—when you see how badly I feel!

MURRAY. (*in acute confusion—stammering*) Look here, Miss Carmody, I didn't mean to— Listen—don't feel mad at me, please. I was only talking. I'm like that. You mustn't take it seriously.

EILEEN. (*still resentful*) I don't see how you can talk—when you've just said you had no family of your own, really.

MURRAY. (*eager to return to her good graces*) Of course I don't know. I was just talking regardless for the fun of it.

EILEEN. (*after a pause*) Hasn't either of your sisters any children?

MURRAY. One of them has—two squally little brats.

EILEEN. (*disapprovingly*) You don't like babies?

MURRAY. (*bluntly*) No. (*Then with a grin at her shocked face*) I don't get them. They're something I can't seem to get acquainted with.

EILEEN. (*with a smile, indulgently*) You're a funny person. (*Then with a superior motherly air*) No wonder you couldn't understand how badly I feel. (*With a tender smile*) I've four of them—my brothers and sisters—though they're not what you'd call babies, except to me. I've been a mother to them now for a whole year—ever since our mother died. (*Sadly*) And I don't know how they'll ever get along while I'm away.

MURRAY. (*cynically*) Oh, they'll— (*He checks what he was going to say and adds lamely*)—get along somehow.

EILEEN. (*with the same superior tone*) It's easy for you to say that. You don't know how children grow to depend on you for everything. You're not a woman.

MURRAY. (*with a grin*) Are you? (*Then with a chuckle*) You're as old as the pyramids, aren't you? I feel like a little boy. Won't you adopt me, too?

EILEEN. (*flushing, with a shy smile*) Someone ought to. (*Quickly changing the subject*) Do you know, I can't get over what you said about hating your work so? I should think it would be wonderful— to be able to write things.

MURRAY. My job had nothing to do with writing. To write—really write—yes, that's something worth trying for. That's what I've always meant to have a stab at. I've run across ideas enough for stories—that sounded good to me, anyway. (*With a forced laugh*) But—like everything else—I never got down to it. I started one or two—but—either I thought I didn't have the time or— (*He shrugs his shoulders.*)

EILEEN. Well, you've plenty of time now, haven't you?

MURRAY. (*instantly struck by this suggestion*) You mean— I could write up here? (*She nods. His face lights up with enthusiasm*) Say! That is an idea! Thank you! I'd never have had sense enough to have thought of that myself. (EILEEN *flushes with pleasure*) Sure there's time—nothing but time up here—

EILEEN. Then you seriously think you'll try it?

MURRAY. (*determinedly*) Yes. Why not? I've got to try and do something real sometime, haven't I? I've no excuse not to, now. My mind isn't sick.

EILEEN. (*excitedly*) That'll be wonderful!

MURRAY. (*confidently*) Listen. I've had ideas for a series of short stories for the last couple of years—small town experiences, some of them actual. I know that life too darn well. I ought to be able to write about it. And if I can sell one—to the *Post,* say—I'm sure they'd take the others, too. And then— I should worry! It'd be easy sailing. But you must promise to help—play critic for me—read them and tell me where they're rotten.

EILEEN. (*pleased but protesting*) Oh, no, I'd never dare. I don't know anything—

MURRAY. Yes, you do. And you started me off on this thing, so you've got to back me up now. (*Suddenly*) Say, I wonder if they'd let me have a typewriter up here?

EILEEN. It'd be fine if they would. I'd like to have one, too—to practice.

MURRAY. I don't see why they wouldn't allow it. You're not sick enough to be kept in bed, I'm sure of that.

EILEEN. I— I don't know—

MURRAY. Here! None of that! You just think you're not and you won't be. Say, I'm keen on that typewriter idea.

EILEEN. (*eagerly*) And I could type your stories after you've written them! I *could* help that way.

MURRAY. (*smiling*) But I'm quite able— (*Then seeing how interested she is he adds hurriedly*) That'd be great! I've always been a bum at a machine. And I'd be willing to pay whatever— (MISS GILPIN *enters from the rear and walks toward them.*)

EILEEN. (*quickly*) Oh, no! I'd be glad to get the practice. I wouldn't accept— (*She coughs slightly.*)

MURRAY. (*with a laugh*) Maybe, after you've read my stuff, you won't type it at any price.

MISS GILPIN. Miss Carmody, may I speak to you for a moment, please? (*She takes* EILEEN *aside and talks to her in low tones of admonition.* EILEEN'S *face falls. She nods a horrified acquiescence.* MISS GILPIN *leaves her and goes into the office, rear.*)

MURRAY. (*as* EILEEN *comes back—noticing her perturbation— kindly*) Well? Now, what's the trouble?

EILEEN. (*her lips trembling*) She told me I mustn't forget to shield my mouth with my handkerchief when I cough.

MURRAY. (*consolingly*) Yes, that's one of the rules, you know.

EILEEN. (*falteringly*) She said they'd give me—a—cup to carry around— (*She stops, shuddering.*)

MURRAY. (*easily*) It's not as bad as it sounds. They're only little paste-board things you carry in your pocket.

EILEEN. (*as if speaking to herself*) It's so horrible. (*She holds out her hand to* MURRAY) I'm to go to my room now. Good-night, Mr. Murray.

MURRAY. (*holding her hand for a moment—earnestly*) Don't mind your first impressions here. You'll look on everything as a matter of course in a few days. I felt your way at first. (*He drops her hand and shakes his finger at her*) Mind your guardian, now! (*She forces a trembling smile*) See you at breakfast. Good-night. (EILEEN *goes out to the hall in rear.* MISS HOWARD *comes in from the door just after her,* *carrying a glass of milk.*)

MISS HOWARD. Almost bedtime, Mr. Murray. Here's your diet. (*He* *takes the glass. She smiles at him provokingly*) Well, is it love at first sight?

MURRAY. (*with a grin*) Sure thing! You can consider yourself heartlessly jilted. (*He turns and raises his glass toward the door through* *which* EILEEN *has just gone, as if toasting her.*)

> "A glass of milk, and thou
>   Coughing beside me in the wilderness—
>   Ah—wilderness were Paradise enow!"

(*He takes a sip of milk.*)

MISS HOWARD. (*peevishly*) That's old stuff, Mr. Murray. A patient at Saranac wrote that parody.

MURRAY. (*maliciously*) Aha, you've discovered it's a parody, have you, you sly minx! (MISS HOWARD *turns from him huffily and walks* *back towards the office, her chin in the air.*)

CURTAIN

ACT TWO—SCENE ONE

THE *assembly room of the main building of the sanatorium—early in the morning of a fine day in June, four months later. The room is large, light and airy, painted a fresh white. On the left forward, an armchair. Farther back, a door opening on the main hall. To the rear of this door a pianola on a raised platform. In back of the pianola, a door leading into the office. In the rear wall, a long series of French windows looking out on the lawn, with wooded hills in the far background. Shrubs in flower grow immediately outside the windows. Inside, there is a row of potted plants. In the right wall, rear, four windows. Farther forward, a long, well-filled bookcase, and a doorway leading into the dining room. Following the walls, but about five feet out from them a stiff line of chairs placed closely against each other forms a sort of right-angled auditorium of which the large, square table that stands at center, forward, would seem to be the stage.*

From the dining room comes the clatter of dishes, the confused murmur of many voices, male and female—all the mingled sounds of a crowd of people at a meal.

After the curtain rises, DOCTOR STANTON *enters from the hall, followed by a visitor,* MR. SLOAN, *and the assistant physician,* DOCTOR SIMMS. DOCTOR STANTON *is a handsome man of forty-five or so with a grave, care-lined, studious face lightened by a kindly, humorous smile. His gray eyes, saddened by the suffering they have witnessed, have the sympathetic quality of real understanding. The look they give is full of companionship, the courage-renewing, human companionship of a hope which is shared. He speaks with a slight Southern accent, soft and slurring.* DOCTOR SIMMS *is a tall, angular young man with a long, sallow face and a sheepish, self-conscious grin.* MR. SLOAN *is fifty, short and stout, well dressed—one of the successful business men whose endowments have made the Hill Farm a possibility.*

STANTON. (*as they enter*) This is the general assembly room, Mr. Sloan—where the patients of both sexes are allowed to congregate together after meals, for diets, and in the evening.

SLOAN. (*looking around him*) Couldn't be more pleasant, I must say. (*He walks where he can take a peep into the dining room*) Ah, they're all at breakfast, I see.

STANTON. (*smiling*) Yes, and with no lack of appetite, let me tell you. (*With a laugh of proud satisfaction*) They'd sure eat us out of house and home at one sitting, if we'd give them the opportunity.

SLOAN. (*with a smile*) That's fine. (*With a nod toward the dining room*) The ones in there are the sure cures, aren't they?

STANTON. (*a shadow coming over his face*) Strictly speaking, there are no sure cures in this disease, Mr. Sloan. When we permit a patient to return to take up his or her activities in the world, the patient is what we call an arrested case. The disease is overcome, quiescent; the wound is healed over. It's then up to the patient to so take care of himself that this condition remains permanent. It isn't hard for them to do this, usually. Just ordinary, bull-headed common sense—added to what they've learned here—is enough. And the precautions we teach them to take don't diminish their social usefulness in the slightest, either, as I can prove by our statistics of former patients. (*With a smile*) It's rather early in the morning for statistics, though.

MR. SLOAN. (*with a wave of the hand*) Oh, you needn't. Your reputation in that respect, Doctor— (STANTON *inclines his head in acknowledgment.* SLOAN *jerks his thumb toward the dining room*) But the ones in there *are* getting well, aren't they?

STANTON. To all appearances, yes. You don't dare swear to it, though. Sometimes, just when a case looks most favorable, there's a sudden, unforeseen breakdown and they have to be sent back to bed, or, if it's very serious, back to the Infirmary again. These are the ex-

71

ceptions, however, not the rule. You can bank on most of those eaters being out in the world and usefully employed within six months.

SLOAN. You couldn't say more than that. (*Abruptly*) But—the unfortunate ones—do you have many deaths?

STANTON. (*with a frown*) No. We're under a very hard, almost cruel imperative which prevents that. If, at the end of six months, a case shows no response to treatment, continues to go down hill—if, in a word, it seems hopeless—we send them away, to one of the State Farms if they have no private means. (*Apologetically*) You see, this sanatorium is overcrowded and has a long waiting list most of the time of others who demand their chance for life. We have to make places for them. We have no time to waste on incurables. There are other places for them—and sometimes, too, a change is beneficial and they pick up in new surroundings. You never can tell. But we're bound by the rule. It may seem cruel—but it's as near justice to all concerned as we can come.

SLOAN. (*soberly*) I see. (*His eyes fall on the pianola—in surprise*) Ah—a piano.

STANTON. (*replying to the other's thought*) Yes, the patients play and sing. (*With a smile*) If you'd call the noise they make by those terms. They'd dance, too, if we permitted it. There's only one song taboo—Home, Sweet Home—for obvious reasons.

SLOAN. I see. (*With a final look around*) Did I understand you to say this is the only place where the sexes are permitted to mingle?

STANTON. Yes, sir.

SLOAN. (*with a smile*) Not much chance for a love affair, then.

STANTON. (*seriously*) We do our best to prevent them. We even have a strict rule which allows us to step in and put a stop to any intimacy which grows beyond the casual. People up here, Mr. Sloan, are expected to put aside all ideas except the one—getting well.

SLOAN. (*somewhat embarrassed*) A damn good rule, too, under the circumstances.

STANTON. (*with a laugh*) Yes, we're strictly anti-Cupid, sir, from top to bottom. (*Turning to the door to the hall*) And now, if you don't mind, Mr. Sloan, I'm going to turn you footloose to wander about the grounds on an unconducted tour. Today is my busy morning—Saturday. We weigh each patient immediately after breakfast.

SLOAN. Every week?

STANTON. Every Saturday. You see we depend on fluctuations in weight to tell us a lot about the patient's condition. If they gain, or stay at normal, all's usually well. If they lose week after week, we keep careful watch. It's a sign that something's wrong.

SLOAN. (*with a smile*) Well, you just shoo me off wherever you please and go on with the good work. I'll be glad of a ramble in the open.

STANTON. After the weighing is over, sir, I'll be free to— (*His words are lost as the three go out. A moment later,* EILEEN *enters from the dining room. She has grown stouter, her face has more of a healthy, out-of-door color, but there is still about her the suggestion of being worn down by a burden too oppressive for her strength. She is dressed in shirtwaist and dark skirt. She goes to the armchair, left forward, and sinks down on it. She is evidently in a state of nervous depression; she twists her fingers together in her lap; her eyes stare sadly before her; she clenches her upper lip with her teeth to prevent its trembling. She has hardly regained control over herself when* STEPHEN MURRAY *comes in hurriedly from the dining room and, seeing her at his first glance, walks quickly over to her chair. He is the picture of health, his figure has filled out solidly, his tanned face beams with suppressed exultation.*)

MURRAY. (*excitedly*) Eileen! I saw you leave your table. I've something to tell you. I didn't get a chance last night after the mail came. Just listen, Eileen—it's too good to be true—but in that mail—guess what?

EILEEN. (*forgetting her depression—with an excited smile*) I know! You've sold your story!

MURRAY. (*triumphantly*) Go to the head of the class. What d'you know about that for luck! My first, too—and only the third magazine I sent it to! (*He cuts a joyful caper.*)

EILEEN. (*happily*) Isn't that wonderful, Stephen! But I knew all the time you would. The story's so good.

MURRAY. Well, you might have known but I didn't think there was a chance in the world. And as for being good— (*With superior air*) —wait till I turn loose with the real big ones, the kind I'm going to write. Then I'll make them sit up and take notice. They can't stop me now. And I haven't told you the best part. The editor wrote saying how much he liked the yarn and asked me for more of the same kind.

EILEEN. And you've the three others about the same person—just as good, too! (*She claps her hands delightedly.*)

MURRAY. And I can send them out right away. They're all typed, thanks to you. That's what's brought me luck, I know. I never had a bit by myself. (*Then, after a quick glance around to make sure they are alone, he bends down and kisses her*) There! A token of gratitude —even if it is against the rules.

EILEEN. (*flushing—with timid happiness*) Stephen! You mustn't! They'll see.

MURRAY. (*boldly*) Let them!

EILEEN. But you know—they've warned us against being so much together, already.

MURRAY. Let them! We'll be out of this prison soon. (EILEEN *shakes her head sadly but he does not notice*) Oh, I wish you could leave when I do. We'd have some celebration together.

EILEEN. (*her lips trembling*) I was thinking last night—that you'd be going away. You look so well. Do you think—they'll let you go— soon?

MURRAY. You bet I do. I caught Stanton in the hall last night and asked him if I could go.

EILEEN. (*anxiously*) What did he say?

MURRAY. He only smiled and said: "We'll see if you gain weight tomorrow." As if that mattered now! Why, I'm way above normal as it is! But you know Stanton—always putting you off.

EILEEN. (*slowly*) Then—if you gain today—

MURRAY. He'll let me go. I'm going to insist on it.

EILEEN. Then—you'll leave—?

MURRAY. The minute I can get packed.

EILEEN. (*trying to force a smile*) Oh, I'm so glad—for your sake; but—I'm selfish—it'll be so lonely here without you.

MURRAY. (*consolingly*) You'll be going away yourself before long. (EILEEN *shakes her head. He goes on without noticing, wrapped in his own success*) Oh, Eileen, you can't imagine all it opens up for me —selling that story. I can go straight to New York, and live, and meet real people who are doing things. I can take my time, and try and do the work I hope to. (*Feelingly*) You don't know how grateful I am to you, Eileen—how you've helped me. Oh, I don't mean just the typing, I mean your encouragement, your faith! The stories would never have been written if it hadn't been for you.

EILEEN. (*choking back a sob*) I didn't do—anything.

MURRAY. (*staring down at her—with rough kindliness*) Here, here, that'll never do! You're not weeping about it, are you, silly? (*He pats her on the shoulder*) What's the matter, Eileen? You didn't eat a thing this morning. I was watching you. (*With kindly severity*) That's no way to gain weight, you know. You'll have to feed up. Do you hear what your guardian commands, eh?

EILEEN. (*with dull hopelessness*) I know I'll lose again. I've been losing steadily the past three weeks.

MURRAY. Here! Don't you dare talk that way! Why, you've been picking up wonderfully—until just lately. Even the old Doc has told you how much he admired your pluck, and how much better you were getting. You're not going to quit now, are you?

EILEEN. (*despairingly*) Oh, I don't care! I don't care—now.

MURRAY. Now? What do you mean by that? What's happened to make things any different?

EILEEN. (*evasively*) Oh—nothing. Don't ask me, Stephen.

MURRAY. (*with sudden anger*) I don't have to ask you. I can guess. Another letter from home—or from that ass, eh?

EILEEN. (*shaking her head*) No, it isn't that. (*She looks at him as if imploring him to comprehend.*)

MURRAY. (*furiously*). Of course, you'd deny it. You always do. But don't you suppose I've got eyes? It's been the same damn thing all the time you've been here. After every nagging letter—thank God they don't write often any more!—you've been all in; and after their Sunday visits—you can thank God they've been few, too—you're utterly knocked out. It's a shame!

EILEEN. Stephen!

MURRAY. (*relentlessly*) They've done nothing but worry and torment you and do their best to keep you from getting well.

EILEEN. (*faintly*) You're not fair, Stephen.

MURRAY. Rot! When it isn't your father grumbling about expense, it's the kids, or that stupid housekeeper, or that slick Aleck, Nicholls, with his cowardly lies. Which is it this time?

EILEEN. (*pitifully*) None of them.

MURRAY. (*explosively*) But him, especially—the dirty cad! Oh, I've got a rich notion to pay a call on that gentleman when I leave and tell him what I think of him.

EILEEN. (*quickly*) No—you mustn't ever! He's not to blame. If you knew— (*She stops, lowering her eyes in confusion.*)

MURRAY. (*roughly*) Knew what? You make me sick, Eileen—always finding excuses for him. I never could understand what a girl like you could see— But what's the use? I've said all this before. You're wasting yourself on a— (*Rudely*) Love must be blind. And yet you say you don't love him, really?

EILEEN. (*shaking her head—helplessly*) But I do—like Fred. We've been good friends so many years. I don't want to hurt him—his pride—

MURRAY. That's the same as answering no to my question. Then, if you don't love him, why don't you write and tell him to go to—break it off? (EILEEN *bows her head but doesn't reply. Irritated,* MURRAY *continues brutally*) Are you afraid it would break his heart? Don't be a fool! The only way you could do that would be to deprive him of his meals.

EILEEN. (*springing to her feet—distractedly*) Please stop, Stephen! You're cruel! And you've been so kind—the only real friend I've had up here. Don't spoil it all now.

MURRAY. (*remorsefully*) I'm sorry, Eileen. I won't say another word. (*Irritably*) Still someone ought to say or do something to put a stop to—

EILEEN. (*with a broken laugh*) Never mind. Everything will stop—soon, now!

MURRAY. (*suspiciously*) What do you mean?

EILEEN. (*with an attempt at a careless tone*) Nothing. If you can't see— (*She turns to him with sudden intensity*) Oh, Stephen, if you only knew how wrong you are about everything you've said. It's all true; but it isn't that—any of it—any more— that's— Oh, I can't tell you!

MURRAY. (*with great interest*) Please do, Eileen!

EILEEN. (*with a helpless laugh*) No.

MURRAY. Please tell me what it is! Let me help you.

EILEEN. No. It wouldn't be any use, Stephen.

MURRAY. (*offended*) Why do you say that? Haven't I helped before?

EILEEN. Yes—but this—

MURRAY. Come now! 'Fess up! What is "this"?

EILEEN. No. I couldn't speak of it here, anyway. They'll all be coming out soon.

MURRAY. (*insistently*) Then when? Where?

EILEEN. Oh, I don't know—perhaps never, nowhere. I don't know — Sometime before you leave, maybe.

77

MURRAY. But I may go tomorrow morning—if I gain weight and Stanton lets me.

EILEEN. (*sadly*) Yes, I was forgetting—you were going right away. (*Dully*) Then nowhere I suppose—never. (*Glancing toward the dining room*) They're all getting up. Let's not talk about it any more —now.

MURRAY. (*stubbornly*) But you'll tell me later, Eileen? You must.

EILEEN. (*vaguely*) Perhaps. It depends— (*The patients, about forty in number, straggle in from the dining room by twos and threes, chatting in low tones. The men and women with few exceptions separate into two groups, the women congregating in the left right angle of chairs, the men sitting or standing in the right right angle. In appearance, most of the patients are tanned, healthy, and cheerful looking. The great majority are under middle age. Their clothes are of the cheap, readymade variety. They are all distinctly of the wage-earning class. They might well be a crowd of cosmopolitan factory workers gathered together after a summer vacation. A hollow-chestedness and a tendency to round shoulders may be detected as a common characteristic. A general air of tension, marked by frequent bursts of laughter in too high a key, seems to pervade the throng.* MURRAY *and* EILEEN, *as if to avoid contact with the others, come over to the right in front of the dining-room door.*)

MURRAY. (*in a low voice*) Listen to them laugh. Did you ever notice —perhaps it's my imagination—how forced they act on Saturday mornings before they're weighed?

EILEEN. (*dully*) No.

MURRAY. Can't you tell me that secret now? No one'll hear.

EILEEN. (*vehemently*) No, no, how could I? Don't speak of it! (*A sudden silence falls on all the groups at once. Their eyes, by a common impulse, turn quickly toward the door to the hall.*)

A WOMAN. (*nervously—as if this moment's silent pause oppressed her*) Play something, Peters. They ain't coming yet. (PETERS, *a stupid-looking young fellow with a sly, twisted smirk which gives him the appearance of perpetually winking his eye, detaches himself from a group on the right. All join in with urging exclamations: "Go on, Peters! Go to it! Pedal up, Pete! Give us a rag! That's the boy, Peters!" etc.*)

PETERS. Sure, if I got time. (*He goes to the pianola and puts in a roll. The mingled conversation and laughter bursts forth again as he sits on the bench and starts pedaling.*)

MURRAY. (*disgustedly*) It's sure good to think I won't have to listen to that old tin-pan being banged much longer! (*The music interrupts him—a quick rag. The patients brighten, hum, whistle, sway their heads or tap their feet in time to the tune.* DOCTOR STANTON *and* DOCTOR SIMMS *appear in the doorway from the hall. All eyes are turned on them.*)

STANTON. (*raising his voice*) They all seem to be here, Doctor. We might as well start. (MRS. TURNER, *the matron, comes in behind them— a stout, motherly, capable-looking woman with gray hair. She hears* STANTON'S *remark.*)

MRS. TURNER. And take temperatures after, Doctor?

STANTON. Yes, Mrs. Turner. I think that's better today.

MRS. TURNER. All right, Doctor. (STANTON *and the assistant go out.* MRS. TURNER *advances a step or so into the room and looks from one group of patients to the other, inclining her head and smiling benevolently. All force smiles and nod in recognition of her greeting.* PETERS, *at the pianola, lets the music slow down, glancing questioningly at the matron to see if she is going to order it stopped. Then, encouraged by her smile, his feet pedal harder than ever.*)

MURRAY. Look at old Mrs. Grundy's eyes pinned on us! She'll accuse us of being too familiar again, the old wench!

EILEEN. Ssshh. You're wrong. She's looking at me, not at us.

MURRAY. At you? Why?

EILEEN. I ran a temperature yesterday. It must have been over a hundred last night.

MURRAY. (*with consoling scepticism*) You're always suffering for

79

trouble, Eileen. How do you know you ran a temp? You didn't see the stick, I suppose?

EILEEN. No—but—I could tell. I felt feverish and chilly. It must have been way up.

MURRAY. Bosh! If it was you'd have been sent to bed.

EILEEN. That's why she's looking at me. (*Piteously*) Oh, I do hope I won't be sent back to bed! I don't know what I'd do. If I could only gain this morning. If my temp has only gone down! (*Hopelessly*) But I feel— I didn't sleep a wink—thinking—

MURRAY. (*roughly*) You'll persuade yourself you've got leprosy in a second. Don't be a nut! It's all imagination, I tell you. You'll gain. Wait and see if you don't. (EILEEN *shakes her head. A metallic rumble and jangle comes from the hallway. Everyone turns in that direction with nervous expectancy.*)

MRS. TURNER. (*admonishingly*) Mr. Peters!

PETERS. Yes, ma'am. (*He stops playing and rejoins the group of men on the right. In the midst of a silence broken only by hushed murmurs of conversation,* DOCTOR STANTON *appears in the hall doorway. He turns to help his assistant wheel in a Fairbanks scale on casters. They place the scale against the wall immediately to the rear of the doorway.* DOCTOR SIMMS *adjusts it to a perfect balance.*)

DOCTOR STANTON. (*takes a pencil from his pocket and opens the record book he has in his hand*) All ready, Doctor?

DOCTOR SIMMS. Just a second, sir.

MURRAY. (*with a nervous smile*) Well, we're all set. Here's hoping!

EILEEN. You'll gain, I'm sure you will. You look so well.

MURRAY. Oh—I—I wasn't thinking of myself, I'm a sure thing. I was betting on you. I've simply got to gain today, when so much depends on it.

EILEEN. Yes, I hope you— (*She falters brokenly and turns away from him.*)

DOCTOR SIMMS. (*straightening up*) All ready, Doctor.

STANTON. (*nods and glances at his book—without raising his voice—*

distinctly) Mrs. Abner. (*A middle-aged woman comes and gets on the scales.* SIMMS *adjusts it to her weight of the previous week which* STANTON *reads to him from the book in a low voice, and weighs her.*)

MURRAY. (*with a relieved sigh*) They're off. (*Noticing* EILEEN's *downcast head and air of dejection*) Here! Buck up, Eileen! Old Lady Grundy's watching you—and it's your turn in a second. (EILEEN *raises her head and forces a frightened smile.* MRS. ABNER *gets down off the scales with a pleased grin. She has evidently gained. She rejoins the group of women, chattering volubly in low tones. Her exultant "gained half a pound" can be heard. The other women smile their perfunctory congratulations, their eyes absent-minded, intent on their own worries.* STANTON *writes down the weight in the book.*)

STANTON. Miss Bailey. (*A young girl goes to the scales.*)

MURRAY. Bailey looks badly, doesn't she?

EILEEN. (*her lips trembling*) She's been losing, too.

MURRAY. Well, *you're* going to gain today. Remember, now!

EILEEN. (*with a feeble smile*) I'll try to obey your orders. (MISS BAILEY *gets down off the scales. Her eyes are full of despondency although she tries to make a brave face of it, forcing a laugh as she joins the women. They stare at her with pitying looks and murmur consoling phrases.*)

EILEEN. She's lost again. Oh, I wish I didn't have to get weighed—

STANTON. Miss Carmody. (EILEEN *starts nervously.*)

MURRAY. (*as she leaves him*) Remember now! Break the scales! (*She walks quickly to the scales, trying to assume an air of defiant indifference. The balance stays down as she steps up.* EILEEN's *face shows her despair at this.* SIMMS *weighs her and gives the poundage in a low voice to* STANTON. EILEEN *steps down mechanically, then hesitates as if not knowing where to turn, her anguished eyes flitting from one group to another.*)

MURRAY. (*savagely*) Damn! (DOCTOR STANTON *writes the figures in his book, glances sharply at* EILEEN, *and then nods significantly to* MRS. TURNER *who is standing beside him.*)

STANTON. (*calling the next*) Miss Doeffler. (*Another woman comes to be weighed.*)

MRS. TURNER. Miss Carmody! Will you come here a moment, please?

EILEEN. (*her face growing very pale*) Yes, Mrs. Turner. (*The heads of the different groups bend together. Their eyes follow* EILEEN *as they whisper.* MRS. TURNER *leads her down front, left. Behind them the weighing of the women continues briskly. The great majority have gained. Those who have not have either remained stationary or lost a negligible fraction of a pound. So, as the weighing proceeds, the general air of smiling satisfaction rises among the groups of women. Some of them, their ordeal over, go out through the hall doorway by twos and threes with suppressed laughter and chatter. As they pass behind* EILEEN *they glance at her with pitying curiosity.* DOCTOR STANTON's *voice is heard at regular intervals calling the names in alphabetical order: Mrs. Elbing, Miss Finch, Miss Grimes, Miss Haines, Miss Hayes, Miss Jutner, Miss Linowski, Mrs. Marini, Mrs. McCoy, Miss McElroy, Miss Nelson, Mrs. Nott, Mrs. O'Brien, Mrs. Olson, Miss Paul, Miss Petrovski, Mrs. Quinn, Miss Robersi, Mrs. Stattler, Miss Unger.*)

MRS. TURNER. (*putting her hand on* EILEEN's *shoulder—kindly*) You're not looking so well, lately, my dear, do you know it?

EILEEN (*bravely*) I feel—fine. (*Her eyes, as if looking for encouragement, seek* MURRAY *who is staring at her worriedly.*)

MRS. TURNER. (*gently*) You lost weight again, you know.

EILEEN. I know—but—

MRS. TURNER. This is the fourth week.

EILEEN. I— I know it is—

MRS. TURNER. I've been keeping my eye on you. You seem—worried. Are you upset about—something we don't know?

EILEEN. (*quickly*) No, no! I haven't slept much lately. That must be it.

MRS. TURNER. Are you worrying about your condition? Is that what keeps you awake?

EILEEN. No.

MRS. TURNER. You're sure it's not that?

EILEEN. Yes, I'm sure it's not, Mrs. Turner.

MRS. TURNER. I was going to tell you if you were: Don't do it! You can't expect it to be all smooth sailing. Even the most favorable cases have to expect these little setbacks. A few days' rest in bed will start you on the right trail again.

EILEEN. (*in anguish, although she has realized this was coming*) Bed? Go back to bed? Oh, Mrs. Turner!

MRS. TURNER. (*gently*) Yes, my dear, Doctor Stanton thinks it best. So when you go back to your cottage—

EILEEN. Oh, please—not today—not right away!

MRS. TURNER. You had a temperature and a high pulse yesterday, didn't you realize it? And this morning you look quite feverish. (*She tries to put her hand on* EILEEN's *forehead but the latter steps away defensively.*)

EILEEN. It's only—not sleeping last night. Oh, I'm sure it'll go away.

MRS. TURNER. (*consolingly*) When you lie still and have perfect rest, of course it will.

EILEEN. (*with a longing look over at* MURRAY) But not today—please, Mrs. Turner.

MRS. TURNER. (*looking at her keenly*) There is something upsetting you. You've something on your mind that you can't tell me, is that it? (EILEEN *maintains a stubborn silence.*) But think—can't you tell me? (*With a kindly smile*) I'm used to other people's troubles. I've been playing mother-confessor to the patients for years now, and I think I've usually been able to help them. Can't you confide in me, child? (EILEEN *drops her eyes but remains silent.* MRS. TURNER *glances meaningly over at* MURRAY *who is watching them whenever he thinks the matron is not aware of it—a note of sharp rebuke in her voice*) I think I can guess your secret. You've let other notions become more important to you than the idea of getting well. And you've no excuse for it. After I had to warn you a month ago, I expected *that* silliness to stop instantly.

EILEEN (*her face flushed—protesting*) Nothing like that has anything to do with it.

MRS. TURNER. (*sceptically*) What is it that has, then?

EILEEN. (*lying determinedly*) It's my family. They keep writing—and worrying me—and— That's what it is, Mrs. Turner.

MRS. TURNER (*not exactly knowing whether to believe this or not—probing the girl with her eyes*) Your father?

EILEEN. Yes, all of them. (*Suddenly seeing a way to discredit all of the matron's suspicions—excitedly*) And principally the young man I'm engaged to—the one who came to visit me several times—

MRS. TURNER. (*surprised*) So—you're engaged? (EILEEN *nods*. MRS. TURNER *immediately dismisses her suspicions*) Oh, pardon me. I didn't know that, you see, or I wouldn't—(*She pats* EILEEN *on the shoulder comfortingly*) Never mind. You'll tell me all about it, won't you?

EILEEN. (*desperately*) Yes. (*She seems about to go on but the matron interrupts her.*)

MRS. TURNER. Oh, not here, my dear. Not now. Come to my room—let me see—I'll be busy all morning—sometime this afternoon. Will you do that?

EILEEN. Yes. (*Joyfully*) Then I needn't go to bed right away?

MRS. TURNER. No—on one condition. You mustn't take any exercise. Stay in your recliner all day and rest and remain in bed tomorrow morning.

EILEEN. I promise, Mrs. Turner.

MRS. TURNER. (*smiling in dismissal*) Very well, then. I'll see you this afternoon.

EILEEN. Yes, Mrs. Turner. (*The matron goes to the rear where* MISS BAILEY *is sitting with* MRS. ABNER. *She beckons to* MISS BAILEY *who gets up with a scared look, and they go to the far left corner of the room.* EILEEN *stands for a moment hesitating—then starts to go to* MURRAY, *but just at this moment* PETERS *comes forward and speaks to* MURRAY.)

PETERS. (*with his sly twisted grin*) Say, Carmody musta lost fierce. Did you see the Old Woman handin' her an earful? Sent her back to bed, I betcha. What d'yuh think?

MURRAY. (*impatiently, showing his dislike*) How the hell do I know?

PETERS. (*sneeringly*) Huh, you don't know nothin' 'bout her, I s'pose? Where d'yuh get that stuff?

MURRAY. (*with cold rage before which the other slinks away*) If it wasn't for other people losing weight you couldn't get any joy out of life, could you? (*Roughly*) Get away from me! (*He makes a threatening gesture.*)

PETERS. (*beating a snarling retreat*) Wait'n' see if yuh don't lose too, yuh stuck-up boob! (*Seeing that* MURRAY *is alone again,* EILEEN *starts toward him but this time she is intercepted by* MRS. ABNER *who stops on her way out. The weighing of the women is now finished, and that of the men, which proceeds much quicker, begins.*)

DOCTOR STANTON. Anderson! (ANDERSON *comes to the scales. The men all move down to the left to wait their turn, with the exception of* MURRAY, *who remains by the dining-room door, fidgeting impatiently anxious for a word with* EILEEN.)

MRS. ABNER. (*taking* EILEEN'S *arm*) Coming over to the cottage, dearie?

EILEEN. Not just this minute, Mrs. Abner. I have to wait—

MRS. ABNER. For the Old Woman? You lost today, didn't you? Is she sendin' you to bed, the old devil?

EILEEN. Yes, I'm afraid I'll have to—

MRS. ABNER. She's a mean one, ain't she? I gained this week—half a pound. Lord, I'm gettin' fat! All my clothes are gittin' too small for me. Don't know what I'll do. Did you lose much, dearie?

EILEEN. Three pounds.

MRS. ABNER. Ain't that awful! (*Hastening to make up for this*

85

thoughtless remark) All the same, what's three pounds? You can git them back in a week after you're resting more. You've been runnin' a temp, too, ain't you? (EILEEN *nods*) Don't worry about it, dearie. It'll go down. Worryin's the worst. Me, I don't never worry none. (*She chuckles with satisfaction—then soberly*) I just been talkin' with Bailey. She's got to go to bed, too, I guess. She lost two pounds. She ain't runnin' no temp though.

STANTON. Barnes! (*Another man comes to the scales.*)

MRS. ABNER. (*in a mysterious whisper*) Look at Mr. Murray, dearie. Ain't he nervous today? I don't know as I blame him, either. I heard the doctor said he'd let him go home if he gained today. Is it true, d'you know?

EILEEN. (*dully*) I don't know.

MRS. ABNER. Gosh, I wish it was me! My old man's missin' me like the dickens, he writes. (*She starts to go*) You'll be over to the cottage in a while, won't you? Me'n' you'll have a game of casino, eh?

EILEEN. (*happy at this deliverance*) Yes, I'll be glad to.

STANTON. Cordero! (MRS. ABNER *goes out.* EILEEN *again starts toward* MURRAY *but this time* FLYNN, *a young fellow with a brick-colored, homely, good-natured face, and a shaven-necked haircut, slouches back to* MURRAY. EILEEN *is brought to a halt in front of the table where she stands, her face working with nervous strain, clasping and unclasping her trembling hands.*)

FLYNN. (*curiously*) Say, Steve, what's this bull about the Doc lettin' yuh beat it if yuh gain today? Is it straight goods?

MURRAY. He said he might, that's all. (*Impatiently*) How the devil did that story get traveling around?

FLYNN. (*with a grin*) Wha' d'yuh expect with this gang of skirts chewin' the fat? Well, here's hopin' yuh come home a winner, Steve.

MURRAY. (*gratefully*) Thanks. (*With confidence*) Oh, I'll gain all right; but whether he'll let me go or not— (*He shrugs his shoulders.*)

FLYNN. Make 'em behave. I wisht Stanton'd ask waivers on me.

(*With a laugh*) I oughter gain a ton today. I ate enough spuds for breakfast to plant a farm.

STANTON. Flynn!

FLYNN. Me to the plate! (*He strides to the scales.*)

MURRAY. Good luck! (*He starts to join* EILEEN *but* MISS BAILEY, *who has finished her talk with* MRS. TURNER, *who goes out to the hall, approaches* EILEEN *at just this moment.* MURRAY *stops in his tracks, fuming. He and* EILEEN *exchange a glance of helpless annoyance.*)

MISS BAILEY (*her thin face full of the satisfaction of misery finding company—plucks at* EILEEN's *sleeve*) Say, Carmody, she sent you back to bed, too, didn't she?

EILEEN. (*absentmindedly*) I suppose—

MISS BAILEY. You suppose? Of course she did. I got to go, too. (*Pulling* EILEEN's *sleeve*) Come on. Let's get out of here. I hate this place, don't you?

STANTON. (*calling the next*) Hopper!

FLYNN. (*shouts to* MURRAY *as he is going out to the hall*) I hit 'er for a two-bagger, Steve. Come on now, Bo, and bring me home! 'Atta boy! (*Grinning gleefully, he slouches out.* DOCTOR STANTON *and all the patients laugh.*)

MISS BAILEY (*with irritating persistence*) Come on, Carmody. You've got to go to bed, too.

EILEEN. (*at the end of her patience—releasing her arm from the other's grasp*) Let me alone, will you? I don't have to go to bed now—not till tomorrow morning.

MISS BAILEY (*in a whining rage*) Why not? You've been running a temp, too, and I haven't! You must have a pull, that's what! It isn't fair. I'll bet you lost more than I did, too! What right have you got—Well, I'm not going to bed if you don't. Wait 'n' see!

EILEEN (*turning away revolted*) Go away! Leave me alone, please.

STANTON. Lowenstein!

MISS BAILEY (*turns to the hall door, whining*) All right for you! I'm going to find out. It isn't square. I'll write home. (*She disappears in the hallway.* MURRAY *strides over to* EILEEN *whose strength seems to have left her and who is leaning weakly against the table.*)

MURRAY. Thank God—at last! Isn't it hell—all these fools! I couldn't get to you. What did Old Lady Grundy have to say to you? I saw her giving me a hard look. Was it about us—the old stuff? (EILEEN *nods with downcast eyes*) What did she say? Never mind now. You can tell me in a minute. It's my turn next. (*His eyes glance toward the scales.*)

EILEEN. (*intensely*) Oh, Stephen, I wish you weren't going away!

MURRAY. (*excitedly*). Maybe I'm not. It's like gambling—if I win—

STANTON. Murray!

MURRAY. Wait here, Eileen. (*He goes to the scales.* EILEEN *keeps her back turned. Her body stiffens rigidly in the intensity of her conflicting emotions. She stares straight ahead, her eyes full of anguish.* MURRAY *steps on the scales nervously. The balance rod hits the top smartly. He has gained. His face lights up and he heaves a great sigh of relief.* EILEEN *seems to sense this outcome and her head sinks, her body sags weakly and seems to shrink to a smaller size.* MURRAY *gets off the scales, his face beaming with a triumphant smile.* DOCTOR STANTON *smiles and murmurs something to him in a low voice.* MURRAY *nods brightly; then turns back to* EILEEN.)

STANTON. Nathan! (*Another patient advances to the scales.*)

MURRAY (*trying to appear casual*) Well—three rousing cheers! Stanton told me to come to his office at eleven. That means a final exam—and release!

EILEEN. (*dully*) So you gained?

MURRAY. Three pounds.

EILEEN. Funny—I lost three. (*With a pitiful effort at a smile*) I hope you gained the ones I lost. (*Her lips tremble*) So you're surely going away.

MURRAY. (*his joy fleeing as he is confronted with her sorrow— slowly*) It looks that way, Eileen.

EILEEN. (*in a trembling whisper broken by rising sobs*) Oh—I'm so glad—you gained—the ones I lost, Stephen— So glad! (*She breaks down, covering her face with her hands, stifling her sobs.*)

MURRAY (*alarmed*) Eileen! What's the matter? (*Desperately*) Stop it! Stanton'll see you!

CURTAIN

ACT TWO—SCENE TWO

MIDNIGHT *of the same day. A crossroads near the sanatorium. The main road comes down forward from the right. A smaller road, leading down from the left, joins it toward left, center.*

Dense woods rise sheer from the grass and bramble-grown ditches at the road's sides. At the junction of the two roads there is a sign-post, its arms pointing toward the right and the left, rear. A pile of round stones is at the road corner, left forward. A full moon, riding high overhead, throws the roads into white shadowless relief and masses the woods into walls of compact blackness. The trees lean heavily together, their branches motionless, unstirred by any trace of wind.

As the curtain rises, EILEEN *is discovered standing in the middle of the road, front center. Her face shows white and clear in the bright moonlight as she stares with anxious expectancy up the road to the left. Her body is fixed in an attitude of rigid immobility as if she were afraid the slightest movement would break the spell of silence and awaken the unknown. She has shrunk instinctively as far away as she can from the mysterious darkness which rises at the road's sides like an imprisoning wall. A sound of hurried footfalls, muffled by the dust, comes from the road she is watching. She gives a startled gasp. Her eyes strain to identify the oncomer. Uncertain, trembling, with fright, she hesitates a second; then darts to the side of the road and crouches down in the shadow.*

STEPHEN MURRAY *comes down the road from the left. He stops by the signpost and peers about him. He wears a cap, the peak of which casts his face into shadow. Finally he calls in a low voice*:

MURRAY. Eileen!

EILEEN. (*coming out quickly from her hiding place—with a glad little cry*) Stephen! At last! (*She runs to him as if she were going to fling her arms about him but stops abashed. He reaches out and takes her hands.*)

MURRAY. It can't be twelve yet. (*He leads her to the pile of stones to the left*) I haven't heard the village clock.

EILEEN. I must have come early. It seemed as if I'd been waiting for ages.

MURRAY. How your hands tremble! Were you frightened?

EILEEN. (*forcing a smile*) A little. The woods are so black and queer looking. I'm all right now.

MURRAY. Sit down. You must rest. (*In a tone of annoyed reproof*) I am going to read you a lecture, young lady. You shouldn't ever have done this—running a temp and— Good heavens, don't you want to get well?

EILEEN. (*dully*) I don't know—

MURRAY. (*irritably*) You make me ill when you talk that way, Eileen. It doesn't sound like you at all. What's come over you lately? I was—knocked out—when I read the note you slipped me after supper. I didn't get a chance to read it until late, I was so busy packing, and by that time you'd gone to your cottage. If I could have reached you any way I'd have refused to come here, I tell you straight. But I couldn't—and I knew you'd be here waiting—and— still, I feel guilty. Damn it, this isn't the thing for you! You ought to be in bed asleep.

EILEEN. (*humbly*) Please, Stephen, don't scold me.

MURRAY. How the devil did you ever get the idea—meeting me here at this ungodly hour?

EILEEN. You'd told me about your sneaking out to go to the village, and I thought there'd be no harm this one night—the last night.

MURRAY. But I'm well. I've been well. It's different. You— Honest, Eileen, you shouldn't lose sleep and tax your strength.

EILEEN. Don't scold me, please. I'll make up for it. I'll rest all the time—after you're gone. I just had to see you some way. (*A clock in the distant village begins striking*) Ssshh! Listen.

MURRAY. That's twelve now. You see I was early. (*In a pause of silence they wait motionlessly until the last mournful note dies in the hushed woods.*)

EILEEN. (*in a stifled voice*) It isn't tomorrow now, is it? It's today— the day you're going.

MURRAY. (*something in her voice making him avert his face and kick at the heap of stones on which she is sitting—brusquely*) Well, I hope you took precautions so you wouldn't be caught sneaking out.

EILEEN. I did just what you'd told me you did—stuffed the pillows under the clothes so the watchman would think I was there.

MURRAY. None of the patients on your porch saw you leave, did they?

EILEEN. No. They were all asleep.

MURRAY. That's all right, then. I wouldn't trust any of that bunch of women. They'd be only too tickled to squeal on you. (*There is an uncomfortable pause.* MURRAY *seems waiting for her to speak. He looks about him at the trees, up into the moonlit sky, breathing in the fresh night air with a healthy delight.* EILEEN *remains with downcast head, staring at the road*) It's beautiful tonight, isn't it? Worth losing sleep for.

EILEEN. (*dully*) Yes. (*Another pause—finally she murmurs faintly*) Are you leaving early?

MURRAY. The ten-forty. Leave the San at ten, I guess.

EILEEN. You're going home?

MURRAY. Home? No. But I'm going to see my sisters—just to say hello. I've got to, I suppose.

91

EILEEN. I'm sure—I've often felt—you're unjust to your sisters. (*With conviction*) I'm sure they must both love you.

MURRAY. (*frowning*) Maybe, in their own way. But what's love without a glimmer of understanding—a nuisance! They've never seen the real me and never wanted to.

EILEEN. (*as if to herself*) What is—the real you? (MURRAY *kicks at the stones impatiently without answering*. EILEEN *hastens to change the subject*) And then you'll go to New York?

MURRAY. (*interested at once*) Yes. You bet.

EILEEN. And write more?

MURRAY. Not in New York, no. I'm going there to take a vacation and really enjoy myself for a while. I've enough money for that as it is and if the other stories you typed sell—I'll be as rich as Rockefeller. I might even travel— No, I've got to make good with my best stuff first. I know what I'll do. When I've had enough of New York, I'll rent a place in the country—some old farmhouse—and live alone there and work. (*Lost in his own plans—with pleasure*) That's the right idea, isn't it?

EILEEN. (*trying to appear enthused*) It ought to be fine for your work. (*After a pause*) They're fine, those stories you wrote here. They're—so much like you. I'd know it was you wrote them even if —I didn't know.

MURRAY. (*pleased*) Wait till you read the others I'm going to do! (*After a slight pause—with a good-natured grin*) Here I am talking about myself again! But you don't know how good it is to have your dreams coming true. It'd make an egotist out of anyone.

EILEEN. (*sadly*) No. I don't know. But I love to hear you talk of yours.

MURRAY. (*with an embarrassed laugh*) Thanks. Well, I've certainly told you all of them. You're the only one— (*He stops and abruptly changes the subject*) You said in your note that you had something important to tell me. (*He sits down beside her, crossing his legs*) Is it about your interview with Old Mrs. Grundy this afternoon?

EILEEN. No, that didn't amount to anything. She seemed mad because I told her so little. I think she guessed I only told her what I did so she'd let me stay up, maybe—your last day—and to keep her from thinking what she did—about us.

MURRAY. (*quickly, as if he wishes to avoid this subject*) What is it you wanted to tell me, then?

EILEEN. (*sadly*) It doesn't seem so important now, somehow. I suppose it was silly of me to drag you out here, just for that. It can't mean anything to you—much.

MURRAY. (*encouragingly*) How do you know it can't?

EILEEN. (*slowly*) I only thought—you might like to know.

MURRAY. (*interestedly*) Know what? What is it? If I can help—

EILEEN. No. (*After a moment's hesitation*) I wrote to him this afternoon.

MURRAY. Him?

EILEEN. The letter you've been advising me to write.

MURRAY. (*as if the knowledge of this alarmed him—haltingly*) You mean—Fred Nicholls?

EILEEN. Yes.

MURRAY. (*after a pause—uncomfortably*) You mean—you broke it all off?

EILEEN. Yes—for good. (*She looks up at his averted face. He remains silent. She continues apprehensively*) You don't say anything. I thought—you'd be glad. You've always told me it was the honorable thing to do.

MURRAY. (*gruffly*) I know. I say more than my prayers, damn it! (*With sudden eagerness*) Have you mailed the letter yet?

EILEEN. Yes. Why?

MURRAY. (*shortly*) Humph. Oh—nothing.

EILEEN. (*with pained disappointment*) Oh, Stephen, you don't think I did wrong, do you—now—after all you've said?

MURRAY. (*hurriedly*) Wrong? No, not if you were convinced it was the right thing to do yourself—if you know you don't love him.

93

But I'd hate to think you did it just on my say-so. I shouldn't— I didn't mean to interfere. I don't know enough about your relations for my opinion to count.

EILEEN. (*hurt*) You know all there is to know.

MURRAY. I know you've been frank. But him—I don't know him. He may be quite different from my idea. That's what I'm getting at. I don't want to be unfair to him.

EILEEN. (*bitterly scornful*) You needn't worry. You weren't unfair. And you needn't be afraid you were responsible for my writing. I'd been going to for a long time before you ever spoke.

MURRAY. (*with a relieved sigh*) I'm glad of that—honestly, Eileen. I felt guilty. I shouldn't have knocked him behind his back without knowing him at all.

EILEEN. You said you could read him like a book from his letters I showed you.

MURRAY. (*apologetically*) I know. I'm a fool.

EILEEN. (*angrily*) What makes you so considerate of Fred Nicholls all of a sudden? What you thought about him was right.

MURRAY. (*vaguely*) I don't know. One makes mistakes.

EILEEN. (*assertively*) Well, I know! You needn't waste pity on him. He'll be only too glad to get my letter. He's been anxious to be free of me ever since I was sent here, only he thought it wouldn't be decent to break it off himself while I was sick. He was afraid of what people would say about him when they found it out. So he's just gradually stopped writing and coming for visits, and waited for me to realize. And if I didn't, I know he'd have broken it off himself the first day I got home. I've kept persuading myself that, in spite of the way he's acted, he did love me as much as he could love anyone, and that it would hurt him if I— But now I know that he never loved me, that he couldn't love anyone but himself. Oh, I don't hate him for it. He can't help being what he is. And all people seem to be—like that, mostly. I'm only going to remember that he and I grew up together, and that he was kind to me then when he thought he liked me—and forget all the rest. (*With agitated impatience*) Oh, Stephen, you know all this I've said about him. Why don't you admit it? You've read his letters.

MURRAY. (*haltingly*) Yes, I'll admit that was my opinion—only I wanted to be sure you'd found out for yourself.

EILEEN. (*defiantly*) Well, I have! You see that now, don't you?

MURRAY. Yes; and I'm glad you're free of him, for your own sake. I knew he wasn't the person. (*With an attempt at a joking tone*) You must get one of the right sort—next time.

EILEEN. (*springing to her feet with a cry of pain*) Stephen! (*He avoids her eyes which search his face pleadingly.*)

MURRAY. (*mumbling*) He wasn't good enough—to lace your shoes —nor anyone else, either.

EILEEN. (*with a nervous laugh*) Don't be silly. (*After a pause during which she waits hungrily for some words from him—with a sigh of despair—faintly*) Well, I've told you—all there is. I might as well go back.

MURRAY. (*not looking at her—indistinctly*) Yes. You mustn't lose too much sleep. I'll come to your cottage in the morning to say good-by. They'll permit that, I guess.

EILEEN. (*stands looking at him, imploringly, her face convulsed with anguish, but he keeps his eyes fixed on the rocks at his feet. Finally she seems to give up and takes a few uncertain steps up the road toward the right—in an exhausted whisper*) Good night Stephen.

MURRAY. (*his voice choked and husky*) Good night, Eileen.

EILEEN. (*walks weakly up the road but, as she passes the signpost, she suddenly stops and turns to look again at* MURRAY *who has not moved or lifted his eyes. A great shuddering sob shatters her pent-up emotions. She runs back to* MURRAY, *her arms outstretched, with a choking cry*) Stephen!

MURRAY. (*startled, whirls to face her and finds her arms thrown around his neck—in a terrified tone*) Eileen!

EILEEN. (*brokenly*) I love you, Stephen—you! That's what I wanted to tell! (*She gazes up into his eyes, her face transfigured by the joy and pain of this abject confession.*)

MURRAY. (*wincing as if this were the thing he had feared to hear*) Eileen!

EILEEN. (*pulling down his head with fierce strength and kissing him passionately on the lips*) I love you! I will say it! There! (*With sudden horror*) Oh, I know I shouldn't kiss you! I mustn't! You're all well—and I—

MURRAY. (*protesting frenziedly*) Eileen! Damn it! Don't say that! What do you think I am! (*He kisses her fiercely two or three times until she forces a hand over her mouth.*)

EILEEN. (*with a hysterically happy laugh*) No! Just hold me in your arms—just a little while—before—

MURRAY. (*his voice trembling*) Eileen! Don't talk that way! You're —it's killing me. I can't stand it!

EILEEN. (*with soothing tenderness*) Listen, dear—listen—and you won't say a word— I've so much to say—till I get through—please, will you promise?

MURRAY. (*between clinched teeth*) Yes—anything, Eileen!

EILEEN. Then I want to say—I know your secret. You don't love me— Isn't that it? (MURRAY *groans*) Ssshh! It's all right, dear. You can't help what you don't feel. I've guessed you didn't—right along. And I've loved you—such a long time now—always, it seems. And you've sort of guessed—that I did—didn't you? No, don't speak! I am sure you've guessed—only you didn't want to know—that—did you? —when you didn't love me. That's why you were lying—but I saw, I knew! Oh, I'm not blaming you, darling. How could I—never! You mustn't look so—so frightened. I know how you felt, dear. I've—I've watched you. It was just a flirtation for you at first. Wasn't it? Oh, I know. It was just fun, and— Please don't look at me so. I'm not hurting you, am I? I wouldn't for worlds, dear—you know—hurt you! And then afterwards—you found we could be such good friends—

helping each other—and you wanted it to stay just like that always, didn't you?—I know—and then I had to spoil it all—and fall in love with you—didn't I? Oh, it was stupid—I shouldn't—I couldn't help it, you were so kind and—and different—and I wanted to share in your work and—and everything. I knew you wouldn't want to know I loved you—when you didn't—and I tried hard to be fair and hide my love so you wouldn't see—and I did, didn't I, dear? You never knew till just lately—maybe not till just today—did you?—when I knew you were going away so soon—and couldn't help showing it. You never knew before, did you? Did you?

MURRAY. (*miserably*) No. Oh, Eileen—Eileen, I'm so sorry!

EILEEN. (*in heartbroken protest*) Sorry? Oh no, Stephen, you mustn't be! It's been beautiful—all of it—for me! That's what makes your going—so hard. I had to see you tonight—I'd have gone—crazy —if I didn't know you knew, if I hadn't made you guess. And I thought—if you knew about my writing to Fred—that—maybe—it'd make some difference. (MURRAY *groans—and she laughs hysterically*) I must have been crazy—to think that—mustn't I? As if that could— when you don't love me. Sshh! Please! Let me finish. You mustn't feel sad—or anything. It's made me happier than I've ever been— loving you—even when I did know—you didn't. Only now—you'll forgive me telling you all this, won't you, dear? Now, it's so terrible to think I won't see you any more. I'll feel so—without anybody.

MURRAY. (*brokenly*) But I'll—come back. And you'll be out soon— and then—

EILEEN. (*brokenly*) Sshh! Let me finish. You don't know how alone I am now. Father—he'll marry that housekeeper—and the children— they've forgotten me. None of them need me any more. They've found out how to get on without me—and I'm a drag—dead to them —no place for me home any more—and they'll be afraid to have me back—afraid of catching—I know she won't want me back. And Fred—he's gone—he never mattered, anyway. Forgive me, dear—

worrying you—only I want you to know how much you've meant to me—so you won't forget—ever—after you've gone.

MURRAY. (*in grief-stricken tones*) Forget? Eileen! I'll do anything in God's world—

EILEEN. I know—you like me a lot even if you can't love me—don't you? (*His arms tighten about her as he bends down and forces a kiss on her lips again*) Oh, Stephen! That was for good-by. You mustn't come tomorrow morning. I couldn't bear having you—with people watching. But you'll write after—often—won't you? (*Heartbrokenly*) Oh, please do that, Stephen!

MURRAY. I will! I swear! And when you get out I'll—we'll—I'll find something— (*He kisses her again.*)

EILEEN. (*breaking away from him with a quick movement and stepping back a few feet*) Good-by, darling. Remember me—and perhaps—you'll find out after a time—I'll pray God to make it so! Oh, what am I saying? Only—I'll hope—I'll hope—till I die!

MURRAY. (*in anguish*) Eileen!

EILEEN. (*her breath coming in tremulous heaves of her bosom*) Remember, Stephen—if ever you want—I'll do anything—anything you want—no matter what—I don't care—there's just you and—don't hate me, dear. I love you—love you—remember! (*She suddenly turns and runs away up the road.*)

MURRAY. Eileen! (*He starts to run after her but stops by the sign-post and stamps on the ground furiously, his fists clenched in impotent rage at himself and at Fate.*) Christ!

CURTAIN

ACT THREE

Scene—*Four months later. An isolation room at the Infirmary with a sleeping porch at the right of it. Late afternoon of a Sunday toward the end of October. The room, extending two-thirds of the distance from left to right, is, for reasons of space economy, scantily furnished with the bare necessities—a bureau with mirror in the left corner, rear—two straight-backed chairs—a table with a glass top in the center. The floor is varnished hardwood. The walls and furniture are painted white. On the left, forward, a door to the hallway. On the right, rear, a double glass door opening on the porch. Farther front two windows. The porch, a screened-in continuation of the room, contains only a single iron bed painted white, and a small table placed beside the bed.*

The woods, the leaves of the trees rich in their autumn coloring, rise close about this side of the Infirmary. Their branches almost touch the porch on the right. In the rear of the porch they have been cleared away from the building for a narrow space, and through this opening the distant hills can be seen with the tree tops glowing in the sunlight.

As the curtain rises, EILEEN *is discovered lying in the bed on the porch, propped up into a half-sitting position by pillows under her back and head. She seems to have grown much thinner. Her face is pale and drawn with deep hollows under her cheek-bones. Her eyes are dull and lusterless. She gazes straight before her into the wood with the unseeing stare of apathetic indifference. The door from the hall in the room behind her is opened and* MISS HOWARD *enters followed by* BILL CARMODY, MRS. BRENNAN, *and* MARY. CARMODY'S *manner is unwontedly sober and subdued. This air of respectable sobriety is further enhanced by a black suit, glaringly new and stiffly pressed, a new black derby hat, and shoes polished like a mirror. His expression*

99

is full of a bitter, if suppressed, resentment. His gentility is evidently forced upon him in spite of himself and correspondingly irksome. MRS. BRENNAN *is a tall, stout woman of fifty, lusty and loud-voiced, with a broad, snub-nosed, florid face, a large mouth, the upper lip darkened by a suggestion of mustache, and little round blue eyes, hard and restless with a continual fuming irritation. She is got up regardless in her ridiculous Sunday-best.* MARY *appears tall and skinny-legged in a starched, outgrown frock. The sweetness of her face has disappeared, giving way to a hangdog sullenness, a stubborn silence, with sulky, furtive glances of rebellion directed at her stepmother.*

MISS HOWARD. (*pointing to the porch*) She's out there on the porch.

MRS. BRENNAN. (*with dignity*) Thank you, ma'am.

MISS HOWARD. (*with a searching glance at the visitors as if to appraise their intentions*) Eileen's been very sick lately, you know, so be careful not to worry her about anything. Do your best to cheer her up.

CARMODY. (*mournfully*) We'll try to put life in her spirits, God help her. (*With an uncertain look at* MRS. BRENNAN) Won't we, Maggie?

MRS. BRENNAN. (*turning sharply on* MARY *who has gone over to examine the things on the bureau*) Come away from that, Mary. Curiosity killed a cat. Don't be touchin' her things. Remember what I told you. Or is it admirin' your mug in the mirror you are? (*Turning to* MISS HOWARD *as* MARY *moves away from the bureau, hanging her head—shortly*) Don't you worry, ma'am. We won't trouble Eileen at all.

MISS HOWARD. Another thing. You mustn't say anything to her of what Miss Gilpin just told you about her being sent away to the State Farm in a few days. Eileen isn't to know till the very last minute. It would only disturb her.

CARMODY. (*hastily*) We'll not say a word of it.

MISS HOWARD. (*turning to the hall door*) Thank you. (*She goes out, shutting the door.*)

MRS. BRENNAN. (*angrily*) She has a lot of impudent gab, that one, with her don't do this and don't do that! (*Gazing about the room critically*) Two sticks of chairs and a table! They don't give much for the money.

CARMODY. Catch them! It's a good thing she's clearin' out of this and her worse off after them curin' her eight months than she was when she came. She'll maybe get well in the new place.

MRS. BRENNAN. (*indifferently*) It's God's will, what'll happen. (*Irritably*) And I'm thinkin' it's His punishment she's under now for having no heart in her and never writin' home a word to you or the children in two months or more. If the doctor hadn't wrote us himself to come see her, we'd have been no wiser.

CARMODY. Whisht. Don't be blamin' a sick girl.

MARY. (*who has drifted to one of the windows at right—curiously*) There's somebody in bed out there. Is it Eileen?

MRS. BRENNAN. Don't be goin' out there till I tell you, you imp! (*Coming closer to him and lowering her voice*) Are you going to tell her about it?

CARMODY. (*pretending ignorance*) About what?

MRS. BRENNAN. About what, indeed! About our marryin' two weeks back, of course. What else?

CARMODY. (*uncertainly*) Yes—I disremembered she didn't know. I'll have to tell her, surely.

MRS. BRENNAN. (*flaring up*) You speak like you wouldn't. Are you afraid of a slip of a girl? Well, then, I'm not! I'll tell her to her face soon enough.

CARMODY. (*angry in his turn—assertively*) You'll not, now! Keep your mouth out of this and your rough tongue! I tell you I'll tell her.

MRS. BRENNAN. (*satisfied*) Let's be going out to her, then. (*They move toward the door to the porch*) And keep your eye on your watch. We mustn't miss the train. Come with us, Mary, and remember to keep your mouth shut. (*They go out on the porch and stand just outside the door waiting for* EILEEN *to notice them; but the girl in bed continues to stare into the woods, oblivious to their presence.*)

MRS. BRENNAN. (*nudging* CARMODY *with her elbow—in a harsh whisper*) Glory be, it's bad she's lookin'. The look on her face'd frighten you. Speak to her, you! (EILEEN *stirs uneasily as if this whisper had disturbed her unconsciously.*)

CARMODY. (*wetting his lips and clearing his throat huskily*) Eileen.

EILEEN. (*startled, turns and stares at them with frightened eyes. After a pause she ventures uncertainly as if she were not sure but what these figures might be creatures of her dream*) Father. (*Her eyes shift to* MRS. BRENNAN'S *face and she shudders*) Mrs. Brennan.

MRS. BRENNAN. (*quickly—in a voice meant to be kindly*) Here we are, all of us, come to see you. How is it you're feelin' now, Eileen? (*While she is talking she advances to the bedside, followed by* CARMODY, *and takes one of the sick girl's hands in hers.* EILEEN *withdraws it as if stung and holds it out to her father.* MRS. BRENNAN'S *face flushes angrily and she draws back from the bedside.*)

CARMODY. (*moved—with rough tenderness patting her hand*) Ah, Eileen, sure it's a sight for sore eyes to see you again! (*He bends down as if to kiss her, but, struck by a sudden fear, hesitates, straightens himself, and shamed by the understanding in* EILEEN'S *eyes, grows red and stammers confusedly*) How are you now? Sure it's the picture of health you're lookin'. (EILEEN *sighs and turns her eyes away from his with a resigned sadness.*)

MRS. BRENNAN. What are you standin' there for like a stick, Mary? Haven't you a word to say to your sister?

EILEEN. (*twisting her head around and seeing* MARY *for the first time—with a glad cry*) Mary! I—why I didn't see you before! Come here. (MARY *approaches gingerly with apprehensive side glances at* MRS. BRENNAN *who watches her grimly.* EILEEN'S *arms reach out for her hungrily. She grasps her about the waist and seems trying to press the unwilling child to her breast.*)

MARY. (*fidgeting nervously—suddenly in a frightened whine*) Let me go! (EILEEN *releases her, looks at her face dazedly for a second, then falls back limply with a little moan and shuts her eyes.* MARY, *who has stepped back a pace, remains fixed there as if fascinated with fright by her sister's face. She stammers*) Eileen—you look so—so funny.

EILEEN. (*without opening her eyes—in a dead voice*) You, too! I never thought you— Go away, please.

MRS. BRENNAN. (*with satisfaction*) Come here to me, Mary, and don't be botherin' your sister. (MARY *avoids her stepmother but retreats to the far end of the porch where she stands shrunk back against the wall, her eyes fixed on* EILEEN *with the same fascinated horror.*)

CARMODY. (*after an uncomfortable pause, forcing himself to speak*) Is the pain bad, Eileen?

EILEEN. (*dully—without opening her eyes*) There's no pain. (*There is another pause—then she murmurs indifferently*) There are chairs in the room you can bring out if you want to sit down.

MRS. BRENNAN. (*sharply*) We've not time to be sittin'. We've the train back to catch.

EILEEN. (*in the same lifeless voice*) It's a disagreeable trip. I'm sorry you had to come.

CARMODY. (*fighting against an oppression he cannot understand, bursts into a flood of words*) Don't be talking of the trip. Sure we're glad to take it to get a sight of you. It's three months since I've had a look at you and I was anxious. Why haven't you written a line to us? You could do that without trouble, surely. Don't you ever think of us at all any more? (*He waits for an answer but* EILEEN *remains silent with her eyes closed.* CARMODY *starts to walk up and down talking with an air of desperation*) You're not asking a bit of news from home. I'm thinkin' the people out here have taken all the thought of us out of your head. We're all well, thank God. I've another good job on the streets from Murphy and one that'll last a long time, praise be! I'm needin' it surely, with all the expenses—but no matter. Billy had a raise from his old skinflint of a boss a month back. He's gettin' seven a week now and proud as a turkey. He was comin' out with us today

103

but he'd a date with his girl. Sure, he's got a girl now, the young bucko! What d'you think of him? It's old Malloy's girl he's after—the pop-eyed one with glasses, you remember—as ugly as a blind sheep, only he don't think so. He said to give you his love. (EILEEN *stirs and sighs wearily, a frown appearing for an instant on her forehead*) And Tom and Nora was comin' out too, but Father Fitz had some doin's or other up to the school, and he told them to be there, so they wouldn't come with us, but they sent their love to you too. They're growin' so big you'd not know them. Tom's no good at the school. He's like Billy was. I've had to take the strap to him often. He's always playin' hookey and roamin' the streets. And Nora—(*With pride*) There's the divil for you! Up to everything she is and no holdin' her high spirits. As pretty as a picture, and the smartest girl in her school, Father Fitz says. Am I lyin', Maggie?

MRS. BRENNAN. (*grudgingly*) She's smart enough—and too free with her smartness.

CARMODY. (*pleased*) Ah, don't be talkin'! She'll know more than the lot of us before she's grown even. (*He pauses in his walk and stares down at* EILEEN, *frowning*) Are you sick, Eileen, that you're keepin' your eyes shut without a word out of you?

EILEEN. (*wearily*) No. I'm tired, that's all.

CARMODY. (*resuming his walk*) And who else is there, let me think? Oh, Mary—she's the same as ever, you can see for yourself.

EILEEN. (*bitterly*) The same? Oh, no!

CARMODY. She's grown, you mean? I suppose. You'd notice, not seeing her so long? (*He can think of nothing else to say but walks up and down with a restless, uneasy expression.*)

MRS. BRENNAN. (*sharply*) What time is it gettin'?

CARMODY. (*fumbles for his watch*) Half past four, a bit after.

MRS. BRENNAN. We'll have to leave soon. It's a long jaunt down the hill in that buggy. (*She catches his eye and makes violent signs to him to tell* EILEEN *what he has come to tell.*)

CARMODY. (*after an uncertain pause—clenching his fists and clearing his throat*) Eileen.

EILEEN. Yes.

CARMODY. (*irritably*) Can't you open your eyes on me? It's like talkin' to myself I am.

EILEEN. (*looking at him—dully*) What is it?

CARMODY. (*stammering—avoiding her glance*) It's this, Eileen— me and Maggie—Mrs. Brennan, that is—we—

EILEEN. (*without surprise*) You're going to marry her?

CARMODY. (*with an effort*) Not goin' to. It's done.

EILEEN. (*without a trace of feeling*) Oh, so you've been married already? (*Without further comment, she closes her eyes.*)

CARMODY. Two weeks back we were, by Father Fitz. (*He stands staring down at his daughter, irritated, perplexed and confounded by her silence, looking as if he longed to shake her.*)

MRS. BRENNAN. (*angry at the lack of enthusiasm shown by* EILEEN) Let us get out of this, Bill. It's little she's caring about you, and little thanks she has for all you've done for her and the money you've spent.

CARMODY. (*with a note of pleading*) Is that a proper way to be treatin' your father, Eileen, after what I've told you? Is it nothin' to you you've a good, kind woman now for mother?

EILEEN. (*fiercely, her eyes flashing open on him*) No, No! Never!

MRS. BRENNAN. (*plucking at* CARMODY's *elbow. He stands looking at* EILEEN *helplessly, his mouth open, a guilty flush spreading over his face*) Come out of here, you big fool, you! Is it to listen to insults to your livin' wife you're waiting?

CARMODY. (*turning on her threateningly*) Will you shut your gab?

EILEEN. (*with a moan*) Oh, go away. Father! Please! Take her away!

MRS. BRENNAN. (*pulling at his arm*) Take me away this second or I'll never speak again to you till the day I die!

CARMODY. (*pushes her violently away from him—raging, his fist uplifted*) Shut your gab, I'm saying!

MRS. BRENNAN. The devil mend you and yours then! I'm leavin' you. (*She starts for the door.*)

CARMODY. (*hastily*) Wait a bit, Maggie. I'm coming. (*She goes into the room, slamming the door, but once inside she stands still, trying to listen.* CARMODY *glares down at his daughter's pale twitching face with closed eyes. Finally he croaks in a whining tone of fear*) Is your last word a cruel one to me this day, Eileen? (*She remains silent. His face darkens. He turns and strides out of the door.* MARY *darts after him with a frightened cry of "Papa."* EILEEN *covers her face with her hands and a shudder of relief runs over her body.*)

MRS. BRENNAN. (*as* CARMODY *enters the room—in a mollified tone*) So you've come, have you? Let's go, then! (CARMODY *stands looking at her in silence, his expression full of gloomy rage. She bursts out impatiently*) Are you comin' or are you goin' back to her? (*She grabs* MARY's *arm and pushes her toward the door to the hall*) Are you comin' or not, I'm asking?

CARMODY. (*somberly—as if to himself*) There's something wrong in the whole of this—that I can't make out. (*With sudden fury he brandishes his fists as though defying someone and growls threateningly*) And I'll get drunk this night—dead, rotten drunk! (*He seems to detect disapproval in* MRS. BRENNAN's *face for he shakes his fist at her and repeats like a solemn oath*) I'll get drunk if my soul roasts for it—and no one in the whole world is strong enough to stop me! (MRS. BRENNAN *turns from him with a disgusted shrug of her shoulders and hustles* MARY *out of the door.* CARMODY, *after a second's pause, follows them.* EILEEN *lies still, looking out into the woods with empty, desolate eyes.* MISS HOWARD *comes into the room from the hall and goes to the porch, carrying a glass of milk in her hand.*)

MISS HOWARD. Here's your diet, Eileen. I forgot it until just now. Did you have a nice visit with your folks?

EILEEN. (*forcing a smile*) Yes.

MISS HOWARD. I hope they didn't worry you over home affairs?

EILEEN. No. (*She sips her milk and sets it back on the table with a shudder of disgust.*)

MISS HOWARD. (*with a smile*) What a face! You'd think you were taking poison.

EILEEN. (*with deep passion*) I wish it was poison!

MISS HOWARD. (*jokingly*) Oh, come now! That isn't a nice way to feel on the Sabbath. (*With a meaning smile*) I've some news that'll cheer you up, I bet. (*Archly*) Guess who's here on a visit?

EILEEN. (*startled—in a frightened whisper*) Who?

MISS HOWARD. Mr. Murray. (EILEEN *closes her eyes wincingly for a moment and a shadow of pain comes over her face*) He came just about the time your folks did. I saw him for a moment, not to speak to. (*Beaming—with a certain curiosity*) What do you think of that for news?

EILEEN. (*trying to conceal her agitation and assume a casual tone*) He must have come to be examined.

MISS HOWARD. (*with a meaning laugh*) Oh, I'd hardly say that was his main reason. (*In business-like tones*) Well, I've got to get back on the job. (*She turns to the door calling back jokingly*) He'll be in to see you of course, so look your prettiest. (*She goes out and shuts the door to the porch.* EILEEN *gives a frightened gasp and struggles up in bed as if she wanted to call the nurse to return. Then she lies back in a state of great nervous excitement, twisting her head with eager, fearful glances toward the door, listening, clasping and unclasping her thin fingers on the white spread. As* MISS HOWARD *walks across the room to the hall door, it is opened and* STEPHEN MURRAY *enters. A great change is visible in his face. It is much thinner and the former healthy tan has faded to a sallow pallor. Puffy shadows of sleeplessness and dissipation are marked under his heavy-lidded eyes. He is dressed in a well-fitting, expensive, dark suit, a white shirt with a soft collar and bright-colored tie.*)

MISS HOWARD. (*with pleased surprise, holding out her hand*) Hello, Mr. Murray.

MURRAY. (*shaking her hand—with a forced pleasantness*) How are you, Miss Howard?

MISS HOWARD. Fine as ever. It certainly looks natural to see you around here again—not that I hope you're here to stay, though. (*With a smile*) I suppose you're on your way to Eileen now. Well, I won't keep you. I've oodles of work to do. (*She opens the hall door. He starts for the porch*) Oh, I was forgetting— Congratulations! I've read those stories—all of us have. They're great. We're all so proud of you. You're one of our graduates, you know.

MURRAY. (*indifferently*) Oh,—that stuff.

MISS HOWARD. (*gaily*) Don't be so modest. Well, see you later, I hope.

MURRAY. Yes. Doctor Stanton invited me to stay for supper and I may—

MISS HOWARD. Fine! Be sure to! (*She goes out.* MURRAY *walks to porch door and steps out. He finds* EILEEN's *eyes waiting for him. As their eyes meet she gasps involuntarily and he stops short in his tracks. For a moment they remain looking at each other in silence.*)

EILEEN. (*dropping her eyes—faintly*) Stephen.

MURRAY. (*much moved, strides to her bedside and takes her hands awkwardly*) Eileen. (*Then after a second's pause in which he searches her face and is shocked by the change illness has made—anxiously*) How are you feeling, Eileen? (*He grows confused by her gaze and his eyes shift from hers, which search his face with wild yearning.*)

EILEEN. (*forcing a smile*) Oh, I'm all right. (*Eagerly*) But you, Stephen? How are you? (*Excitedly*) Oh, it's good to see you again! (*Her eyes continue fixed on his face pleadingly, questioningly.*)

MURRAY. (*haltingly*) And it's sure great to see you again, Eileen. (*He releases her hand and turns away*) And I'm fine and dandy. I look a little done up, I guess, but that's only the result of too much New York.

EILEEN. (*sensing from his manner that whatever she has hoped for*

*from his visit is not to be, sinks back on the pillows, shutting her eyes
hopelessly, and cannot control a sigh of pain.*)

MURRAY. (*turning to her anxiously*) What's the matter, Eileen?
You're not in pain, are you?

EILEEN. (*wearily*) No.

MURRAY. You haven't been feeling badly lately, have you? Your letters suddenly stopped—not a line for the past three weeks—and I—

EILEEN. (*bitterly*) I got tired of writing and never getting any
answer, Stephen.

MURRAY. (*shamefaced*) Come, Eileen, it wasn't as bad as that.
You'd think I never—and I did write, didn't I?

EILEEN. Right after you left here, you did, Stephen. Lately—

MURRAY. I'm sorry, Eileen. It wasn't that I didn't mean to—but—
in New York it's so hard. You start to do one thing and something
else interrupts you. You never seem to get any one thing done when
it ought to be. You can understand that, can't you, Eileen?

EILEEN. (*sadly*) Yes. I understand everything now.

MURRAY. (*offended*) What do you mean by everything? You said
that so strangely. You mean you don't believe— (*But she remains
silent with her eyes shut. He frowns and takes to pacing up and down
beside the bed*) Why have they got you stuck out here on this isolation porch, Eileen?

EILEEN. (*dully*) There was no room on the main porch, I suppose.

MURRAY. You never mentioned in any of your letters—

EILEEN. It's not very cheerful to get letters full of sickness. I wouldn't
like to, I know.

MURRAY. (*hurt*) That isn't fair, Eileen. You know I— How long
have you been back in the Infirmary?

EILEEN. About a month.

MURRAY. (*shocked*) A month! But you were up and about—on exercise, weren't you—before that?

EILEEN. No. I had to stay in bed while I was at the cottage.

MURRAY. You mean—ever since that time they sent you back—the day before I left?

EILEEN. Yes.

MURRAY. But I thought from the cheery tone of your letters that you were—

EILEEN. (*uneasily*) Getting better? I am, Stephen. I'm strong enough to be up now but Doctor Stanton wants me to take a good long rest this time so that when I get up again I'll be sure— (*She breaks off impatiently*) But don't let's talk about it. I'm all right. (MURRAY *glances down at her face worriedly. She changes the subject*) You've been over to see Doctor Stanton, haven't you?

MURRAY. Yes.

EILEEN. Did he examine you?

MURRAY. Yes. (*Carelessly*) Oh, he found me O.K.

EILEEN. I'm glad, Stephen. (*After a pause*) Tell about yourself— what you've been doing. You've written a lot lately, haven't you?

MURRAY. (*frowning*) No. I haven't been able to get down to it— somehow. There's so little time to yourself once you get to know people in New York. The sale of the stories you typed put me on easy street as far as money goes, so I've felt no need— (*He laughs weakly*) I guess I'm one of those who have to get down to hard pan before they get the kick to drive them to hard work.

EILEEN. (*surprised*) Was it hard work writing them up here? You used to seem so happy just in doing them.

MURRAY. I was—happier than I've been before or afterward. (*Cynically*) But—I don't know—it was a new game to me then and I was chuck full of illusions about the glory of it. (*He laughs half-heartedly*) Now I'm hardly a bit more enthusiastic over it than I used to be over newspaper work. It's like everything else, I guess. When you've got it, you find you don't want it.

EILEEN. (*looking at him wonderingly—disturbed*) But isn't just the writing itself worth while?

MURRAY. (*as if suddenly ashamed of himself—quickly*) Yes. Of course it is. I'm talking like a fool. I'm sore at everything because I'm dissatisfied with my own cussedness and laziness—and I want to pass the buck. (*With a smile of cheerful confidence*) It's only a fit. I'll come out of it all right and get down to brass tacks again.

EILEEN. (*with an encouraging smile*) That's the way you ought to feel. It'd be wrong—I've read the two stories that have come out so far over and over. They're fine, I think. Every line in them sounds like you, and at the same time sounds natural and like people and things you see every day. Everybody thinks they're fine, Stephen.

MURRAY. (*pleased but pretending cynicism*) Then they must be rotten. (*Then with self-assurance*) Well, I've plenty more of those stories in my head. (*Spiritedly*) And I'll make them so much better than what I've done so far, you won't recognize them. (*Smiling*) Darn it, do you know just talking about it makes me feel as if I could sit right down now and start in on one. Is it the fact I've worked here before—or is it seeing you, Eileen? (*Gratefully*) I really believe it's you. I haven't forgotten how you helped me before.

EILEEN. (*in a tone of pain*) Don't, Stephen. I didn't do anything.

MURRAY. (*eagerly*) Yes, you did. You made it possible. And since I've left the San, I've looked forward to your letters to boost up my spirits. When I felt down in the mouth over my own idiocy, I used to reread them, and they always were good medicine. I can't tell you how grateful I've felt, honestly!

EILEEN. (*faintly*) You're kind to say so, Stephen—but it was nothing, really.

MURRAY. And I can't tell you how I've missed those letters for the past three weeks. They left a big hole in things. I was worried about you—not having heard a word. (*With a smile*) So I came to look you up.

EILEEN. (*faintly—forcing an answering smile*) Well, you see now I'm all right.

MURRAY. (*concealing his doubt*) Yes, of course you are. Only I'd a darn sight rather see you up and about. We could take a walk, then

—through the woods. (*A wince of pain shadows* EILEEN's *face. She closes her eyes.* MURRAY *continues softly, after a pause*) You haven't forgotten that last night—out there—Eileen?

EILEEN. (*her lips trembling—trying to force a laugh*) Please, please don't remind me of that, Stephen. I was so silly and so sick, too. My temp was so high it must have made me—completely crazy—or I'd never dreamed of doing such a stupid thing. My head must have been full of wheels because I don't remember anything I did or said, hardly.

MURRAY. (*his pride taken down a peg by this—in a hurt tone*) Oh! Well—I haven't forgotten and I never will, Eileen. (*Then his face clears up as if a weight had been taken off his conscience*) Well—I rather thought you wouldn't take it seriously—afterward. You were all up in the air that night. And you never mentioned it in your letters—

EILEEN. (*pleadingly*) Don't talk about it! Forget it ever happened. It makes me feel— (*With a half-hysterical laugh*) like a fool!

MURRAY. (*worried*) All right, Eileen. I won't. Don't get worked up over nothing. That isn't resting, you know. (*Looking down at her closed eyes—solicitously*) Perhaps all my talking has tired you out? Do you feel done up? Why don't you try and take a nap now?

EILEEN. (*dully*) Yes, I'd like to sleep.

MURRAY. (*clasps her hands gently*) I'll leave you then. I'll drop back to say good-by and stay awhile before I go. I won't leave until the last train. (*As she doesn't answer*) Do you hear, Eileen?

EILEEN. (*weakly*) Yes. You'll come back—to say good-by.

MURRAY. Yes. I'll be back sure. (*He presses her hand and after a kindly glance of sympathy down at her face, tiptoes to the door and goes into the room, shutting the door behind him. When she hears the door shut* EILEEN *struggles up in bed and stretches her arms after him with an agonized sob* "Stephen!" *She hides her face in her hands and sobs brokenly.* MURRAY *walks across to the hall door and is about to go out when the door is opened and* MISS GILPIN *enters.*)

MISS GILPIN. (*hurriedly*) How do you do, Mr. Murray. Doctor Stanton just told me you were here.

MURRAY. (*as they shake hands—smiling*) How are you, Miss Gilpin?

MISS GILPIN. He said he'd examined you, and that you were O.K. I'm glad. (*Glancing at him keenly*) You've been talking to Eileen?

MURRAY. Just left her this second. She wanted to sleep for a while.

MISS GILPIN. (*wonderingly*) Sleep? (*Then hurriedly*) It's too bad. I wish I'd known you were here sooner. I wanted very much to talk to you before you saw Eileen. (*With a worried smile*) I still think I ought to have a talk with you.

MURRAY. Certainly, Miss Gilpin.

MISS GILPIN. (*takes a chair and places it near the hall door*) Sit down. She can't hear us here. Goodness knows this is hardly the place for confidences, but there are visitors all over and it'll have to do. Did you close the door tightly? She mustn't hear me above all. (*She goes to the porch door and peeps out for a moment; then comes back to him with flashing eyes*) She's crying! What have you been saying to her? Oh, it's too late, I know! What has happened out there? Tell me!

MURRAY. (*stammering*) Nothing. She's crying? Why, Miss Gilpin— you know I wouldn't hurt her for worlds.

MISS GILPIN. (*more calmly*) Intentionally, I know you wouldn't. But something has happened. (*Then briskly*) Since you don't seem inclined to confide in me, I'll have to in you. You noticed how badly she looks, didn't you?

MURRAY. Yes, I did.

MISS GILPIN. (*gravely*) She's been going down hill steadily— (*Meaningly*) ever since you left. She's in a very serious state, let me impress you with that. Doctor Stanton has given up hope of her improving here, and her father is unwilling to pay for her elsewhere now he knows there's a cheaper place—the State Farm. So she's to be sent there in a day or so.

MURRAY. (*springing to his feet—horrified*) To the State Farm!

113

MISS GILPIN. Her time here is long past. You know the rule—and she isn't getting better.

MURRAY. (*appalled*) That means—!

MISS GILPIN. (*forcibly*) Death! That's what it means for her!

MURRAY. (*stunned*) Good God, I never dreamed—

MISS GILPIN. In her case, it's certain. She'll die. And it wouldn't do any good to keep her here, either. She'd die here. She'll die anywhere because lately she's given up hope, she hasn't wanted to live any more. She's let herself go—and now it's too late.

MURRAY. Too late? You mean there's no chance—now? (MISS GILPIN *nods.* MURRAY *is overwhelmed—after a pause—stammering*) Isn't there—anything—we can do?

MISS GILPIN. (*sadly*) I don't know. I should have talked to you before. You see, she's seen you now. She knows. (*As he looks mystified she continues slowly*) I suppose you know that Eileen loves you, don't you?

MURRAY. (*as if defending himself against an accusation—with confused alarm*) No—Miss Gilpin. She may have felt something like that —once—but that was long ago before I left the San. She's forgotten all about it since, I know she has. (MISS GILPIN *smiles bitterly*) Why— just now—she said that part of it had all been so silly she felt she'd acted like a fool and didn't ever want to be reminded of it.

MISS GILPIN. She saw that you didn't love her—any more than you did in the days before you left. Oh, I used to watch you then. I sensed what was going on between you. I would have stopped it then out of pity for her, if I could have, if I didn't know that any interference would only make matters worse. (*She sighs—then after a pause*) You'll have to forgive me for speaking to you so boldly on a delicate subject. But, don't you see, it's for her sake. I love Eileen. We all do. (*Averting her eyes from his—in a low voice*) I know how Eileen feels, Mr. Murray. Once—a long time ago—I suffered as she is suffering— from the same mistake. But I had resources to fall back upon that Eileen hasn't got—a family who loved me and understood—friends—

so I pulled through. But it spoiled my life for a long time. (*Looking at him again and forcing a smile*) So I feel that perhaps I have a right to speak for Eileen who has no one else.

MURRAY. (*huskily—much moved*) Say anything you like, Miss Gilpin.

MISS GILPIN. (*after a pause—sadly*) You don't love her—do you?

MURRAY. No—I— I don't believe I've ever thought much of loving anyone—that way.

MISS GILPIN. (*sadly*) Oh, it's too late, I'm afraid. If we had only had this talk before you had seen her! I meant to talk to you frankly and if I found out you didn't love Eileen—there was always the forlorn hope that you might—I was going to tell you not to see her, for her sake—not to let her face the truth. For I'm sure she continued to hope in spite of everything, and always would—to the end—if she didn't see you. I was going to implore you to stay away, to write her letters that would encourage her hope, and in that way she'd never learn the truth. I thought of writing you all this—but—it's so delicate a matter—I didn't have the courage. (*With intense grief*) And now Doctor Stanton's decision to send her away makes everything doubly hard. When she knows *that*—she'll throw everything that holds her to life—out of the window! And think of it—her dying there alone!

MURRAY. (*very pale*) Don't! That shan't happen. I have money enough—I'll make more—to send her any place you think—

MISS GILPIN. That's something—but it doesn't touch the source of her unhappiness. If there were only some way to make her happy in the little time that's left to her! She has suffered so much through you. Oh, Mr. Murray, can't you tell her you love her?

MURRAY. (*after a pause—slowly*) But she'll never believe me, I'm afraid, now.

MISS GILPIN. (*eagerly*) But you must make her believe! And you must ask her to marry you. If you're engaged it will give you the right in her eyes to take her away. You can take her to some private San. There's a small place but a very good one at White Lake. It's not too expensive, and it's a beautiful spot, out of the world, and you can live and work near by. And she'll be happy to the very last. Don't you think that's something you can give in return for her love for you?

MURRAY. (*slowly—deeply moved*) Yes. (*Then determinedly*) But I won't go into this thing by halves. It isn't fair to her. I'm going to marry her—yes, I mean it. I owe her that if it will make her happy.

MISS GILPIN. (*with a sad smile*) She'll never consent—for your sake —until she's well again. And stop and think, Mr. Murray. Even if she did consent to marry you right now the shock—it'd be suicide for her. I'd have to warn her against it myself. I've talked with Dr. Stanton. God knows I'd be the first one to hold out hope if there was any. There isn't. It's merely a case of prolonging the short time left to her and making it happy. You must bear that in mind—as a fact!

MURRAY. (*dully*) All right. I'll remember. But it's hell to realize— (*He turns suddenly toward the porch door*) I'll go out to her now while I feel—that—yes, I know I can make her believe me now.

MISS GILPIN. You'll tell me—later on?

MURRAY. Yes. (*He opens the door to the porch and goes out.* MISS GILPIN *stands for a moment looking after him worriedly. Then she sighs helplessly and goes out to the hall.* MURRAY *steps noiselessly out on the porch.* EILEEN *is lying motionless with her eyes closed.* MURRAY *stands looking at her, his face showing the emotional stress he is under, a great pitying tenderness in his eyes. Then he seems to come to a revealing decision on what is best to do for he tiptoes to the bedside and bending down with a quick movement, takes her in his arms, and kisses her*) Eileen!

EILEEN. (*startled at first, resists automatically for a moment*) Stephen! (*Then she succumbs and lies back in his arms with a happy sigh, putting both hands to the sides of his face and staring up at him adoringly*) Stephen, dear!

MURRAY. (*quickly questioning her before she can question him*)

You were fibbing—about that night—weren't you? You do love me, don't you, Eileen?

EILEEN. (*breathlessly*) Yes—I—but you, Stephen—you don't love me. (*She makes a movement as if to escape from his embrace.*)

MURRAY. (*genuinely moved—with tender reassurance*) Why do you suppose I came away up here if not to tell you I did? But they warned me—Miss Gilpin—that you were still weak and that I mustn't excite you in any way. And I—I didn't want—but I had to come back and tell you.

EILEEN. (*convinced—with a happy laugh*) And is that why you acted so strange—and cold? Aren't they silly to tell you that! As if being happy could hurt me! Why, it's just that, just you I've needed!

MURRAY. (*his voice trembling*) And you'll marry me, Eileen?

EILEEN. (*a shadow of doubt crossing her face momentarily*) Are you sure—you want me, Stephen?

MURRAY. (*a lump in his throat—huskily*) Yes. I do want you, Eileen.

EILEEN. (*happily*) Then I will—after I'm well again, of course. (*She kisses him.*)

MURRAY. (*chokingly*) That won't be long now, Eileen.

EILEEN. (*joyously*) No—not long—now that I'm happy for once in my life. I'll surprise you, Stephen, the way I'll pick up and grow fat and healthy. You won't know me in a month. How can you ever love such a skinny homely thing as I am now! (*With a laugh*) I couldn't if I was a man—love such a fright.

MURRAY. Ssshh!

EILEEN. (*confidently*) But you'll see now. I'll make myself get well. We won't have to wait long, dear. And can't you move up to the town near here where you can see me every day, and you can work and I can help you with your stories just as I used to—and I'll soon be strong enough to do your typing again. (*She laughs*) Listen to me—talking about helping you—as if they weren't all your own work, those blessed stories!—as if I had anything to do with it!

MURRAY. (*hoarsely*) You had! You did! They're yours. (*Trying to calm himself*) But you mustn't stay here, Eileen. You'll let me take you away, won't you?—to a better place—not far away—White Lake, it's called. There's a small private sanatorium there. Doctor Stanton says it's one of the best. And I'll live near by—it's a beautiful spot—and see you every day.

EILEEN. (*in the seventh heaven*) And did you plan out all this for me beforehand, Stephen? (*He nods with averted eyes. She kisses his hair*) You wonderful, kind dear! And it's a small place—this White Lake? Then we won't have so many people around to disturb us, will we? We'll be all to ourselves. And you ought to work so well u there. I know New York wasn't good for you—alone—without me And I'll get well and strong so quick! And you say it's a beautifu place? (*Intensely*) Oh, Stephen, any place in the world would be beautiful to me—if you were with me! (*His face is hidden in the pillow beside her. She is suddenly startled by a muffled sob—anxiously*) Why—Stephen—you're—you're crying! (*The tears start to her own eyes.*)

MURRAY. (*raising his face which is this time alight with a passionate awakening—a revelation*) Oh, I do love you, Eileen! I do! I love you, love you!

EILEEN. (*thrilled by the depths of his present sincerity—but with a teasing laugh*) Why, you say that as if you'd just made the discovery, Stephen!

MURRAY. Oh, what does it matter, Eileen! Oh, what a blind selfish ass I've been! You are my life—everything! I love you, Eileen! I do! I do! And we'll be married— (*Suddenly his face grows frozen with horror as he remembers the doom. For the first time Death confronts him face to face as a menacing reality.*)

EILEEN. (*terrified by the look in his eyes*) What is it, Stephen? What—?

MURRAY. (*with a groan—protesting half aloud in a strangled voice*) No! No! It can't be—! My God! (*He clutches her hands and hides his face in them.*)

EILEEN. (*with a cry*) Stephen! What is the matter? (*Her face suddenly betrays an awareness, an intuitive sense of the truth*) Oh—Stephen— (*Then with a childish whimper of terror*) Oh, Stephen, I'm going to die! I'm going to die!

MURRAY. (*lifting his tortured face—wildly*) No!

EILEEN. (*her voice sinking to a dead whisper*) I'm going to die.

MURRAY. (*seizing her in his arms in a passionate frenzy and pressing his lips to hers*) No, Eileen, no, my love, no! What are you saying? What could have made you think it? You—die? Why, of course, we're all going to die—but— Good God! What damned nonsense! You're getting well—every day. Everyone—Miss Gilpin—Stanton—everyone told me that. I swear before God, Eileen, they did! You're still weak, that's all. They said—it won't be long. You mustn't think that—not now.

EILEEN. (*miserably—unconvinced*) But why did you look at me—that way—with that awful look in your eyes—? (*While she is speaking* MISS GILPIN *enters the room from the hallway. She appears worried, agitated. She hurries toward the porch but stops inside the doorway, arrested by* MURRAY'S *voice.*)

MURRAY. (*takes* EILEEN *by the shoulders and forces her to look into his eyes*) I wasn't thinking about you then— No, Eileen—not you. I didn't mean you—but me—yes, me! I couldn't tell you before. They'd warned me—not to excite you—and I knew that would—if you loved me.

EILEEN. (*staring at him with frightened amazement*) You mean you—you're sick again?

MURRAY. (*desperately striving to convince her*) Yes. I saw Stanton. I lied to you before—about that. It's come back on me, Eileen—you see how I look—I've let myself go. I don't know how to live without you, don't you see? And you'll—marry me now—without waiting—and help me to get well—you and I together—and not mind their lies—what they say to prevent you? You'll do that, Eileen?

EILEEN. I'll do anything for you— And I'd be so happy— (*She breaks*

119

down) But, Stephen, I'm so afraid. I'm all mixed up. Oh, Stephen, I don't know what to believe!

MISS GILPIN. (*who has been listening thunderstruck to* MURRAY's *wild pleading, at last summons up the determination to interfere— steps out on the porch—in a tone of severe remonstrance*) Mr. Murray!

MURRAY. (*starts to his feet with wild, bewildered eyes—confusedly*) Oh—you— (MISS GILPIN *cannot restrain an exclamation of dismay as she sees his face wrung by despair.* EILEEN *turns her head away with a little cry as if she would hide her face in the bedclothes. A sudden fierce resolution lights up* MURRAY's *countenance—hoarsely*) You're just in time, Miss Gilpin! Eileen! Listen! You'll believe Miss Gilpin, won't you? She knows all about it. (EILEEN *turns her eyes questioningly on the bewildered nurse.*)

MISS GILPIN. What—?

MURRAY. (*determinedly*) •Doctor Stanton—he must have told you about me. Eileen doesn't believe me—when I tell her I got T. B. again. She thinks—I don't know what. I know you're not supposed to, but— can't you tell her—?

MISS GILPIN. (*stunned by being thus defiantly confronted—stammeringly*) Mr. Murray! I—I—how can you ask—

MURRAY. (*quickly*) She loves me—and I—I—love her! (*He holds her eyes and speaks with a passion of sincerity that compels belief*) I love her, do you hear?

MISS GILPIN. (*falteringly*) You—love—Eileen?

MURRAY. Yes! I do! (*Entreatingly*) So—tell her—won't you?

MISS GILPIN. (*swallowing hard, her eyes full of pity and sorrow fixed on* EILEEN) Yes—Eileen— (*She turns away slowly toward the door.*)

EILEEN. (*with a little cry of alarmed concern, stretches out her hands to* MURRAY *protectingly*) Poor Stephen—dear! (*He grasps her hands and kisses them.*)

MISS GILPIN. (*in a low voice*) Mr. Murray. May I speak to you?

MURRAY. (*with a look of questioning defiance at her*) Certainly.

MISS GILPIN. (*turns to* EILEEN *with a forced smile*) I won't steal him away for more than a moment, Eileen. (EILEEN *smiles happily.*)

MURRAY. (*follows* MISS GILPIN *into the room. She leads him to the far end of the room near the door to the hall, after shutting the porch door carefully behind him. He looks at her defiantly*) Well?

MISS GILPIN. (*in low, agitated tones*) What has happened? I feel as if I may have done a great wrong to myself—to you—to her—by that lie. And yet—something forced me.

MURRAY. (*moved*) It has saved her—us. Oh, how can I explain what happened? I suddenly saw—how beautiful and sweet and good she is—how I couldn't bear the thought of life without her— That's all. (*Determinedly*) She must marry me at once and I'll take her away—the far West—any place Stanton thinks can help. And she can take care of me—as she thinks—and I know she'll grow well as I seem to grow well. Oh Miss Gilpin, don't you see? No half and half measures can help us—help her. (*Fiercely as if defying her*) But we'll win together. We can! We must! There are things doctors can't value—can't know the strength of! (*Exultantly*) You'll see! I'll make Eileen get well, I tell you! Happiness will cure! Love is stronger than— (*He suddenly breaks down before the pitying negation she cannot keep from her eyes. He sinks on a chair, shoulders bowed, face hidden in his hands, with a groan of despair*) Oh, why did you give me a hopeless hope?

MISS GILPIN. (*putting her hand on his shoulder—with tender compassion—sadly*) Isn't all life just that—when you think of it? (*Her face lighting up with a consoling revelation*) But there must be something back of it—some promise of fulfillment—somehow—somewhere—in the spirit of hope itself.

MURRAY. (*dully*) What do words mean to me now? (*Then suddenly starting to his feet and flinging off her hand with disdainful strength—violently and almost insultingly*) What damned rot! I tell you we'll win! We must! All the verdicts of all the doctors—what do they matter? This is—beyond you! And we'll win in spite of you!

(*Scornfully*) How dare you use the word hopeless—as if it were the last! Come now, confess, damn it! There's always hope, isn't there? What do you *know*? Can you say you *know* anything?

MISS GILPIN. (*taken aback by his violence for a moment, finally bursts into a laugh of helplessness which is close to tears*) I? I know nothing—absolutely nothing! God bless you both! (*She raises her handkerchief to her eyes and hurries out to the hallway without turning her head.* MURRAY *stands looking after her for a moment; then strides out to the porch.*)

EILEEN. (*turning and greeting him with a shy smile of happiness as he comes and kneels by her bedside*) Stephen! (*He kisses her. She strokes his hair and continues in a tone of motherly, self-forgetting solicitude*) I'll have to look out for you, Stephen, won't I? From now on? And see that you rest so many hours a day—and drink your milk when I drink mine—and go to bed at nine sharp when I do—and obey everything I tell you—and—

CURTAIN

GOLD

A Play in Four Acts

1920

CHARACTERS

CAPTAIN ISAIAH BARTLETT, *of the whaling ship "Triton"*

SILAS HORNE, *boatswain of the "Triton"*

BEN CATES

JIMMY KANAKA, *an Islander* } *of the "Triton's" crew*

BUTLER, *cook of the "Triton"*

ABEL, *the ship's boy*

SARAH ALLEN BARTLETT, *the captain's wife*

SUE, *their daughter*

NAT, *their son*

DANIEL DREW, *officer of a freight steamer*

DOCTOR BERRY

GOLD

ACT ONE

Scene—*A small, barren coral island on the southern fringe of the Malay Archipelago. The coral sand, blazing white under the full glare of the sun, lifts in the right foreground to a long hummock a few feet above sea-level. A stunted coco palm rises from the center of this elevation, its bunch of scraggly leaves drooping motionlessly, casting a small circular patch of shadow directly beneath on the ground about the trunk. About a hundred yards in the distance the lagoon is seen, its vivid blue contrasting with the white coral beach which borders its circular outline. The far horizon to seaward is marked by a broad band of purplish haze which separates the bright blue of the water from the metallic gray-blue of the sky. The island bakes. The intensity of the sun's rays is flung back skyward in a quivering mist of heat-waves which distorts the outlines of things, giving the visible world an intangible eerie quality, as if it were floating submerged in some colorless molten fluid.*

As the curtain rises, ABEL *is discovered lying asleep, curled up in the patch of shade beneath the coco palm. He is a runty, undersized boy of fifteen, with a shrivelled old face, tanned to parchment by the sun. He has on a suit of dirty dungarees, man's size, much too large for him, which hang in loose folds from his puny frame. A thatch of brown hair straggles in limp wisps from under the peaked canvas cap he wears. He looks terribly exhausted. His dreams are evidently fraught with terror, for he twitches convulsively and moans with fright.* BUTLER *enters hurriedly, panting, from the right, rear. He is a tall man of over middle age, dressed in the faded remainder of what*

125

was once a brown suit. The coat, the buttons of which have been torn off, hangs open, revealing his nakedness beneath. A cloth cap covers his bald head, with its halo of dirty thin gray hair. His body is emaciated. His face, with its round, blue eyes, is weathered and cracked by the sun's rays. The wreck of a pair of heavy shoes flop about his bare feet. He looks back cautiously, as if he were afraid of being followed; then satisfied that he is not, he approaches the sleeping boy, and bending down, puts his hand on ABEL's *forehead.* ABEL *groans and opens his eyes. He stares about furtively, as if seeking someone whose presence he dreads to find.*

ABEL. (*in a husky voice*) Where's Capt'n and the rest, Butts?

BUTLER. (*in a hoarse, cracked whisper*) On the beach—down there. (*He makes an exhausted gesture, right, and then sinks with a groan at the foot of the tree, leaning back against the trunk, trying vainly to hunch his long legs up so as to be completely in the shade.*)

ABEL. (*with avid eyes*) They ain't found no water yet?

BUTLER. (*shaking his head, his eyes closing wearily*) No. How would they—when there ain't any—not on this devil's island—dry as a bone, my sonny—sand and sun—that's all.

ABEL. (*with a sudden, shrill agony—his lips twitching*) I need a drink of water—something awful! (*With tremulous pleading*) Say, ain't you got 'nother drink left?—honest, ain't you?

BUTLER. (*looking around him cautiously*) Not so loud! (*Fixing his eyes sternly on the boy*) This is a dead secret, mind! You'll swear you won't blab—not to him?

ABEL. Sure, Butts, sure! Gawd strike me dead!

BUTLER. (*takes a pint bottle from the hip-pocket of his pants. It is about half full of water*) He—and the rest—they'd kill me like a dog—and you too, sonny—remember that!

ABEL. Sure! I ain't goin' to tell 'em, Butts. (*Stretching out his hands frenziedly*) Aw, give it to me, Butts! Give me a drink, for Christ's sake!

126

BUTLER. No, you don't! Only a few drops. It's got to last 'til a ship comes past that'll pick us up. That's the only hope. (*Holding the bottle at arm's length from the boy*) Hands down, now—or you don't get a drop! (*The boy lets his hands drop to his sides.* BUTLER *puts the bottle carefully to his lips, and allows the boy two gulps—then snatches it away*) That's all now. More later. (*He takes one gulp himself, and making a tremendous effort of will, jerks the bottle from his lips, and corking it quickly, thrusts it back in his pocket and heaves a shuddering sigh.*)

ABEL. Aw, more! Just another swaller—

BUTLER. (*determinedly*) No!

ABEL. (*crying weakly*) Yuh dirty mutt!

BUTLER. (*quietly*) Don't get riled. It only makes you hotter—and thirstier. (*The boy sinks back exhausted and closes his eyes.* BUTLER *begins to talk in a more assured voice, as if the sip of water had renewed his courage*) That'll save us yet, that bit of water. A lucky notion of mine to think of it—at the last moment. They were just lowering the boats. I could hear you calling to me to hurry and come. But I thought of filling this bottle. It'd been lying there in the galley for two years almost. I'd had it on my hip, full of whisky, that night in Oakland when I was shanghaied. So I filled it out of a bucket before I ran to the boat. Lucky I did, son—for you and me—not for them—damn 'em! (*As if in self-justification*) Why should I tell 'em, eh? Did I ever get anything better than a kick or a curse from one of them? (*Vindictively*) Would they give it to me if they had it? They'd see me in hell first! And besides, it's too late for them. They're mad as hatters right now, the four of them. They ain't had a drop since three nights back, when the water in the cask gave out and we rowed up against this island in the dark. (*Suddenly he laughs queerly*) Didn't you hear them shouting and yelling like lunatics just before I came?

ABEL. I thought I heard something—on'y maybe I was dreamin'.

BUTLER. It's them that are doing the dreaming. I was with them.

(*With rising anger*) He kicked me awake—and every time I tried to get away he beat me back. He's strong yet—(*with threatening vindictiveness*)—but he can't last long, damn him! (*Controlling himself, goes on with his story excitedly*) We went looking for water. Then Jimmy Kanaka saw a boat sunk half under down inside the reef—a Malay canoe, only bigger. They thought there might be something to drink on her. All of a sudden they gave an awful yell. They was all standing about a box they'd forced open, yelling and cursing and out of their heads completely. When I looked I seen the box was full of all sorts of metal junk—bracelets and bands and necklaces that I guess the Malays wear. Nothing but brass and copper, and bum imitations of diamonds and things—not worth a damn! I picked up some of the stuff to make sure. Then I told him straight. "This ain't gold. It's brass and copper—not worth a damn." God, he got wild! I had to run, or he'd knifed me. (*With sudden violence*) It serves 'em right, all that's happened and going to happen. Me shanghaied when I was drunk—taken away from a good job and forced to cook the swill on a rotten whaler! Oh, I'll pay him back for it! His damn ship is wrecked and lost to him—that's the first of it. I'll see him rot and die—and the three with him! But you and me'll be saved! D'you know why I've let you go halves on this water? It's because they kicked and beat you, too. And now we'll get even! (*He sinks back, exhausted by this outburst. They are both silent, leaning with closed eyes against the bole of the tree. A murmur of men's voices comes from the right, rear, and gradually gets nearer.*)

ABEL. (*opening his eyes with a start*) Butts! I hear 'em comin'!

BUTLER. (*listening, wide-eyed, for a moment*) Yes, it's them. (*He gets up weakly.* ABEL *staggers to his feet. They both move to the left.* BUTLER *shades his eyes with his hands and looks toward the beach*) Look! They're dragging along that box of junk with 'em, the damn fools! (*Warningly*) They're crazy as hell. Don't give 'em no chance to pick on you, d'you hear? (*There is a scuffling of heavy footsteps in the sand, and* CAPTAIN BARTLETT *appears, followed by* HORNE, *who in turn is followed by* CATES *and* JIMMY KANAKA. BARTLETT *is a tall, huge-framed figure of a man, dressed in a blue double-breasted coat, pants of the same material, and rubber sea-boots turned down from the knees. In spite of the ravages of hunger and thirst there is still a suggestion of immense strength in his heavy-muscled body. His head is massive, thickly covered with tangled, iron-gray hair. His face is large, bony, and leather-tanned, with a long aquiline nose and a gash of a mouth shadowed by a bristling gray mustache. His broad jaw sticks out at an angle of implacable stubbornness. Bushy gray brows overhang the obsessed glare of his somber dark eyes.* SILAS HORNE *is a thin, parrot-nosed, angular old man, his lean face marked by a life-time of crass lusts and mean cruelty. He is dressed in gray cotton trousers, and a singlet torn open across his hairy chest. The exposed skin of his arms and shoulders and chest has been blistered and seared by the sun. A cap is on his head.* CATES *is squat and broad chested, with thick, stumpy legs and arms. His square, stupid face, with its greedy pig's eyes, is terribly pock-marked. He is gross and bestial, an unintelligent brute. He is dressed in dungaree pants and a dirty white sailor's blouse, and wears a brown cap.* JIMMY KANAKA *is a tall, sinewy, bronzed young Islander. He wears only a loin cloth and a leather belt with a sheath-knife. The last two are staggering beneath the weight of a heavy inlaid chest. The eyes of the three white men are wild. They pant exhaustedly, their legs trembling with weakness beneath them. Their lips are puffed and cracked, their voices muffled by their swollen tongues. But there is a mad air of happiness, of excitement, about their scorched faces.*)

BARTLETT. (*in a crooning, monotonous voice*) It's heavy, I know, heavy—that chest. Up, bullies! Up with her! (*He flings himself in the shade, resting his back against the tree, and points to the sand at his feet.*) Put 'er there, bullies—there where I kin see!

HORNE. (*echoing his words mechanically*) Put 'er there!

CATES. (*in thick, stupid tones*) Aye-aye, sir! Down she goes, Jimmy. (*They set the chest down.*)

129

BARTLETT. Sit down, lads, sit down. Ye've earned your spell of rest. (*The three men throw themselves on the sand in attitudes of spent weariness.* BARTLETT'S *eyes are fixed gloatingly on the chest. There is a silence suddenly broken by* CATES, *who leaps to a kneeling position with a choked cry.*)

CATES. (*his eyes staring at the* CAPTAIN *with fierce insistence*) I want a drink—water! (*The others are startled into a rigid, dazed attention.* HORNE's *lips move painfully in a soundless repetition of the word. There is a pause. Then* BARTLETT *strikes the sides of his head with his fist, as if to drive this obsession from his brain.* BUTLER *and* ABEL *stand looking at them with frightened eyes.*)

BARTLETT. (*having regained control over himself, in a determined voice, deep-toned and menacing*) If ye speak that word again, Ben Cates—if ye say it once again—ye'll be food for the sharks! Ye hear?

CATES. (terrified) Yes, sir. (*He collapses limply on the sand again.* HORNE *and the* KANAKA *relax hopelessly.*)

BARTLETT. (*with heavy scorn*) Are ye a child to take on like a sick woman—cryin' for what ye know we've not got? Can't ye stand up under a little thirst like a man? (*Resolutely*) There'll be water enough —if ye'll wait and keep a stiff upper lip on ye. We'll all be picked up today. I'll stake my word on it. This state o' things can't last. (*His eyes fall on the chest*) Ye ought to be singin' 'stead o' cryin'—after the find we've made. What's the lack of water amount to—when ye've gold before you? (*With mad exultation*) Gold! Enough of it is your share alone to buy ye rum, and wine, and women, too, for the rest o' your life.

CATES. (*straightening up to a sitting posture—his small eyes staring at the box fascinatedly—in a stupid mumble*) Aye—aye—rum and wine!

BARTLETT. (*half closing his eyes as if the better to enjoy his vision*) Aye, rum and wine and women for you and Horne and Jimmy. No more hard work on the dirty sea for ye, bullies, but a full payday in your pockets to spend each day o' the year. (*The three strain their ears, listening eagerly. Even* BUTLER *and* ABEL *advance a step or two toward him, as if they, too, were half hypnotized*) And Cates grumbling because he's thirsty! I'd be the proper one to complain—if complainin' there was to do! Ain't I lost my ship and the work o' two years with her? And what have ye lost, all three, but a few rags o' clothes? (*With savage emphasis*) I tell ye, I be glad the "Triton" went down! (*He taps the box with his fingers*) They's more in this than ever was earned by all the whalin' ships afloat. They's gold—heavy and solid—and diamonds and emeralds and rubies!—red and green, they be.

CATES. (*licking his lips*) Aye, I seen 'em there—and emeralds be green, I know, and sell for a ton of gold!

BARTLETT. (*as if he hadn't heard and was dreaming out loud to himself*) Rum and wine for you three, and rest for me. Aye, I'll rest to home 'til the day I die. Aye, woman, I be comin' home now. Aye, Nat and Sue, your father be comin' home for the rest o' his life! I'll give up whalin' like ye've always been askin' me, Sarah. Aye, I'll go to meetin' with ye on a Sunday like ye've always prayed I would. We'll make the damn neighbors open their eyes, curse 'em! Carriages and silks for ye—they'll be nothin' too good—and for Sue and the boy. I've been dreamin' o' this for years. I never give a damn 'bout the oil—that's just trade—but I always hoped on some voyage I'd pick up ambergris—a whole lot of it—and that's worth gold!

HORNE. (*his head bobbing up from his chest drowsily*) Aye, ambergris! It's costly truck.

BUTLER. (*in a whisper to the boy—cautiously*) There! Wasn't I right? Mad as hatters, all of 'em!

BARTLETT. (*his voice more and more that of a somnambulist*) It's time I settled down to home with ye, Sarah. They's plenty o' big trees on my place, bullies, and shade and green grass, and a cool wind off the sea. (*He shakes off the growing drowsiness and glares about him in a rage*) Hell's fire! What crazy truck be I thinkin' of? (*But he and the others sink back immediately into stupor. After a pause*

131

he begins to relate a tale in a droning voice) Years ago, when I was whalin' out o' New Bedford, a man come to me—Spanish-looking, he was—and wanted to charter my ship and me go shares. He showed me a map o' some island off the coast of South America somewhere. They was a cross marked on it where treasure had been buried by the old pirates. But I was a fool. I didn't believe him. He got old Scott's schooner—finally. She sailed and never was heard o' since. But I've never forgot him and his ma. And often I've thought if I'd 'a' went that vige— (*He straightens up and shouts with aggressive violence*) But here she be! Run right into it—without no map nor nothin'. Gold and diamonds and all—there they be in front o' our eyes! (*To the now alert* JIMMY) Open 'er up, Jimmy!

JIMMY. (*getting up—in his soft voice*) Aye, Captain. (*He reaches down to lift the lid.*)

BARTLETT. (*a sudden change of feeling comes over him, and he knocks* JIMMY's *arm aside savagely*) Hands off, ye dog! I'm takin' care o' this chest, and no man's hand's goin' to touch it but mine!

JIMMY. (*stepping back docilely—in the same unmoved, soft tone*) Aye, Captain. (*He squats down to the left of the chest.*)

BARTLETT. (*seeming suddenly to notice the cook for the first time*) So there you be, eh? (*His voice growing thick with rage*) I ain't forgot what ye said down by the shore there! Lucky for ye I didn't catch ye then! "Brass and copper—junk," ye said—"not gold! Not worth a damn," ye said! Ye blasted son of a liar! (*Looking at* ABEL) Ye've been tellin' that boy your lies too, I kin tell by the look o' him. (*Sternly*) Come here, boy!

ABEL. (*advances with faltering steps*) Y-yes, s-sir?

BARTLETT. Open up that chest! Open it up, ye brat! (*With a desperate movement of fear* ABEL *reaches down and flings open the lid of the chest. As he does so,* BARTLETT's *huge hand fastens on the collar of his coat, and holds him with face bent over the box.* HORNE, CATES, *and* JIMMY KANAKA *pull themselves close, their necks craning for a look inside.*)

BARTLETT. (*shaking the terror-stricken boy*) What d'ye see there, ye little swab? What d'ye see there?

ABEL. Aw—leggo—I'm chokin'!

BARTLETT. (*grimly*) Ye'll choke in earnest if ye don't answer me. What d'ye see? Is it gold? Answer me—is it gold?

ABEL. (*stutteringly*) Yes—sure—gold—I see it!

BARTLETT. (*thrusts him away. The boy staggers and falls to the sand. BARTLETT turns to BUTLER triumphantly*) Ye see, ye liar? Gold! Gold! Even a child can tell it at a look. (*With a somber menace in his tone*) But ye—don't believe—do ye?

BUTLER. (*frightenedly*) Maybe I was wrong, sir. I—didn't—look very careful.

BARTLETT. Come here! (*He stands up, his back against the tree*) Come here!

BUTLER. Yes, sir. (*But he looks about him shiftily, as if to run away.*)

BARTLETT. Jimmy! (*The KANAKA leaps to his feet*) Knife him, Jimmy, if he tries to run.

JIMMY. (*his hand goes to his knife, his dark eyes lighting up with savagery—in his soft voice*) Aye, Captain!

BARTLETT. (*to the trembling cook*) Come here!

BUTLER. (*goes to him with the courage of desperation*) Yes, sir.

BARTLETT. (*pointing to the contents of the chest*) Is it gold—or no?

BUTLER. If I can feel of one—

BARTLETT. Pick one up.

BUTLER. (*picks up a heavy anklet encrusted with colored glass, looks at it for a minute—then feigning great assurance*) I was wrong, Captain. It's gold all right enough—worth all kinds of money, I bet.

BARTLETT. (*with mad triumph*) Ha! Ye've come to your senses, have ye? Too late, ye swab! No share for ye! And here's to teach ye for lyin' to me before! (*His fist jerks out from his side, and BUTLER is knocked sprawling on the sand, where he lies groaning for a moment, the anklet still clutched in his hand. The boy gives a gasp of fright and scampers off, left.*)

BARTLETT. That'll learn ye! (*He sits down beside the chest. The others crouch close.* BARTLETT *shoves in both of his hands—in a tone of mad gloating*) Gold! Better'n whaling, ain't she, boys? Better'n ambergris, even if I ever had luck to find any! (BUTLER *staggers to his feet. He examines the anklet with contemptuous scorn and even bites it to make sure. Then he edges stealthily toward the left. A sudden transformation comes over his face and he glowers at the Captain with hatred, his features distorted with fury.*)

JIMMY KANAKA. (*pointing to* BUTLER) He got him, Captain!

BARTLETT. (*glancing at the cook with contemptuous scorn*) Sneakin' away with that piece o' the gold, be ye? Ye thievin' swine! Ye know right enough it's gold now, don't ye? Well, ye kin keep it—for your share for speakin' the truth that once.

HORNE. (*his cupidity protesting*) Don't give it to him, sir! It's so much the less for us that worked for it when he did nothin'!

BUTLER. (*overcome by hysterical rage—stammering*) Who asked you for it—eh? Who—wants the damn thing? Not me! No! (*Holding the anklet out contemptuously*) Gold? Ha-ha! Gold? Brass, that's what—and pieces of glass! Junk! Not worth a damn. Here! Take it! (*He flings it on the sand before them.* BARTLETT *snatches it up protectingly.*)

BARTLETT. (*in a frenzy*) Jimmy! (*But* BUTLER *runs off left with a terrified cry.* JIMMY *springs to his feet and stands with his hand on his knife, waiting for a further order.*)

JIMMY. (*eagerly*) I go catch—go stick him, Captain?

BARTLETT. (*pausing—with a frown*) No. They's time enough for that—if need be. Sit down. (JIMMY *sits down again with a childish air of sulking.* BARTLETT *stares at the treasure, continuing to frown, as if* BUTLER's *action had made him uneasy, bewildered and confused him. He mutters half to himself*) Queer! Queer! He threw it back as if 'twas a chunk of mud! He knew—and yet he said he didn't want it. Junk, he called it—and he knows it's gold! He said 'twas gold himself a second back. He's queer. Why would he say junk when he knows it's gold? D'ye think—he don't believe?

HORNE. He was mad because you knocked him down.

BARTLETT. (*shaking his head grimly*) It ain't the first time I've knocked him down; but he never spoke up to me—like that—before. No, it's somethin' else is wrong with him—somethin'.

HORNE. No share for him, you told him, sir. That's what's wrong with him.

BARTLETT. (*again shaking his head*) No. His eyes—It's somethin' he's got in his head—somethin' he's hidin'! His share—maybe he thinks he'll get his share anyway, in spite o' us! Maybe he thinks his share wouldn't be all he wants! Maybe he thinks we'll die o' hunger and thirst before we get picked up—and he'll live—and then—he'll come in for the whole chestful! (*Suddenly springing to his feet in a rage*) Hell's fire! That's it, bullies! That's his sneakin' plan! To watch us die—and steal it from us!

CATES. (*rising to his knees and shaking his hand threateningly above his head*) Tell Jimmy to knife him, sir! Tell Jimmy—I ain't got a knife, or I'd do it myself. (*He totters weakly to his feet.*)

JIMMY. (*eagerly*) You speak, I stick him, Captain. I stick boy, too.

CATES. (*weakening*) I'm weak, but I kin do for him yet. I'm weak—(*His knees sag under him. He pleads piteously*) If I'd only a drink to put some strength in me! If I'd only a sup o' water, I'd do for him! (*Turning, as if to stagger down toward the beach*) There must be water. Let's look again. I'll go look— (*But the effort he makes is too much for his strength and he falls to the sand, panting with open mouth*).

BARTLETT. (*summoning his will—sternly*) Put a clapper on that jaw of yours, Cates, or I'll do it for ye!

CATES. (*blubbering*) If we don't find water—he'll watch us die.

JIMMY. (*insinuatingly*) Better me knife cook fella—kill boy, too!

BARTLETT. Will killin' 'em give us drink, ye fools? (*After a pause, he shakes his head as if to drive off some thought, and mutters*) No more o' that! (*Suddenly, in a tone of sharp command*) No more o' that, I say! We're keepin' no right watch for ships. Go aloft on that tree, Jimmy—and damn quick! (KANAKA *climbs quickly up the bole of the coco palm to the top and looks out on all sides of him. The others rise painfully to their feet and gaze up at him with awakened hope.*)

JIMMY. (*suddenly, in a glad voice*) I see um—see sail, Captain.

CATES. (*waving his arms frenziedly*) Sail—ho!

JIMMY. Look plenty like trade schooner, Captain. She no change course she fetch plenty close by here. She make full sail, she got plenty fella wind out there, she come quick.

HORNE. (*clapping* CATES *on the back*) Headin' straight for us, Cates, d'you hear?

BARTLETT. Come down. (*The Islander slides down.* BARTLETT *exclaims exultantly*) Didn't I tell ye? In the nick o' time. When she makes in close we'll go down to the reef and yell and wave at her. They'll see! The luck's with us today! (*His eyes fall on the treasure and he starts*) But now—what's to do with this chest—the gold?

HORNE. (*quickly*) You ain't going to tell them on the schooner about it?

CATES. They'd claim to share with us.

BARTLETT. (*scornfully*) D'ye think I'm cracked? No, we'll bury it here.

CATES. (*regretfully*) Leave it behind for anyone to find?

BARTLETT. We'll bury it deep, where hell itself won't find it—and we'll make a map o' this island. (*He takes a piece of paper and a stub of pencil from his pocket—pointing to the foot of the tree*) Dig a hole here—you, Horne and Jimmy—and dig it deep. (*The two bend down and commence to hollow out the sand with their hands.* BARTLETT *draws on the paper*) There's the lagoon—and the reef— (*To* CATES, *who is peering over his shoulder*) And here where the tree is, d'ye see, Cates, I'll make a cross where the gold is hid. (*Exultantly*) Oh, all hell'd not stop me from findin' this place again! Let us once get home and I'll fit out a small schooner the four of us can sail, and we'll come back here to dig it up. It won't be long, I swear to ye!

HORNE. (*straightening up*) This deep enough, sir?

JIMMY. (*who has straightened up and is looking off left—suddenly points excitedly*) He look, Captain! Cook fella, he look here! Boy he look, too! They look plenty too much, Captain! (*All four stand staring off at* BUTLER *and the boy, whose presence on the island they have forgotten in their mad excitement.*)

CATES. (*in stupid dismay*) They'll know where it's hid, sir!

HORNE. They'll tell 'em on the schooner!

CATES. (*wildly*) We've got to do for 'em, Captain! Gimme your knife, Jimmy—your knife— (*He stumbles toward the Islander, who pushes him aside brusquely, looking questioningly toward the Captain.*)

BARTLETT. (*who has been standing motionless, as if stunned by this forgotten complication—slowly*) There they be watchin' us, the sneakin' dogs! I was forgettin' they was here. (*Striking his knee with clenched fist*) We've got to do somethin' damn quick! That schooner'll be up soon where they kin sight her—and they'll wave and yell then—and she'll see 'em!

HORNE. And good-by to the gold for us!

JIMMY. (*eagerly*) You say fella word, Captain, me kill um quick. They no make plenty cry for schooner! They keep dam still plenty too much!

BARTLETT. (*looking at the Islander with mad cunning but replying only to* HORNE) Aye, it's good-by to the gold, Horne. That scum of a cook—he's made a mock o' us—sayin' it wasn't gold when he knew it was—he'll tell 'em—he'll get joy o' tellin' 'em!

HORNE. And that scrub of a boy—he's no better. He'll be in with him neck and crop.

CATES. (*hoarsely*) Knife 'em—and be done with it—I say!

BARTLETT. Or, if they don't tell the schooner's skipper it'll only be because they're plannin' to come back themselves—before we kin—

and dig it up. That cook—there's somethin' queer in his mind—somethin' he was hidin'—pretendin' not to believe. What d'ye think, Horne?

HORNE. I think—time's gettin' short—and talkin' won't do no good. (*Insinuatingly*) They'd do for us soon enough if *they* was able.

BARTLETT. Aye, murder was plain in his eyes when he looked at me.

HORNE. (*lowering his voice to a whisper*) Tell Jimmy—Captain Bartlett—is what I say!

BARTLETT. It's agin the law, Silas Horne!

HORNE. The law don't reach to this island.

BARTLETT. (*monotonously*) It's agin the law a captain's sworn to keep wherever he sails. They ain't refused duty—nor mutinied.

HORNE. Who'll know they ain't? They're trying to steal what's yours—that's worse'n mutiny. (*As a final persuasion*) And Jimmy's a heathen and under no laws. And he's stronger'n you are. You couldn't stop 'im.

BARTLETT. Aye—I couldn't prevent—

JIMMY. (*eagerly*) I fix um, Captain, they no tell! (BARTLETT *doesn't answer, but stares at the treasure.* HORNE *makes violent motions to* JIMMY *to go. The Islander stares at his master's face. Then, seeming to read the direct command there, he grunts with satisfaction, and pulling his knife from his sheath, he goes stealthily off left.* CATES *raises himself on his haunches to watch the Islander's movements.* HORNE *and* BARTLETT *sit still in a strained immobility, their eyes on the chest.*)

CATES. (*in an excited whisper*) I see 'em! They're sittin' with their backs this way! (*A slight pause*) There's Jimmy. He's crawlin' on his hands behind 'em. They don't notice—he's right behind—almost atop o' them. (*A pause.* CATES *gives a fiendish grunt*) Ugh! (BUTLER's *muffled cry comes from the left*) Right in the middle of the back! The cook's done! The boy's runnin'! (*There is a succession of quick screams from the boy, the padding of feet running toward them, the fall of a body, and the boy's dying groan.*)

HORNE. (*with satisfaction*) It's done, sir!

BARTLETT. (*slowly*) I spoke no word, remember that, Silas Horne!

HORNE. (*cunningly*) Nor me neither, sir. Jimmy took it on himself. If blame there is—it's on him.

BARTLETT. (*gloomily*) I spoke no word! (JIMMY *returns noiselessly from the left.*)

JIMMY. (*grinning with savage pride*) I fix um fella plenty, Captain. They no tell. They no open mouth plenty too much!

CATES. (*maudlinly*) You're a man, Jimmy—a man with guts to him —even if you're a— (*He babbles incoherently.*)

JIMMY. (*as the Captain does not look at him*) I go climb fella tree, Captain? I make look for schooner?

BARTLETT. (*rousing himself with an effort*) Aye. (*The Islander climbs the tree.*)

HORNE. (*getting to his feet—eagerly*) Where away, Jimmy?

JIMMY. She come, Captain, she come plenty quick.

HORNE. (*looking in the direction* JIMMY *indicates*) I kin see her tops'ls from here, sir. Look!

BARTLETT. (*getting to his feet—stares out to sea*) Aye! There she be —and makin' towards us fast. (*In a flash his somber preoccupation is gone, and he is commander once more. He puts the anklet in his hand into his coat pocket—harshly*) Come down o' that! They's work to do. (JIMMY *clambers down*) Did ye leave—them—lyin' in plain sight on the open sand?

JIMMY. Yes. I no touch um, Captain.

BARTLETT. Then ye'll touch 'em now. Go, bury 'em, cover 'em up with sand. And mind ye make a good job o' it that none'll see. Jump now!

JIMMY. (*obediently*) I go, Captain. (*He hurries off left.*)

BARTLETT. Down to the reef with ye, Horne! (*Giving the prostrate* CATES *a kick*) Up out o' that, Cates! Go with Horne, and when ye see the schooner hull up, wave to 'em, and yell like mad, d'ye hear?

HORNE. Aye, aye, sir!

BARTLETT. I'll stay here and bury the gold. It's best to be quick about it! They may turn a spyglass on us when they raise the island from deck! Off with ye! (*He gives* CATES *another kick.*)

CATES. (*groaning*) I'm sick! (*Incoherently*) Can't—report for duty —this watch. (*With a shout*) Water!

BARTLETT. (*contemptuously*) Ye dog! Give him a hand, Horne.

HORNE. (*putting a hand under his shoulder*) Up, man! We're to signal the schooner. There'll be water on board o' her—barrels of it!

CATES. (*aroused, scrambles to his feet, violently shaking off Horne's hand*) Water aboard o' her! (*His staring eyes catch the schooner's sails on the horizon. He breaks into a staggering run and disappears down toward the beach, right rear, waving his arms wildly and shouting*) Ahoy! Ahoy! Water! (HORNE *walks out quickly after him.*)

BARTLETT. (*after a quick glance around, sinks on his knees beside the chest and shoves both hands into it. From the chest comes a metallic clink as he fingers the pieces in his hands gloatingly*) Ye're safe now! (*In a dreaming tone, his eyes fixed before him in an ecstatic vision*) No more whalin' on the dirty seas! Rest to home! Gold! I've been dreamin' o' it all my life! (*Shaking himself—savagely*) Ye fool! Losin' your senses, be ye? Time ye was pickd up! Lucky! (*He shoves down the lid and places the chest in the hole. He pushes the sand in on top of it, whispering hoarsely*) Lay safe, d'ye hear! For I'll be back for ye! Aye—in spite of hell I'll dig ye up again. (*The voices of* HORNE *and* JIMMY *can be heard from the distance shouting as the curtain falls.*)

ACT TWO

SCENE—*Interior of an old boat-shed on the wharf of the Bartlett place on the California coast. In the rear, a double doorway looking out over the end of the wharf to the bay with the open sea beyond. On the left, two windows, and another door, opening on the dock. Near this door, a cot with blankets and a pillow without a slip. In the center, front, a table with a bottle and glasses on it, and three cane-bottomed chairs. On the right, a fishing dory. Here and there about the shed all sorts of odds and ends pertaining to a ship—old anchors, ropes, tackle, paint-pots, old spars, etc.*

It is late afternoon of a day six months later. Sunlight filters feebly through the stained, cobwebby window panes.

As the curtain rises, BARTLETT *and* SILAS HORNE *are discovered.* HORNE *is in working clothes of paint-stained dungaree. If his sufferings on the island have left any marks on his dry wizened face, they are undiscoverable. In* BARTLETT, *however, the evidence is marked. His hair has turned white. There are deep hollows under his cheek-bones. His jaw and tight-lipped mouth express defiant determination, as if he were fighting back some weakness inside himself, a weakness found in his eyes, which have something in them of fear, of a wishing to avoid other eyes. He is dressed much the same as when on the island. He sits by the table, center, his abstracted gaze bent on the floor before him.*

HORNE. (*who is evidently waiting for the Captain to say something —after a pause, glancing at him uneasily*) I'd best be getting back aboard the schooner, sir. (*Receiving no answer he starts for the door on the left.*)

BARTLETT. (*rousing himself with an effort*) Wait. (*After a pause*)

The full tide's at dawn tomorrow. They know we'll be sailin' then, don't they—Cates and Jimmy?

HORNE. Yes, sir. Oh, they'll be glad o' the word—and me, too, sir. (*With a greedy grin*) It's all we've been talkin' of since ye brought us down here—diggin' up the gold!

BARTLETT. (*passionately*) Aye, the gold! We'll have it before long, now, I reckon. That schooner—the way we've fitted her up—she'd take a man safe to the Pole and back! We'll drop anchor here with the chest on board in six months, unless— (*Hesitates.*)

HORNE. (*uneasily*) What, sir?

BARTLETT. (*brusquely*) The weather, ye fool!

HORNE. We'll trust to luck for that. (*Glancing at the Captain curiously*) And speakin' o' luck, sir—the schooner ain't been christened yet.

BARTLETT. (*betraying a sudden, fierce determination*) She will be!

HORNE. There'd be no luck for a ship sailin' out without a name.

BARTLETT. She'll have a name, I tell ye! She'll be named the "Sarah Allen," and Sarah'll christen her herself.

HORNE. It oughter been done, by rights, when we launched her a month back.

BARTLETT. (*sternly*) I know that as well as ye. (*After a pause*) She wasn't willin' to do it then. Women has queer notions—when they're sick, like. (*Defiantly—as if he were addressing someone outside of the room*) But Sarah'll be willin' now!

HORNE. Yes, sir. (*He again turns to go, as if he were anxious to get away.*)

BARTLETT. Wait! There's somethin' else I want to ask ye. Nat, he's been hangin' round the schooner all his spare time o' late. (*With rising anger*) I hope ye've remembered what I ordered ye, all three. Not a word o' it to him!

HORNE. (*retreating a step—hastily*) No fear o' that, sir!

BARTLETT. It ain't that I'm afeerd to tell him o' the gold, Silas Horne. (*Slowly*) It's them—other things—I'd keep him clear of.

HORNE. (*immediately guessing what he means—reassuringly*) We was all out o' our heads when them things happened, sir.

BARTLETT. Mad? Aye! But I ain't forgot—them two. (*He represses a shudder—then goes on slowly*) Do they ever come back to you—when you're asleep, I mean?

HORNE. (*pretending mystification*) Who's that, sir?

BARTLETT. (*with somber emphasis*) That cook and that boy. They come to me. I'm gettin' to be afeered o' goin' to sleep—not 'feered o' them, I don't mean. (*With sudden defiant bravado*) Not all the ghosts out o' hell kin keep me from a thing I've set my mind on. (*Collecting himself*) But I've waked up talkin' out loud—and I'm afeerd there might be someone hear me.

HORNE. (*uneasily—with an attempt to be reassuring*) You ain't all cured o' that sun and thirst on the island yet, sir.

BARTLETT. (*evidently reassured—with an attempt at conviviality*) Sit down a bit, Horne, and take a grog. (HORNE *does so.* BARTLETT *pours out a half-tumbler full of rum for himself and shoves the bottle over to* HORNE.)

HORNE. Luck to our vige, sir.

BARTLETT. Aye, luck! (*They drink.* BARTLETT *leans over and taps* HORNE *on the arm*) Aye, it takes time to get cured o' thirst and sun! (*Somberly—after a pause*) I spoke no word, Silas Horne, d'ye remember?

HORNE. Nor me. Jimmy did it alone. (*Craftily*) We'd all three swear Bible oaths to that in any court. And even if ye'd given the word, there ain't no good thinkin' more o' it, sir. Didn't they deserve all they got? Wasn't they plottin' on the sly to steal the gold?

BARTLETT. (*his eyes gleaming*) Aye!

HORNE. And when you said he'd get no share of it, didn't he lie to your face that it wasn't gold?

BARTLETT. (*with sudden rage*) Aye, brass and junk, he said, the lyin' scum! That's what he keeps sayin' when I see him in sleep! He didn't believe—an' then he owned up himself 'twas gold! He knew! He

143

lied a-purpose! (*Rising to his feet—with confident defiance*) They deserved no better nor they got. Let 'em rot! (*Pours out another drink for himself and* HORNE.)

HORNE. Luck, sir! (*They drink. There is a knock at the door on the left followed by* MRS. BARTLETT's *voice calling feebly*, "Isaiah! Isaiah!" BARTLETT *starts but makes no answer.* HORNE *turns to him questioningly*) It's Mrs. Bartlett, sir. Shall I open the door?

BARTLETT. No. I ain't aimin' to see her—yet awhile. (*Then with sudden reasonless rage*) Let her in, damn ye! (HORNE *goes and unhooks the door.* MRS. BARTLETT *enters. She is a slight, slender little woman of fifty. Sickness, or the inroads of a premature old age, have bowed her shoulders, whitened her hair, and forced her to walk feebly with the aid of a cane. A resolute spirit still flashes from her eyes, however, and there is a look of fixed determination on her face. She stands gazing at her husband. There is something accusing in her stare.*)

BARTLETT. (*avoiding her eyes—brusquely*) Well? What is it ye want o' me, Sarah?

MRS. B. I want to speak with you alone, Isaiah.

HORNE. I'll be gettin' back aboard, sir. (*Starts to go.*)

BARTLETT. (*in a tone almost of fear*) Wait. I'm goin' with ye. (*Turning to his wife—with a certain rough tenderness*) Ye oughtn't to walk down the hill here, Sarah. The doctor told ye to rest in the house and save your strength.

MRS. B. I want to speak to you alone, Isaiah.

BARTLETT. (*very uneasily*) I've got to work on the schooner, Sarah.

MRS. B. She'll be sailin' soon?

BARTLETT. (*suddenly turning on her defiantly*) Tomorrow at dawn!

MRS. B. (*with her eyes fixed accusingly on his*) And you be goin' with her?

BARTLETT. (*in the same defiant tone*) Yes, I be! Who else'd captain her?

MRS. B. On a craft without a name.

BARTLETT. She'll have that name!

144

MRS. B. No.

BARTLETT. She'll have that name, I tell ye!

MRS. B. No.

BARTLETT. (*thoroughly aroused, his will tries to break hers, but finds her unbending. He mutters menacingly*) Ye'll see! We'll talk o' that later, you and me. (*Without a further glance at his wife he strides past her and disappears through the doorway, followed by* HORNE. MRS. BARTLETT *sinks down in the chair by the table. She appears suddenly weak and crushed. Then from outside comes a girl's laughing voice.* MRS. BARTLETT *does not seem to hear, nor to notice* SUE *and* DREW *when they enter.* SUE *is a slender, pretty girl of about twenty, with large blue eyes, reddish-brown hair, and a healthy, sun-tanned, out-of-door complexion. In spite of the slightness of her figure there is a suggestion of great vitality and nervous strength about her.* DREW *is a well-set-up, tall young fellow of thirty. Not in any way handsome, his boyish face, tanned to a deep brown, possesses an engaging character of healthy, cheerful forcefulness that has its compelling charm. There would be no chance of mistaking him for anything but the ship's officer he is. It is written on his face, his walk, his voice, his whole bearing.*)

SUE. (*as they enter*) He'll either be here or on the schooner, Danny. (*Then she sees her mother, with startled amazement*) Ma! Good heavens, what are you doing here? Don't you know you shouldn't—

MRS. B. (*with a start—turning to her daughter with a forced smile*) There, Sue, now! Don't go scoldin' me! (*Then seeing* DREW—*in a tone of forced gayety*) And if there ain't Danny Drew—back home to port at last! You can kiss an old woman, Danny—without makin' her jealous, I reckon.

DREW. (*kissing her—with a smile*) It certainly seems good to see you again—and be back again myself.

MRS. B. We read in the paper where your ship'd reached San Francisco. Sue's been on pins and needles ever since.

SUE. (*protestingly*) Ma!

DREW. (*with a grin*) It's a long time to be away from Sue—four

145

months. You remember, Ma, I left just after the big excitement here —when Captain Bartlett turned up after we'd all heard the "Triton" was wrecked and given him up for lost.

MRS. B. (*her face clouding—in a tone of deep sorrow*) Yes. (DREW *is surprised and glances at* SUE *questioningly. She sighs.* MRS. BARTLETT *gets to her feet with difficulty, assisted by* DREW.)

SUE. We'll help you back to the house.

MRS. B. Shucks! I'm sick o' the house. I need sun and fresh air, and today's so nice I couldn't stay indoors. I'm goin' to set out on the wharf and watch your Pa workin' on the schooner. Ain't much time left to see her, Sue. They're sailin' tomorrow at dawn, your Pa says.

SUE. Tomorrow? Then you're going to christen her?

MRS. B. (*with grim determination*) No, I ain't, Sue! (*Catching* DREW'S *glance fixed on her with puzzled curiosity, she immediately attempts to resume her joking tone*) Shucks! Here's Danny wonderin' what silliness we're talkin' of. It's just this, Danny. Captain Bartlett, he's got a crazy notion in his head that just because his ship was wrecked last vige he'll give up whalin' for life. He's fitted out this little schooner for tradin' in the Islands. More money in that, he says. But I don't agree with no such lunatic notions, and I'm not goin' to set my approval on his craziness by christenin' his ship with my name, like he wants me to. He'd ought to stick to whalin', like he's done all his life. Don't you think so, Danny?

DREW. (*embarrassed*) Why, sure—he's rated one of the smartest whaling skippers here on the coast—and I should think—

MRS. B. Just what I tell him—only he's that stubborn. I'd best get out quick while it's still sunny and warm. It's damp in here for an old body. (DREW *helps her to the door on the left, opens it, and the two go out, followed by* SUE, *who carries a chair. After a pause,* SUE *and* DREW *return.* SUE *carefully shuts the door after them. Her face is troubled.*)

DREW. (*looks at her for a minute, then comes and puts his arm around her and kisses her*) What's the trouble, Sue?

SUE. (*trying to force a smile*) Nothing, Danny.

DREW. Oh, yes there is! No use putting me off that way. Why, I felt it hanging about in the air ever since I looked at your Ma.

SUE. Yes, she's failed terribly since you saw her last.

DREW. Oh, I don't mean just sickness—only—did you notice how she had to—force herself—to joke about things? She used to be so cheerful natural. (*Scratching his head in honest puzzlement*) But—that ain't what I mean, either. What is it, Sue? Maybe I can help somehow. You look worried, too. Pshaw! You can tell me, can't you?

SUE. Why, yes, Danny—of course—only I'm just as puzzled as you over what it comes from. It's something between Pa and Ma—something only the two of them know. It all seemed to start one morning after you'd left—about a week after he'd come home with those three awful men. During that first week he acted all right—just like he used to—only he'd get talking kind of wild now and then about being glad the Triton was lost, and promising we'd all be millionaires once he started making trips on the schooner. Ma didn't seem to mind his going in for trading then. Then, the night of the day he bought the schooner, something must have happened between them. Neither of them came down to breakfast. I went up to Ma, and found her so sick we sent for the doctor. He said she'd suffered a great shock of some kind, although she wouldn't tell him a word. I found Pa down in this shed. He'd moved that cot down here, and said he'd have to sleep here after that because he wanted to be near the schooner. It's been that way ever since. He's slept down here and never come up to the house except at mealtimes. He's never been alone with Ma one second since then, I don't believe. And she—she's been trying to corner him, to get him alone. I've noticed it, although she does her best to hide it from Nat and me. And she's been failing, growing weaker and sicker looking every day. (*Breaking down*) Oh, Danny, these last months have been terrible!

DREW. (*soothing her*) There! It'll all come out right.

SUE. I'm sure that's why she's crept down here today. She's bound she'll see him alone.

DREW. (*frowning*) Seems to me it must be all your Pa's fault, Sue—whatever it is. Have you tried to talk to him?

SUE. Yes—a good many times; but all he's ever said was: "There's things you wouldn't take interest in, Sue. You'll know when it's time to know"—and then he'd break off by asking me what I'd like most to have in the world if he had piles of money. And then, one time, he seemed to be terribly afraid of something, and he said to me: "You hustle up and marry Danny, Sue. You marry him and get out of this."

DREW. (*with an affectionate grin*) I surely wish you'd take his advice, Sue! (*He kisses her.*)

SUE. (*with intense longing*) Oh, I wish I could, Danny.

DREW. I've quite considerable saved now, Sue, and it won't be so long before I get my own ship, I'm hoping, now that I've got my master's certificate. I was hoping at the end of this voyage—

SUE. So was I, Danny—but it can't be this time. With Ma so weak, and no one to take care of her but me— (*Shaking her head—in a tone of decision*) I couldn't leave home now, Danny. It wouldn't be right. I couldn't feel really happy—until this thing—whatever it is—is settled between Pa and Ma and they're just as they used to be again. (*Pleadingly*) You understand, don't you, Danny?

DREW. (*soberly*) Why—surely I do, Sue. (*He pats her hand*) Only, it's hard waiting. (*He sighs.*)

SUE. I know. It's just as hard for me.

DREW. I thought maybe I could help; but this isn't anything anyone outside your family could mix in. (SUE *shakes her head. He goes on gloomily after a pause*) What's the matter with Nat? Seems as if he ought to be able to step in and talk turkey to your Pa.

SUE. (*slowly*) You'll find Nat changed, too, Danny—changed terribly. He's caught the disease—whatever it is. You know how interested in his work he's been ever since they put him in the designing department down in the shipyard?

DREW. Yes.

SUE. (*with emphasis*) Well, all that's changed. He hates it now, or at

148

least he says he does. And when he comes home, he spends all his time prowling around the dock here, talking with those three awful men. And what do you think he told me only the other day? That he was bound he'd throw up his job and make this voyage on the schooner. He even asked me to ask Pa to let him go.

DREW. Your Pa don't want him to, eh?

SUE. Why, of course not! Leave a fine position he worked so hard to get just for this crazy notion! The terrible part is, he's got Ma worried to death—as if she wasn't upset enough already. She's so afraid he'll go—that Pa'll let him at the last moment.

DREW. Maybe I can help after all. I can talk to Nat.

SUE. (*shaking her head*) He's not the same Nat, Danny.

DREW. (*trying to be consoling*) Pshaw, Sue! I think you just get to imagining things. (*As he finishes speaking, the door in the rear opens and* NAT *appears. He is a tall, loose-framed boy of eighteen, who bears a striking resemblance to his father. His face, like his father's, is large and bony, with deepset black eyes, an aquiline nose, and a wide, thin-lipped mouth. There is no suggestion in* NAT, *however, of the older man's physical health and great strength. He appears an indoor product, undeveloped in muscle, with a sallow complexion and stooped shoulders. His thick hair is a deep black. His voice recalls his father's, hollow and penetrating. He is dressed in a gray flannel shirt and cor-duroy trousers.* DREW *calls out to him heartily*) Hello, Nat! Speak of the Devil! Sue and I were just talking about you. (*He goes toward* NAT, *his hand outstretched.*)

NAT. (*comes toward them, meets* DREW, *and shakes his hand with evident pleasure*) Hello, Danny! You're a sight for sore eyes! (*His manner undergoes a sudden change. He casts a quick, suspicious glance from* DREW *to his sister*) You were talking about me? what about?

SUE. (*quickly—with a warning glance at* DREW) About your work down at the shipyard.

NAT. (*disgustedly*) Oh, that. (*In a tone of reasonless irritation*) For

God's sake, Sue, let me alone about my work. Don't I have to live with the damn thing all day, without your shoving it in my face the minute I get home? I want to forget it—get away!

DREW. Go to sea, eh?

NAT. (*suspiciously*) Maybe. Why? What do you mean? (*Turning to his sister—angrily*) What have you been telling Danny?

SUE. I was talking about the schooner—telling him she sails tomorrow.

NAT. (*dumfounded*) Tomorrow? (*Overcome by sudden, nervous excitement*) It can't be. How do you know? Who told you?

SUE. Ma. Pa told her.

NAT. Then she's been talking to him—telling him not to take me, I'll bet. (*Angrily*) Oh, I wish Ma'd mind her own business!

SUE. Nat!

NAT. Well, Sue, how would you like it? I'm not a little boy any more. I know what I want to do. I want to go with them. I want to go more than I've ever wanted anything else in my life before. He—he doesn't want me. He's afraid I— But I think I can force him to— (*He glances at* DREW's *amazed face and stops abruptly—sullenly*) Where is Pa?

SUE. He's aboard the schooner.

NAT. (*disappointedly*) Then it's no good trying to see him now.

DREW. Sounds funny to hear you talking about going to sea. Why, you always used—

NAT. This is different.

DREW. You want to see the Islands, I suppose?

NAT. (*suspiciously*) Maybe. Why not?

DREW. What group is your Pa heading for first?

NAT. (*more suspiciously*) You'll have to ask him. Why do you want to know? (*Abruptly*) You better be getting up to the house, Sue— if we're to have any supper. Danny must be hungry. (*He turns his back on them. They exchange meaning glances.*)

SUE. (*with a sigh*) It must be getting late. Come on, Danny. You can see Pa later on. (*They go toward the door in the rear*) Aren't you coming, Nat?

NAT. No. I'll wait. (*Impatiently*) Go ahead. I'll be up before long.

DREW. See you later, then, Nat.

NAT. Yes. (*They go out, rear.* NAT *paces up and down in a great state of excitement. The door on the left is opened and* BARTLETT *enters. Father and son stand looking at one another for a second.* NAT *takes a step backward as if in fear, then straightens up defiantly.*)

BARTLETT. (*slowly*) Is this the way ye mind my orders, boy? I've told ye time an' again not to be sneakin' and spyin' around this wharf.

NAT. I'm not sneaking and spying. I wanted to talk to you, Pa.

BARTLETT. (*sits down by the table*) Well, here I be.

NAT. Sue said the schooner sails tomorrow.

BARTLETT. Aye!

NAT. (*resolutely*) I want to go with you, Pa.

BARTLETT. (*briefly—as if dismissing the matter*) Ye can't. I've told ye that before. Let this be the last time ye ask it.

NAT. But why? Why can't I go?

BARTLETT. Ye've your own work to do—good work. Attend to that and leave me to mine.

NAT. But you always wanted me to go on voyages to learn whaling with you.

BARTLETT. This be different.

NAT. (*with excited indignation*) Yes, this is different! Don't I know it? Do you think you can hide that from me? It is different, and that's why I want to go.

BARTLETT. Ye can't, I say.

NAT. (*pleadingly*) But why not, Pa? I can do a man's work on a ship, or anywhere else.

BARTLETT. (*roughly*) Your place is here, with Sue and your Ma, and here you'll stay.

NAT. (*angrily*) That isn't any reason. But I know your real one. You're afraid—

151

BARTLETT. (*with a touch of uneasiness—forcing a scornful laugh*) Afeerd! Afeerd o' what? Did ye ever know me to be afeerd?

NAT. Afraid of what I might find out if I went with you.

BARTLETT. (*with the same forced, uneasy scorn*) And what d'ye think ye'd find out, Nat?

NAT. First of all that it's not a trading venture you're going on. Oh, I'm not a fool! That story is all right to fool the neighbors and girls like Sue. But I know better.

BARTLETT. What d'ye know?

NAT. You're going for something else.

BARTLETT. What would that be?

NAT. I don't know—exactly. Something—on that island.

BARTLETT. (*he gets to his feet with a forced burst of laughter*) Ye fool of a boy! Ye got that notion out o' some fool book ye've been reading, didn't ye? And I thought ye'd growed to be a man! (*More and more wild in his forced scorn*) Ye'll be tellin' me next it's buried treasure I be sailin after—pirates' gold buried on that island—all in a chest— and a map to guide me with a cross marked on it where the gold is hid! And then they be ghosts guardin' it, ben't they—spirits o' murdered men? They always be, in the books. (*He laughs scornfully.*)

NAT. (*gazing at him with fascinated eyes*) No, not that last. That's silly—but I did think you might have found—

BARTLETT. (*laughing again*) Treasure? Gold? (*With forced sternness*) Nat, I be ashamed of ye. Ye've had schoolin', and ye've been doin' a man's work in the world, and doin' it well, and I'd hoped ye'd take my place here to home when I be away, and look after your Ma and Sue. But ye've owned up to bein' a little better nor a boy in short britches, dreamin' o' pirates' gold that never was 'cept in books.

NAT. But you—you're to blame. When you first came home you did nothing but talk mysteriously of how rich we'd all be when the schooner got back.

BARTLETT. (*roughly*) But what's that to do with silly dreams? It's in the line o' trade I meant.

NAT. But why be so mysterious about trade? There's something you're hiding. You can't say no because I feel it.

BARTLETT. (*insinuatingly—with a crafty glance at his son*) Supposin' in one of them Eastern trading ports I'd run across a bit o' business with a chance for a fortune in it for a man that wasn't afeerd of the law, and could keep his mouth shut?

NAT. (*disappointed*) You mean illegal trading?

BARTLETT. I mean what I mean, Nat—and I'd be a fool to tell an overgrown boy, or two women—or any man in the world, for the matter o' that—what I do mean.

NAT. (*turning toward the door in the rear—disgustedly*) If it's only that, I don't want to hear it. (*He walks toward the door—stops and turns again to his father*) No, I don't believe it. That's not like you. You're not telling the truth, Pa.

BARTLETT. (*rising to his feet—with a savage sternness in which there is a wild note of entreaty*) I've listened to your fool's talk enough. Get up to the house where ye belong! I'll stand no more o' your meddling in business o' mine. I've been patient with ye, but there's an end to that! Take heed o' what I'm sayin', if ye know what's good for ye! (*With a sort of somber pride*) I'll stand alone in this business and finish it out alone if I go to hell for it. Ye hear me?

NAT. (*alarmed by this outburst—submissively*) Yes, Pa.

BARTLETT. Then see that ye heed. (*After a pause—as* NAT *lingers*) They'll be waitin' for ye at the house.

NAT. All right. I'll go. (*He turns to the doorway on the left, but before he gets to it, the door is pushed open and* MRS. BARTLETT *enters.* NAT *stops, startled*) Ma!

MRS. BARTLETT. (*with a forced smile*) Run along, Nat. It's all right. I want to speak with your Pa.

BARTLETT. (*uneasily*) Ye'd best go up with Nat, Sarah. I've work to do.

MRS. BARTLETT. (*fixing her eyes on her husband*) I want to talk with you alone, Isaiah.

BARTLETT. (*grimly—as if he were accepting a challenge*) As ye like, then.

MRS. BARTLETT. (*dismissing* NAT *with a feeble attempt at a smile*) Tell Sue I'll be comin' up directly, Nat.

NAT. (*hesitates for a moment, looking from one to the other uneasily*) All right, Ma. (*He goes out.*)

BARTLETT. (*waits for* NAT *to get out of hearing*) Won't ye set, Sarah? (*She comes forward and sits by the table. He sits by the other side.*)

MRS. BARTLETT. (*shuddering as she sees the bottle on the table*) Will drinkin' this poison make you forget, Isaiah?

BARTLETT. (*gruffly*) I've naught to forget—leastways naught that's in your mind. But they's things about the stubborn will o' woman I'd like to forget. (*They look at each other across the table. There is a pause. Finally he cannot stand her accusing glance. He looks away, gets to his feet, walks about, then sits down again, his face set determinedly—with a grim smile*) Well, here we be, Sarah—alone together for the first time since—

MRS. BARTLETT. (*quickly*) Since that night, Isaiah.

BARTLETT. (*as if he hadn't heard*) Since I come back to you, almost. Did ye ever stop to think o' how strange it be we'd ever come to this? I never dreamed a day 'd come when ye'd force me to sleep away from ye, alone in a shed like a mangy dog!

MRS. BARTLETT. (*gently*) I didn't drive you away, Isaiah. You came o' your own will.

BARTLETT. Because o' your naggin' tongue, woman—and the wrong ye thought o' me.

MRS. BARTLETT. (*shaking her head, slowly*) It wasn't me you ran from, Isaiah. You ran away from your own self—the conscience God put in you that you think you can fool with lies.

BARTLETT. (*starting to his feet—angrily*) Lies?

MRS. BARTLETT. It's the truth, Isaiah, only you be too weak to face it.

BARTLETT. (*with defiant bravado*) Ye'll find I be strong enough to face anything, true or lie! (*Then protestingly*) What call have ye to think evil o' me, Sarah? It's mad o' ye to hold me to account for things I said in my sleep—for the damned nightmares that set me talkin' wild when I'd just come home and my head was still cracked with the thirst and the sun I'd borne on that island. Is that right, woman, to be blamin' me for mad dreams?

MRS. BARTLETT. You confessed the rest of what you said was true—of the gold you'd found and buried there.

BARTLETT. (*with a sudden fierce exultation*) Aye—that be true as Bible, Sarah. When I've sailed back in the schooner, ye'll see for yourself. There be a big chest o' it, yellow and heavy, and fixed up with diamonds, emeralds and sech, that be worth more, even, nor the gold. We'll be rich, Sarah—rich like I've always dreamed we'd be! There'll be silks and carriages for ye—all the woman's truck in the world ye've a mind to want—and all that Nat and Sue'll want, too.

MRS. BARTLETT. (*with a shudder*) Are you tryin' to bribe me, Isaiah—with a treasure that's cursed by God?

BARTLETT. (*as if he hadn't heard*) D'ye remember long ago, how I'd talk to ye o' findin' ambergris, a pile o' it on one vige that'd make us rich? Ye used to take interest then, and all the vige with me ye'd be hopin' I'd find it, too.

MRS. BARTLETT. That was my sin o' greed that I'm bein' punished for now.

BARTLETT. (*again as if he hadn't heard*) And now when the gold's come to us at last—bigger nor I ever dreamed on—ye drive me away from ye and say it's cursed.

MRS. BARTLETT. (*inexorably*) Cursed with the blood o' the man and boy ye murdered!

BARTLETT. (*in a mad rage*) Ye lie, woman! I spoke no word!

MRS. BARTLETT. That's what you kept repeatin' in your sleep, night after night that first week you was home, till I knew the truth, and could bear no more. "I spoke no word!" you kept sayin', as if 'twas your own soul had you at the bar of judgment. And "That cook, he didn't believe 'twas gold," you'd say, and curse him.

BARTLETT. (*wildly*) He was lyin', the thief! Lyin' so's he and the boy could steal the gold. I made him own up he was lyin'. What if it's all true, what ye heard? Hadn't we the right to do away with two thieves? And we was all mad with thirst and sun. Can ye hold madmen to account for the things they do?

MRS. BARTLETT. You wasn't so crazed but you remember.

BARTLETT. I remember I spoke no word, Sarah—as God's my judge!

MRS. BARTLETT. But you could have prevented it with a word, couldn't you, Isaiah? That heathen savage lives in the fear of you. He'd not have done it if—

BARTLETT. (*gloomily*) That's woman's talk. There be three o' us can swear in any court I spoke no word.

MRS. BARTLETT. What are courts? Can you swear it to yourself? You can't, and it's that's drivin' you mad, Isaiah. Oh, I'd never have believed it of you for all you said in sleep, if it wasn't for the way you looked and acted out of sleep. I watched you that first week, Isaiah, till the fear of it had me down sick. I had to watch you, you was so strange and fearful to me. At first I kept sayin', 'twas only you wasn't rid o' the thirst and the sun yet. But then, all to once, God gave me sight, and I saw 'twas guilt written on your face, in the queer stricken way you acted, and guilt in your eyes. (*She stares into them*) I see it now, as I always see it when you look at me. (*She covers her face with her hands with a sob.*)

BARTLETT. (*his face haggard and drawn—hopelessly, as if he were too beaten to oppose her further—in a hoarse whisper*) What would ye have me do, Sarah?

MRS. BARTLETT. (*taking her hands from her face—her eyes lighting up with religious fervor*) Confess your sin, Isaiah! Confess to God and men, and make your peace and take your punishment. Forget that gold that's cursed and the voyage you be settin' out on, and make your peace. (*Passionately*) I ask you to do this for my sake and the children's, and your own most of all! I'll get down on my knees, Isaiah, and pray you to do it, as I've prayed to God to send you His grace! Confess and wash your soul of the stain o' blood that's on it. I ask you that, Isaiah—and God asks you—to make your peace with Him.

BARTLETT. (*his face tortured by the inward struggle—as if the word strangled him*) Confess and let someone steal the gold! (*This thought destroys her influence over him in a second. His obsession regains possession of him instantly, filling him with rebellious strength. He laughs harshly*) Ye'd make an old woman o' me, would ye, Sarah?—an old, Sunday go-to-meetin' woman snivelin' and prayin' to God for pardon? Pardon for what? Because two sneakin' thieves are dead and done for? I spoke no word, I tell ye—but if I had, I'd not repent it. What I've done I've done, and I've never asked pardon o' God or men for ought I've done, and never will. Confess, and give up the gold I've dreamed of all my life that I've found at last? By thunder, ye must think I'm crazed!

MRS. BARTLETT. (*seeming to shrivel up on her chair as she sees she has lost—weakly*) You be lost, Isaiah—and no one can stop you.

BARTLETT. (*triumphantly*) Aye, none'll stop me. I'll go my course alone. I'm glad ye see that, Sarah.

MRS. BARTLETT. (*feebly trying to get to her feet*) I'll go to home.

BARTLETT. Ye'll stay, Sarah. Ye've had your say, and I've listened to ye; now I'll have mine and ye listen to me. (MRS. BARTLETT *sinks back in her chair exhaustedly.* BARTLETT *continues slowly*) The schooner sails at dawn on the full tide. I ask ye again and for the last time, will ye christen her with your name afore she sails?

MRS. BARTLETT. (*firmly*) No.

BARTLETT. (*menacingly*) Take heed, Sarah, o' what ye're sayin'! I'm your husband ye've sworn to obey. By right I kin order ye, not ask.

MRS. BARTLETT. I've never refused in anything that's right—but this be wicked wrong.

BARTLETT. It's only your stubborn woman's spite makes ye refuse. Ye've christened every ship I've ever been skipper on, and it's brought me luck o' a kind, though not the luck I wanted. And ye'll christen this one with your own name to bring me the luck I've always been seekin'.

MRS. BARTLETT. (*resolutely*) I won't, Isaiah.

BARTLETT. Ye will, Sarah, for I'll make ye. Ye force me to it.

MRS. BARTLETT. (*again trying to get up*) Is this the way you talk to me who've been a good wife to you for more than thirty years?

BARTLETT. (*commandingly*) Wait! (*Threateningly*) If ye don't christen her afore she sails, I'll take Nat on the vige along with me. (MRS. BARTLETT *sinks back in her chair, stunned*) He wants to go, ye know it. He's asked me a hundred times. He s'spects—'bout the gold —but he don't know for sartin. But I'll tell him the truth o' it, and he'll come with me, unless—

MRS. BARTLETT. (*looking at him with terror-stricken eyes—imploringly*) You won't do that, Isaiah? You won't take Nat away from me and drag him into sin? I know he'll go if you give him the word, in spite of what I say. (*Pitifully*) You be only frightenin' me! You can't be so wicked cruel as that.

BARTLETT. I'll do it, I take my oath—unless—

MRS. BARTLETT. (*with hysterical anger*) Then I'll tell him myself—of the murders you did, and—

BARTLETT. (*grimly*) And I'll say 'twas done in fair fight to keep them from stealin' the gold! I'll tell him yours is a woman's notion, and he'll believe me, not you. He's his father's son, and he's set to go. Ye know it, Sarah. (*She falls back in the chair hopelessly staring at him with horrified eyes. He turns away and adds after a pause*) So ye'll christen the "Sarah Allen" in the mornin' afore she sails, won't ye, Sarah?

MRS. BARTLETT. (*in a terrified tone*) Yes—if it's needful to save Nat— and God'll forgive me when He sees my reason. But you— Oh, Isaiah! (*She shudders and then breaks down, sobbing.*)

BARTLETT. (*after a pause, turns to her humbly as if asking forgiveness*) Ye mustn't think hard o' me that I want your name. It's because it's a good woman's name, and I know it'll bring luck to our vige. I'd find it hard to sail without it—the way things be.

MRS. BARTLETT. (*getting to her feet—in a state of feverish fear of him*) I'm going to home.

BARTLETT. (*going to her*) I'll help ye to the top o' the hill, Sarah.

MRS. BARTLETT. (*shrinking from him in terror*) No. Don't you touch me! Don't you touch me! (*She hobbles quickly out of the door in the rear, looking back frightenedly over her shoulder to see if he is following as the curtain falls.*)

ACT THREE

Scene—*Dawn of the following morning—exterior of the* BARTLETT *home, showing the main entrance, facing left, toward the harbor. On either side of the door, two large windows, their heavy green shutters tightly closed. In front of the door, a small porch, the roof supported by four white columns. A flight of three steps goes up to this porch from the ground. Two paths lead to the steps through the straggly patches of grass, one around the corner of the house to the rear, the other straight to the left to the edge of the cliff where there is a small projecting iron platform, fenced in by a rail. The top of a steel ladder can be seen. This ladder leads up the side of the cliff from the shore below to the platform. The edge of the cliff extends from the left corner front, half-diagonally back to the right, rear center.*

In the gray half-light of the dawn, HORNE, CATES, *and* JIMMY KANAKA *are discovered.* HORNE *is standing on the steel platform looking down at the shore below.* CATES *is sprawled on the ground nearby.* JIMMY *squats on his haunches, his eyes staring out to sea as if he were trying to pierce the distance to the warm islands of his birth.* CATES *wears dungarees,* JIMMY *dungaree pants and a black jersey,* HORNE *the same as in Act Two.*

CATES. (*with sluggish indifference*) Ain't she finished with it yet?

HORNE. (*irritably*) No, damn her! I kin see 'em all together on the wharf at the bow o' the schooner.

CATES. (*after a pause*) Funny, ain't it—his orderin' us to come up here and wait till it's all done.

HORNE. There's nothin' funny to me that he does no more. He's still out o' his head, d'ye know that, Cates?

CATES. (*stupidly*) I ain't noticed nothin' diff'rent 'bout him.

HORNE. (*scornfully*) He axed me if I ever seen them two in my sleep—that cook and the boy o' the "Triton." Said he did often.

CATES. (*immediately protesting uneasily as if he had been accused*) They was with us in the boat b'fore we fetched the island, that's all 'bout 'em I remember. I was crazy, after.

HORNE. (*looking at him with contempt*) I'll not call ye a liar, Cates, but—a hell of a man ye be! You wasn't so out o' your head that ye forgot the gold, was ye?

CATES. (*his eyes glistening*) Any man'd remember that, even if he was crazy.

HORNE. (*with a greedy grin*) Aye. That's the one thing I see in my sleep. (*There is the faint sound of cries from the beach below.* HORNE *starts and turns to look down again*) They must 'a' finished it. (CATES *and* JIMMY *come to the edge to look down.*)

JIMMY. (*suddenly—with an eager childish curiosity*) That falla wife Captain she make strong falla spell on ship, we sail fast, plenty good wind?

HORNE. (*contemptuously*) Aye, that's as near as ye'll come to it. She's makin' a spell. Ye stay here, Jimmy, and tell us when the Old Man is comin'. (JIMMY *remains looking down.* HORNE *motions* CATES *to follow him, front—then in a low voice, disgustedly*) Did ye hear that damn fool nigger?

CATES. (*grumblingly*) Why the hell is the Old Man givin' him a full share? One piece o' it'd be enough for a nigger like him.

HORNE. (*craftily*) There's a way to get rid o' him—if it comes to that. He knifed them two, ye remember.

CATES. Aye.

HORNE. The two o' us can take oath to that.

CATES. Aye.

HORNE. (*after a calculating look into his companion's greedy eyes—meaningly*) We're two sane men, Cates—and the other two to share is a lunatic and a nigger. The skipper's showed me where there's a copy o' this map o' the island locked up in the cabin—in case anything happens to him I'm to bring back the gold to his woman, he says. (*He laughs harshly*) Catch me! The fool! I'll be open with ye, Cates. If I could navigate and find the island myself I wouldn't wait for a cracked man to take me there. No, be damned if I would! Me and you'd chance it alone some way or other.

CATES. (*greedily*) The two o' us—share and share alike! (*Then shaking his head warningly*) But he's a hard man to git the best on.

HORNE. (*grimly*) And I be a hard man, too.

JIMMY. (*turning to them*) Captain, he come. (CATES *and* HORNE *separate hastily.* BARTLETT *climbs into sight up the ladder to the platform. He is breathing heavily but his expression is one of triumphant exultation.*)

BARTLETT. (*motions with his arms*) Down with ye and git aboard. The schooner's got a name now—a name that'll bring us luck. We'll sail on this tide.

HORNE. Aye—aye, sir.

BARTLETT. I got to wait here till they climb up the path. I'll be aboard afore long. See that ye have her ready to cast off by then.

HORNE. Aye—aye, sir. (*He and* CATES *disappear down the ladder.* JIMMY *lingers, looking sidewise at his Captain.*)

BARTLETT. (*noticing him—gruffly*) What are ye waitin' for?

JIMMY. (*volubly*) That old falla wife belong you, Captain, she make strong falla spell for wind blow plenty? She catch strong devil charm for schooner, Captain?

BARTLETT. (*scowling*) What's that, ye brown devil? (*Then suddenly laughing harshly*) Yes—a strong spell to bring us luck. (*Roughly*) Git aboard, ye dog! Don't let her find ye here with me. (JIMMY *disappears hurriedly down the ladder.* BARTLETT *remains at the edge looking down after him. There is a sound of voices from the right and presently* MRS. BARTLETT, SUE, DREW *and* NAT *enter, coming around the house from the rear.* NAT *and* DREW *walk at either side of* MRS. BARTLETT, *who is in a state of complete collapse, so that they are practically carrying her.* SUE *follows, her handkerchief to her eyes.*

NAT *keeps his eyes on the ground, his expression fixed and gloomy.* DREW *casts a glance of angry indignation at the Captain, who, after one indifferent look at them, has turned back to watch the operations on the schooner below.*)

BARTLETT. (*as they reach the steps of the house—intent on the work below—makes a megaphone of his hands and shouts in stentorian tones*) Look lively there, Horne!

SUE. (*protestingly*) Pa!

BARTLETT. (*wheels about. When he meets his daughter's eyes he controls his angry impatience and speaks gently*) What d'ye want, Sue?

SUE. (*pointing to her mother who is being assisted through the door —her voice trembling*) You mustn't shout. She's very sick.

BARTLETT. (*dully, as if he didn't understand*) Sick?

SUE. (*turning to the door*) Wait. I'll be right back. (*She enters the house. As soon as she is gone all of* BARTLETT'S *excitement returns. He paces up and down with nervous impatience.* NAT *comes out of the house.*)

NAT. (*in a tone of anxiety*) Ma seems bad. I'm going for the doctor.

BARTLETT. (*as if he hadn't heard—draws* NAT'S *attention to the schooner*) Smart lines on that schooner, boy. She'll sail hell bent in a breeze. I knowed what I was about when I bought her.

NAT. (*staring down fascinatedly*) How long will the voyage take?

BARTLETT. (*preoccupied*) How long?

NAT. (*insinuatingly*) To get to the island.

BARTLETT. Three months at most—with fair luck. (*Exultantly*) And I'll have luck now!

NAT. Then in six months you may be back—with *it*?

BARTLETT. Aye, with— (*Stopping abruptly, turns and stares into his son's eyes—angrily*) With what? What boy's foolishness be ye talkin'?

NAT. (*pleading fiercely*) I want to go, Pa! There's no good in my staying here any more. I can't think of anything but—

BARTLETT. (*sternly, to conceal his uneasiness*) Keep clear o' this, boy, I've warned ye!

SUE. (*appearing in doorway—indignantly*) Nat! Haven't you gone for the doctor yet?

NAT. (*shamefacedly*) I forgot.

SUE. Forgot!

NAT. (*starting off*) I'm going, Sue. (*Then over his shoulder*) You won't sail before I come back, Pa. (BARTLETT *does not answer.* NAT *stands miserably hesitating.*)

SUE. Nat! For heaven's sake! (NAT *hurries off around the corner of the house, rear.* SUE *comes to her father who is watching her with a queer, humble, hunted expression.*)

BARTLETT. Well, Sue?

SUE. (*her voice trembling*) Oh, Pa, how could you drag Ma out of bed to christen your old boat—when you knew how sick she's been!

BARTLETT. (*avoiding her eyes*) It's only weakness. She'll get well o' it soon.

SUE. Pa! How can you say things like that—as if you didn't care! (*Accusingly*) The way you've acted ever since you've been home almost, anyone would think—you *hated* her!

BARTLETT. (*wincing*) No!

SUE. Oh, Pa, what is it that has come between you? Can't you tell me? Can't I help to set things right again?

BARTLETT. (*mumblingly*) Nothin'—nothin' ye kin help—nor me.

SUE. But things can't go on like this. Don't you see it's killing Ma?

BARTLETT. She'll forget her stubborn notions, now I be sailin' away.

SUE. But you're not—not going for a while now, are you?

BARTLETT. Ain't I been sayin' I'd sail at dawn today?

SUE. (*looking at him for a moment with shocked amazement*) But —you can't mean—right now!

BARTLETT. (*keeping his face averted*) Aye—or we'll miss this tide.

SUE. (*putting her hands on his shoulders and trying to look into his face*) Pa! You can't mean that! (*His face is set with his obsessed deter-*

mination. She lets her hands fall with a shudder) You can't be as cruel
as that! Why, I thought, of course, you'd put off— (*Wildly*) You
have, haven't you, Pa? You did tell those men you couldn't sail when
you saw how sick Ma was, didn't you—when she fainted down on the
wharf?

BARTLETT. (*implacably*) I said I was sailin' by this tide!

SUE. Pa! (*Then pleadingly*) When the doctor comes and you hear
what he says—

BARTLETT. (*roughly*) I ain't stoppin' on his word nor any man's.
(*Intensely*) That schooner's been fit to sail these two weeks past. I
been waitin' on her stubborn will, (*He gestures toward the house*)
eatin' my heart out day and night. Then I swore I'd sail today. I tell
ye, Sue, I got a feelin' in my bones if I don't put out now I never will.
Aye, I feel it deep down inside me. (*In a tone of superstitious awe*)
And when she christened the schooner—jest to the minute, mind ye!—
a fair breeze sprung up and come down out o' the land to blow her
out to sea—like a sign o' good luck.

SUE. (*aroused to angry indignation*) Oh, I can't believe you're the
same man who used to be my father!

BARTLETT. Sue!

SUE. To talk cold-bloodedly of sailing away on a long voyage when
Ma's inside—dying for all you seem to know or care! You're not the
father I love! You've changed into someone else—hateful and cruel—
and I hate him, I hate him! (*She breaks down, sobbing hysterically.*)

BARTLETT. (*who has listened to her with a face suddenly stricken by
fear and torturing remorse*) Sue! Ye don't know what ye be sayin',
do ye?

SUE. I do! And I hate those three awful men who make you act
this way. I hate the schooner! I wish she and they were at the bottom
of the sea!

BARTLETT. (*frenziedly—putting his hand over her mouth to stop
her words*) Stop, girl! Don't ye dare—

SUE. (*shrinking away from him—frightenedly*) Pa!

BARTLETT. (*bewilderedly, pleading for forgiveness*) Don't heed that, Sue—I didn't mean—ye git me so riled—I'd not hurt ye for all the gold in the world. But don't ye talk wrong o' things ye can't know on.

SUE. Oh, Pa, what kind of things must they be—when you're ashamed to tell them!

BARTLETT. Ye'll know all they be to know—and your Ma and Nat, too—when I come back from this vige. Oh, ye'll be glad enough then—when ye see with your own eyes! Ye'll bless me then 'stead o' turning agin me! (*Hesitating for a second—then somberly*) On'y now—till it's all over and done—ye'd best keep clear o' it.

SUE. (*passionately*) I don't want to know anything about it. What I do know is that you can't sail now. Haven't you any heart at all? Can't you see how bad Ma is?

BARTLETT. It's the sight o' me sickens her.

SUE. No. She called your name just a while ago—the only word she's spoken since she christened the ship.

BARTLETT. (*desperately*) I got to git away from her, I tell ye, Sue! She's been houndin' me ever since I got back—houndin' me with her stubborn tongue till she's druv me mad, a'most! Ye've been on'y givin' thought to her, not me. It's for her sake as much as my own I'm goin'—for her and you and Nat. (*With a sudden return of his old resolution*) I've made up my mind, I tell ye, and in the end ye'll know I be right. (*A hail in* HORNE's *voice comes thinly up from the shore below.* BARTLETT *starts, his eyes gleaming*) Ye hear! It's Horne hailin' me to come. They're ready to cast off. I'll git aboard. (*He starts for the ladder.*)

SUE. Pa! After all I've said—without one word of good-by to Ma! (*Hysterically*) Oh, what can I do, what can I say to stop you! She hasn't spoken but that one call for you. She hardly seems to breathe. If it weren't for her eyes I'd believe she was dead—but her eyes look for you. She'll die if you go, Pa!

BARTLETT. No!

SUE. You might just as well kill her now in cold blood as murder her that way!

BARTLETT. (*shaken—raising his hands as if to put them over his ears to shut out her words—hoarsely*) No! Ye lie!

DREW. (*appearing at the doorway, his face working with grief and anger—harshly*) Captain Bartlett! (*Then lowering his voice as he sees* SUE) Mrs. Bartlett is asking to see you, Captain, before you go.

SUE. There! Didn't I tell you, Pa!

BARTLETT. (*struggling with himself—dully*) She's wantin' to hound me again, that be all.

SUE. (*seeing him weakening—grasps his hand persuasively*) Pa! Come with me. She won't hound you. How silly you are! Come! (*Hesitatingly, head bowed, he follows her toward the door.*)

BARTLETT. (*As he comes to* DREW *he stops and looks into the young man's angry, accusing face. He mutters half mockingly*) So ye, too, be agin me, Danny!

DREW. (*unable to restrain his indignation*) What man that's a real man wouldn't be against you, sir?

SUE. (*frightenedly*) Danny! Pa!

BARTLETT. (*in a sudden rage draws back his fist threateningly.* DREW *stares into his eyes unflinchingly—*BARTLETT *controls himself with an effort and lets his arm fall to his side—scornfully*) Big words from a boy, Danny. I'll forget them this time—on account o' Sue. (*He turns to her*) I'm goin' in to her to please ye, Sue—but if ye think any words that she kin say'll change my mind, ye make a mistake—for I be sailin' out as I planned I would in spite o' all hell! (*He walks resolutely into the house.* SUE *follows him after exchanging a hopeless glance with* DANNY.)

DREW. (*to himself—with a shudder*) He's mad, damn him! (*He paces up and down.* HORNE *appears on the ladder from below, followed by* CATES.)

HORNE. (*coming forward and addressing* DREW) Is the skipper about?

DREW. (*curtly*) He's in the house. You can't speak to him now.

HORNE. She's ready to cast off. I hailed him from below but I s'pect he didn't hear. (*As* DREW *makes no comment—impatiently*) If he don't shake a leg, we'll miss the tide. There's a bit o' fair breeze, too.

DREW. (*glancing at him resentfully*) Don't count on his sailing today. It's just as likely he'll change his mind.

HORNE. (*angrily*) Change his mind again? After us waitin' and wastin' time for weeks! (*To* CATES *in a loud tone so* DREW *can hear*) What did I tell ye, Cates? He's crazy as hell.

DREW. (*sharply*) What's that?

HORNE. I was tellin' Cates the skipper's not right in his head. (*Angrily*) What man in his senses'd do the way he does?

DREW. (*letting his resentment escape him*) That's no lie, damn it!

HORNE. (*surprised*) Aye, ye've seen it, too, have ye? (*After a pause*) Now I axe ye, as a sailor, how'd ye like to be puttin' out on a vige with a cracked man for skipper? (SUE *comes out of the door, stops with a shudder of disgust as she sees the two sailors, and stands listening. They do not notice her presence.*)

DREW. It seems to me a crazy voyage all round. (*With sudden interest as if a new idea had come to him*) But you know all about it, don't you—what the Captain plans to do on this voyage—and all that?

HORNE. (*dryly*) Aye, as well as himself—but I'm tellin' no man.

DREW. And I'm not asking. What I want to find out is: Do you know enough about this business to make this one voyage alone and attend to everything—in case the Captain can't go?

HORNE. (*exchanging a quick glance with* CATES—*trying to hide his eagerness*) Aye, I could do as well as any many alive. He could trust me for it—and I'd make more money for him than he's likely to make with his head out o' gear. (*Then scowling*) On'y trouble is, who'd captain her if he ain't goin'?

DREW. (*disappointedly*) Then you don't know navigation enough for that?

HORNE. I've never riz above bo'sun. (*Then after a pause in which he appears to be calculating something—curiously*) Why d'ye ask me them questions? (*Insinuatingly—almost in a whisper*) It can't be done 'less we got an officer like you aboard.

DREW. (*angrily*) Eh? What're you driving at?

SUE. (*who has been listening with aroused interest*) Danny! (*She comes down to him.* HORNE *and* CATES *bob their heads respectfully and move back near the platform.* HORNE *watches* SUE *and* DREW *out of the corner of his eye*) Danny, I've been listening to what you were saying, but I don't understand. What are you thinking of?

DREW. (*excitedly*) I was thinking— Listen, Sue! Seems to me your Pa's out of his right mind. Something's got to be done to keep him home in spite of himself. Even leaving your Ma out of it, he's not in any fit state to take a ship to sea; and I was thinking if we could fix it some way so that fellow Horne could take her out on this voyage—

SUE. But, Danny, Pa'd never give in to that.

DREW. I wasn't thinking he would. We—you'd have to give the word—and keep him in the house somehow—and then when he did come out it'd be too late. The schooner'd be gone.

SUE. (*disturbed, but showing that this plan has caught her mind*) But—he'd never forgive—

DREW. When he's back in his right mind again, he would. (*Earnestly*) You can't let him sail, and wreck his ship and himself in the bargain, likely. Then, there's your Ma—

SUE. No, no, we can't let him. (*With a glance at* HORNE *and* CATES) But I don't trust those men.

DREW. No more do I; but it would be better to chance them than— (*Suddenly interrupting himself—with a shrug of his shoulders*) But I was forgetting. None of them can navigate.

SUE. But didn't I hear him say—if they had an officer on board— like you—

DREW. Yes, but where'll you find one at a second's notice?

SUE. (*meaningly*) And you told me, didn't you, that you'd just got your master's papers.

DREW. (*looking at her with stunned astonishment*) Sue! D'you mean—

SUE. (*a light coming over her face*) Oh, Danny, we could trust you! He'd trust you! And after he'd calmed down I know he wouldn't mind so much. Oh, Danny, it'll break my heart to have you go, to send you away just after you've come back. But I don't see any other way. I wouldn't ask—if it wasn't for Ma being this way—and him— Oh, Danny, can't you see your way to do it—for my sake?

DREW. (*bewilderedly*) Why, Sue, I—I never thought— (*Then as he sees the look of disappointment which comes over her face at his hesitancy—resolutely*) Why sure, Sue, I'll do it—if you want me to. I'll do it if it can be done. But we've got to hustle. You've got to keep him in the house some way if he aims to come out. And I'll talk to them. (SUE *goes to the doorway.* DREW *goes over to* HORNE *and* CATES.)

SUE. (*after listening*) He's still in with Ma. It's all right.

DREW. (*to* HORNE) How would you like me for skipper on this one voyage? Listen here. Miss Sue's decided her father isn't in a fit state to captain this trip.

HORNE. That's no lie.

CATES. (*to* HORNE *protestingly*) But if we git ketched the Old Man'll take it out o' our hides, not his'n.

HORNE. (*savagely—with a meaning look at* CATES) Shut up, ye fool!

DREW. (*impatiently*) I'll shoulder all that risk, man!

SUE. (*earnestly*) No harm will come to any of you, I promise you.

HORNE. (*in the tone of one clinching a bargain*) Then we'll chance it. (*Warningly*) But it's got to be done smart, sir.

DREW. I've got to get my dunnage. I'll be right back and we'll tumble aboard. (*He goes into the house.* SUE *follows him in.*)

CATES. (*with stupid anger*) This is a hell of a mess we're gettin' in, if ye axe me.

HORNE. And I tell ye it's a great stroke o' luck.

CATES. He'll be aboard to spy on us.

HORNE. Leave me to fool him. And when the time comes to git rid o' him, I'll find a means some way or other.

CATES. (*stupidly*) S'long as he don't git no share o' the gold—

HORNE. (*contemptuously*) Share, ye dumbhead! I'd see him in hell first—and send him there myself. (DREW *comes out of the house carrying his bag which he hands to* CATES. SUE *follows him.*)

DREW. Look lively now!

HORNE. Aye—aye, sir. (*He and* CATES *clamber hurriedly down the ladder.*)

SUE. (*throwing her arms around his neck and kissing him*) Good-by, Danny. It's so fine of you to do this for us! I'll never forget—

DREW. (*tenderly*) Ssssh! It's nothing, Sue.

SUE. (*tearfully*) Oh, Danny, I hope I'm doing right! I'll miss you so dreadfully! But you'll come back just as soon as you can—

DREW. Of course!

SUE. Danny! Danny! I love you so!

DREW. And I guess you know I love you, don't you? (*Kisses her*) And we'll be married when I come back this time *sure?*

SUE. Yes—yes—Danny—sure!

DREW. I've got to run. Good-by, Sue.

SUE. Good-by, dear. (*They kiss for the last time and he disappears down the ladder. She stands at the top, sobbing, following him with her eyes.* NAT *comes around the house from the rear and goes to the front door.*)

NAT. (*seeing his sister*) Sue! He hasn't gone yet, has he? (*She doesn't hear him. He hesitates in the doorway for a moment, listening for the sound of his father's voice from inside. Then, very careful to make no noise, he tiptoes carefully into the house.* SUE *waves her hand to* DREW *who has evidently now got aboard the ship. Then she covers her face with her hands, sobbing.* NAT *comes out of the house again and goes to his sister. As she sees him approaching, she dries her eyes hastily, trying to smile.*)

SUE. Did you get the doctor, Nat?

NAT. Yes, he's coming right away, he promised. (*Looking at her face*) What—have you been crying?

SUE. No. (*She walks away from the edge of the cliff, drawing him with her.*)

NAT. Yes, you have. Look at your eyes.

SUE. Oh, Nat, everything's so awful. (*She breaks down again.*)

NAT. (*trying to comfort her in an absent-minded way*) There, don't get worked up. Ma'll be all right as soon as the doctor comes. (*Then curiously*) Pa's inside with her. They were arguing—have they made it up, d'you think?

SUE. Oh, Nat, I don't know.

NAT. The strain's been too much for him—waiting and hiding his secret from all of us. What do you suppose it is, Sue?

SUE. (*wildly*) I don't know and I don't care!

NAT. Well, there's something— (*Starts for the platform.* SUE *does her best to interpose to hold him back*) Are they all ready on the schooner? He'll have to hurry if she's going to sail on this tide. (*With sudden passion*) Oh, I've got to go! I can't stay here! (*Pleadingly*) Don't you think, Sue, if you were to ask him for me he'd— You're the only one he seems to act sane with or care about any more.

SUE. No! I won't! I can't!

NAT. (*angrily*) Haven't you any sense? Wouldn't it be better for everyone if I went in his place?

SUE. No. You know that's a lie. Ma would lose her mind if you went.

NAT. And I'll lose mine if I stay! (*Half aware of* SUE's *intention to keep him from looking down at the schooner—irritably*) What are you holding my arm for, Sue? I want to see what they're doing. (*He pushes her aside and goes to the platform—excitedly*) Hello, they've got the fores'l and mains'l set. They're setting the stays'l. (*In amazement*) Why—they're casting off! She's moving away from the wharf! (*More and more excitedly*) I see four of them on board! Who—who is that, Sue?

SUE. It's Danny.

NAT. (*furiously*) Danny! What right has he—when I can't! Sue, call Pa! They're sailing, I tell you, you little fool!

SUE. (*trying to calm him—her voice trembling*) Nat! Don't be such a donkey! Danny's only going a little way—just trying the boat to see how she sails while they're waiting for Pa.

NAT. (*uncertainly*) Oh. (*Then bitterly*) I was never allowed to do even that—his own son! Look, Sue, that must be Danny at the stern waving.

SUE. (*brokenly*) Yes. (*She waves her handkerchief over her head—then breaks down, sobbing again. There is the noise of* BARTLETT'S *voice from inside and a moment later he appears in the doorway. He seems terribly shattered, at the end of his tether. He hesitates uncertainly, looking about him wildly as if he didn't know what to do or where to go.*)

SUE. (*after one look at his face, runs to him and flings her arms about his neck*) Pa! (*She weeps on his shoulder.*)

BARTLETT. Sue, ye did wrong beggin' me to see her. I knowed it'd do no good. Ye promised she'd not hound me—"Confess," she says—when they be naught to tell that couldn't be swore to in any court. "Don't go on this vige," she says, "there be the curse o' God on it." (*With a note of baffled anguish*) She kin say that after giving the ship her own name! (*With wild, haggard defiance*) But curse or no curse, I be goin'! (*He moves toward the platform,* SUE *clinging to his arm.*)

SUE. (*frightenedly*) Pa! Go back in the house, won't you?

BARTLETT. I be sorry to go agin your will, Sue, but it's got to be. Ye'll know the reason some day—and be glad o' it. And now good-by to ye. (*With a sudden strange tenderness he bends and kisses his daughter. Then as she seems about to protest further, his expression becomes stern and inflexible*) No more o' talk, Sue! I be bound out. (*He takes her hand off his arm and strides to the platform. One look down at the harbor and he stands transfixed—in a hoarse whisper*)

What damned trick be this? (*He points to the schooner and turns to* NAT *bewilderedly*) Ain't that my schooner, boy—the "Sarah Allen"—reachin' toward the p'int?

NAT. (*surprised*) Yes, certainly. Didn't you know? Danny's trying her to see how she sails while they're waiting for you.

BARTLETT. (*with a tremendous sigh of relief*) Aye. (*Then angrily*) He takes a lot o' rope to himself without askin' leave o' me. Don't he know they's no time to waste on boy's foolin'? (*Then with admiration*) She sails smart, don't she, boy? I knowed she'd show a pair o' heels.

NAT. (*with enthusiasm*) Yes, she's a daisy! Say, Danny's taking her pretty far out, isn't he?

BARTLETT. (*anxiously*) He'd ought to come about now if he's to tack back inside the p'int. (*Furiously*) Come about, damn ye! The swab! That's what comes o' steamer trainin'. I'd sooner trust Sue to sail her nor him. (*Waves his arm and shouts*) Come about!

NAT. (*bitterly*) He seems to be heading straight for the open sea. He's taking quite a sail, it seems to me.

BARTLETT. (*as if he couldn't believe his eyes*) He's passed the p'int—and now—headin' her out to sea—so'east by east. By God, that be the course I charted for her! (SUE *bursts out sobbing. He wheels on her, his mouth fallen open, his face full of a stupid despair*) They be somethin' wrong here. What be it, Sue? What be it, Nat? (*His voice has begun to quiver with passion*) That schooner—she's sailin' without me— (*He suddenly springs at* NAT *and grabs him by the throat—with hoarse fury, shaking him*) What be it, ye whelp? It's your doin'—because I wouldn't let ye go. Answer me!

SUE. (*rushing to them with a scream*) Pa! (*She tugs frantically at his hands.* BARTLETT *lets them fall to his side, stepping back from* NAT *who sinks weakly to the ground, gasping for breath.* BARTLETT *stands looking at him wildly.*)

SUE. Nat didn't know it, Pa. It's all my fault. I had to do it. There was no other way—

BARTLETT. (*raging*) What d'ye mean, girl? What is it ye've done? Tell me, I say! Tell me or I'll—

SUE. (*unflinchingly*) You had to be stopped from going some way. So I asked Danny if he wouldn't make the trip in your place. He's just got his captain's papers—and oh, Pa, you can trust him, you know that! That man Horne said he knows about everything you wanted done, and he promised to tell Danny, and Danny'll come back—

BARTLETT. (*chokingly*) So—that be it— (*Shaking his clenched fist at the sky as if visualizing the fate he feels in all of this*) Curse ye! Curse ye! (*He subsides weakly, his strength spent, his hand falls limply at his side.*)

MRS. BARTLETT. (*appears in the doorway. Her face is pale with anguish. She gives a cry of joy when she sees her son*) Nat! (*Then with a start of horror as her eyes fall on her husband*) Isaiah! (*He doesn't seem to hear*) Then—you ain't sailed yet?

SUE. (*going to her—gently*) No, Ma, he isn't going to sail. He's going to stay home with you. But the schooner's gone. See. (*She points and her mother's eyes turn seaward.*)

BARTLETT. (*aloud to himself—in a tone of groping superstitious awe and bewildered fear*) They be somethin' queer—somethin' wrong— they be a curse in this somewhere—

MRS. BARTLETT. (*turning accusing eyes on him—with a sort of fanatical triumph*) I'm glad to hear you confess that, Isaiah. Yes, there be a curse—God's curse on the wicked sinfulness o' men—and I thank God He's saved you from the evil of that voyage, and I'll pray Him to visit His punishment and His curse on them three men on that craft you forced me to give my name— (*She has raised her hand as if calling down retribution on the schooner she can dimly see.*)

SUE. (*terrified*) Ma!

BARTLETT. (*starting toward his wife with an insane yell of fury*) Stop it, I tell ye! (*He towers over her with upraised fist as if to crush her.*)

SUE. Pa!

NAT. (*starting to his feet from where he has been sitting on the ground—hoarsely*) Pa! For God's sake!

MRS. BARTLETT. (*gives a weak, frightened gasp*) Would you murder me too, Isaiah? (*She closes her eyes and collapses in* SUE's *arms.*)

SUE. (*tremblingly*) Nat! Help me! Quick! We must carry her to bed. (*They take their mother in their arms, carrying her inside the house.*)

BARTLETT. (*while they are doing this, rushes in his mad frenzy to the platform over the edge of the cliff. He puts his hands to his mouth, megaphone-fashion, and yells with despairing rage*) Ahoy! Ahoy! "Sarah Allen!" Put back! Put back! (*As the curtain falls.*)

ACT FOUR

Scene—*About nine o'clock of a moonlight night one year later—*
Captain bartlett's *"cabin," a room erected on the top of his house
as a lookout post. The interior is fitted up like the cabin of a sailing
vessel. On the left, forward, a porthole. Farther back, the stairs of the
companionway. Still farther, two more portholes. In the rear, left, a
marble-topped sideboard. In the rear, center, a door opening on stairs
which lead to the lower house. A cot with a blanket is placed against
the wall to the right of door. In the right wall, five portholes. Directly
under them, a wooden bench. In front of the bench, a long table with
two chairs placed, one in front, one to the left of it. A cheap, dark-
colored rug is on the floor. In the ceiling, midway from front to rear,
a skylight extending from opposite the door to above the left edge of
the table. In the right extremity of the skylight is placed a floating
ship's compass. The light from the binnacle sheds down over this
and seeps into the room, casting a vague globular shadow of the compass on the floor. Moonlight creeps in through the portholes on the
right. A lighted lantern is on the table.*

As the curtain rises, sue *and* doctor berry *are discovered sitting by
the table. The doctor is a man of sixty or so, hale and hearty-looking,
his white hair and mustache setting off his ruddy complexion. His
blue eyes have a gentle expression, his smile is kindly and sympathetic. His whole manner toward* sue *is that of the old family doctor
and friend, not the least of whose duties is to play father-confessor
to his patients. She is dressed in deep mourning. She looks much
older. But there is an excited elation in her face at present, her eyes are
alight with some unexpected joy.*

SUE. (*excitedly*) And here is Danny's letter, Doctor—to prove it's all true. (*She takes a letter from the bosom of her dress and holds it out to him.*)

DOCTOR. (*takes it with a smile, patting her hand*) I can't say how glad I am, Susan. Coming after we'd all given him up for lost—it's like a miracle.

SUE. (*smiling happily*) Read what he says.

DOCTOR. (*hesitating—playfully*) I don't know that it's right for me—love letters at my age!

SUE. I want you to read it. (*He reaches in his pocket for his spectacles.* SUE *continues gratefully*) As if I could have any secrets from you after all you've done for us since Ma died. You've been the only friend— (*She stops, her lips trembling.*)

DOCTOR. Tut-tut. (*He adjusts his spectacles and peers at her over them*) Who wouldn't be of all the service he could to a brave girl like you? This past year—with your mother's death—and then the news of the schooner being reported lost—not many could have stood it—living in this house with him the way he is—even if he was their father.

SUE. (*glancing up at the skylight—apprehensively*) Ssshh! He might hear you.

DOCTOR. (*listening intently*) Not him. There he goes pacing up and down, looking out to sea for that ship that will never come back! (*Shaking himself*) Brrr! This house of mad dreams!

SUE. Don't you think Pa'll come to realize the schooner is lost as time goes by and she doesn't come back?

DOCTOR. No, your father won't let himself look the facts in the face. If he did, probably the shock of it would kill him. That darn dream of his has become his life. No, Susan, as time goes on he'll believe in it harder and harder. After observing him for the past year—and I speak for his own sake, too, as his good friend for twenty years or more—my final advice is the same: Send him to an asylum.

SUE. (*with a shudder*) No, Doctor.

DOCTOR. (*shaking his head*) You'll have to come to it in time. He's getting worse. No one can tell—he might get violent—

SUE. How can you say that? You know how gentle and sane he is with me.

DOCTOR. You're his one connecting link with things as they are—but that can't last. Eh, well, my dear, one thing you've got to realize: Your father and Nat must be separated somehow. Nat's going to pieces. I'll bet he doesn't believe that schooner is lost any more than your father does.

SUE. You mean he still hopes it may not be true. That's only natural. He's in San Francisco now tracing down the report again. He saw in the papers where the British freighter that found the derelict was there and he went to talk with the people on board. I'm hoping he'll come back fully convinced, with the whole thing out of his mind.

DOCTOR. (*shaking his head—gravely*) I've watched him and talked with him. You've got to persuade Nat to go away, Susan.

SUE. (*helplessly*) I don't know— (*Then brightening*) Just now it's enough to know Danny's alive and coming back. Read his letter, Doctor.

DOCTOR. Yes, yes, let's see. (*He takes the letter from the envelope.*)

SUE. Poor Danny! He's been through terrible things.

DOCTOR. Hmm! Rangoon.

SUE. Yes, he's still in the hospital there. You'll see.

DOCTOR. (*reads the letter—grunts with astonishment—angrily*) By Gad! The damn scoundrels!

SUE. (*shuddering*) Yes, wasn't it hideous—those awful men stabbing him and leaving him for dead in that out of the way native settlement! And then he was laid up for four months there waiting for a vessel to touch and take him back to civilization. And then, think of it, getting the fever on top of all that and nearly dying in the hospital in Rangoon!

DOCTOR. A terrible time of it! He's lucky to be alive. Hmm. I see he foresaw the wreck of the schooner. (*Folding the letter and putting*

179

it back) He doesn't seem to have found out what the purpose of that mad trip was. Horne hid it from him to the last, he says. Well, it's queer—damn queer. But I'm glad to know those wretches have gone to their final accounting.

SUE. (*with a shudder*) I was always afraid of them. They looked like—murderers. (*At a noise from below they both start. Steps can be heard climbing the stairs.* SUE *jumps to her feet frightenedly*) Why—do you hear—who can that be? (*There is a soft rap on the door. The* DOCTOR *jumps to his feet.* SUE *turns to him with a half-hysterical laugh*) Shall I open? I don't know why—but I'm afraid.

DOCTOR. Tut-tut! I'll see who it is. (*He opens the door and* NAT *is discovered on the stairs outside*) Why hello, boy. You gave us a scare. Susan thought it was a ghost knocking.

NAT. (*comes into the room. He has aged, grown thin, his face gaunt and drawn from continual mental strain, his eyes moody and pre-occupied. He glances up at the skylight apprehensively, then turns to* SUE) I didn't find you downstairs so I— (*Then to the* DOCTOR) Yes, you do grow to look for ghosts in this house, don't you? (*Again glancing upward*) He's up there as usual, I suppose—looking for a ship that'll never, never come now!

DOCTOR. (*with a grunt of approval*) I'm glad to hear you acknowledge that.

SUE. (*who is just recovering from her fright*) But, Nat, I didn't expect you— Did you find out—?

NAT. Yes, I talked with several of the men who were on board at the time. They said they steamed in so close to the schooner it was easy to read the name with the naked eye. All agreed—"Sarah Allen," Harborport. They even remembered how her taffrail was painted. There's no chance for mistake. The "Sarah Allen" is gone. (*With great emphasis*) And I'm glad—damn glad! I feel free again, and I can go back to work—but not here. I've got to go away—start new altogether.

SUE. (*happily, coming and putting her arms around him*) It's so good to hear you talk like your old self again.

DOCTOR. (*earnestly*) Yes, Nat, by Gad, that's sound sense. Get out of this.

NAT. (*giving him a queer look*) I suppose you thought I was doomed, eh?—like him. (*He makes a motion upward—then with an uncertain laugh*) A doctor's always looking for trouble where there isn't any. (*In a tone of finality*) Well, it's all over, anyway.

SUE. (*snatching the letter from the table*) Oh, I was forgetting, Nat. Read this. I got it yesterday.

NAT. (*turns it over in his hands suspiciously*) Who from?

SUE. Open it and see.

NAT. (*does so and turns over the pages to read the signature—he gives a start—hoarsely*) Danny! It can't be! But it's his writing sure enough! (*He exclaims with a sudden wild exultation*) Then they must have been lying to me!

SUE. No, the "Sarah Allen" was wrecked all right, but that was afterwards. Read it. You'll see. (NAT *sinks back on a chair, evidently depressed by this information. He starts to read the letter with unconcealed indifference, then becomes engrossed, excited, the paper trembling in his hands. The* DOCTOR *shakes his head at* SUE *indicating his disapproval of her giving him the letter.* NAT *finishes and springs to his feet—angrily.*)

NAT. The stupid fool! He let Horne pull the wool over his eyes in fine shape.

SUE. (*indignantly*) Nat!

NAT. (*unheedingly*) Oh, if I could only have gone in his place! I knew the kind Horne was. He couldn't have played that trick on me. I'd have forced the secret out of him if I had to— (*He raises his clenched fist in a gesture of threat like his father's—then lets it fall and sits down again—disgustedly*) But what's the use? And what's the use of this? (*Tosses the letter contemptuously on the table*) He might just as well not have written.

SUE. (*snatching up the letter—deeply hurt*) Aren't you even glad to hear Danny's alive?

NAT. (*turning to her at once—with remorseful confusion*) Yes—yes —of course, Sue—I don't have to say that, do I? What I mean is, he never found out from Horne—and we're no wiser.

DOCTOR. (*briskly—with a significant glance at* SUE) Well, Susan— Nat—I've got to run along— (*Meaningly*) I'll be over again tomorrow, Susan.

SUE. Yes, do come. (*Goes with him to the door*) Can you see your way?

DOCTOR. Yes. Good night.

SUE. Good night. (*She closes the door and comes back to* NAT. *The* DOCTOR's *footsteps die out.*)

NAT. (*savagely*) That damned old fool! What is he doing, sneaking around here all the time? I've grown to hate the sight of him.

SUE. Nat! You can't mean that. Think of how kind he's been.

NAT. Yes—kindness with a purpose.

SUE. Don't be silly. What purpose could he have except wanting to help us?

NAT. To find out things, of course, you simpleton. To pump Pa when he's not responsible for what he's saying.

SUE. (*indignantly*) Nat!

NAT. Much good it's done him! I know Pa. Sane or not, he won't tell *that* to anyone—not even you or me, Sue. (*With sudden fury*) I'm going away—but before I go I'm going to make him tell me! He's been so afraid I'd find out, so scared to speak to me even—locking himself up here. But I'll make him tell—yes, I will!

SUE. Careful, Nat. He'll hear you if you shout like that.

NAT. But we have a right to know—his own children. What if he dies without ever speaking?

SUE. (*uneasily*) Be sensible, Nat. There's nothing to tell except in your imagination. (*Taking his arm—persuasively*) Come on downstairs. I'll get you something to eat. You must be starved, aren't you?

NAT. No—I don't know—I suppose I ought to be. (*He gets to his feet and glances around with a shudder*) What a place for him to build to wait in—like the cabin of a ship sunk deep under the sea—like the "Sarah Allen's" cabin as it is now, probably. (*With a shiver*) There's a chill comes over you. No wonder he's mad. (*He listens*) Hear him. A year ago today she sailed. I wonder if he knows that. Back and forth, always staring out to sea for the "Sarah Allen." Ha-ha! God! It would be funny if it didn't make your flesh creep. (*Brusquely*) Come on. Let's leave him and go down where there's light and warmth. (*They go down the stairs, closing the door behind them. There is a pause. Then the door of the companionway above is heard being opened and shut. A gust of wind sweeps down into the room.* BARTLETT *stamps down the stairs. The madness which has taken almost complete possession of him in the past year is clearly stamped on his face, particularly in his eyes which seem to stare through and beyond objects with a hunted, haunted expression. His movements suggest an automaton obeying invisible wires. They are quick, jerky, spasmodic. He appears to be laboring under a state of extraordinary excitement. He stands for a second at the foot of the stairs, peering about him suspiciously. Then he goes to the table and sits down on the edge of a chair, his chin supported on his hands.*)

BARTLETT. (*takes a folded piece of paper from his pocket and spreads it out on the table in the light of the lantern—pointing with his finger—mumblingly*) Where the cross be—ye'll not forget that, Silas Horne. Ye had a copy o' this—no chance for a mistake, bullies—the gold's there, restin' safe—back to me and we'll share it fair and square. A year ago today—ye remember the orders I wrote ye, Horne. (*Threateningly*) Ye'll not be gone more nor a year or I'll—and if ye make port to home here at night, hang a red and a green light at the mainm'st head so I'll see ye comin'. A red and a green— (*He springs up suddenly and goes to a porthole to look out at the sea—disappointedly*) No lights be there—but they'll come. The year be up today and ye've got to come or I'll— (*He sinks back on the chair, his head in his hands. Suddenly he starts and stares straight in front of him as if he saw something in the air—with angry defiance*) Aye, there ye be again—the two o' ye! Makin' a mock o' me! Brass and junk, ye say, not worth a damn! Ye don't believe, do ye? I'll show ye! (*He springs to his feet and makes a motion as if grabbing someone by the throat and shaking them—savagely*) Ye lie! Is it gold or no? Answer me! (*With a mocking laugh*) Aye, ye own up to it now, right enough. Too late, ye swabs! No share for ye! (*He sinks back on the chair again—after a pause, dully*) Jimmy's gone. Let them rot. But I spoke no word, Silas Horne, remember! (*Then in a tone of fear*) Be ye dyin', Sarah? No, ye must live—live to see your ship come home with the gold—and I'll buy ye all in the world ye set your heart on. No, not ambergris, Sarah—gold and diamonds and sech! We're rich at last! (*Then with great anguish*) What woman's stubborn talk be this? Confess, ye say? But I spoke no word, I swear to ye! Why will ye hound me and think evil o' what I done? Men's business, I tell ye. They would have killed us and stolen the gold, can't ye see? (*Wildly*) Enough o' talk, Sarah! I'll sail out in spite o' ye! (*He gets to his feet and paces up and down the room. The door in the rear is opened and* NAT *re-enters. He glances at his father, then looks down the stairs behind him cautiously to see if he is followed. He comes in and closes the door behind him carefully.*)

NAT. (*in a low voice*) Pa! (*Then as his father does not appear to notice his presence—louder*) Pa!

BARTLETT. (*stops short and stares at his son as if he were gradually awakening from a dream—slowly*) Be that ye, Nat?

NAT. (*coming forward*) Yes. I want to talk with you.

BARTLETT. (*struggling to bring his thoughts under control*) Talk? Ye want to talk—to me? Men's business—no room for a boy in it—keep clear o' this.

NAT. (*defiantly*) That's what you've always said. But I won't be put off any longer. I won't, do you hear?

BARTLETT. (*angrily*) I've ordered ye not to set foot in this cabin o' mine. Git below where ye belong. Where's Sue? I told her to keep ye away.

NAT. She can't prevent me this time. I've made up my mind. Listen, Pa. I'm going away tomorrow.

BARTLETT. (*uncertainly*) Goin' away?

NAT. Yes, and I'm never coming back. I'm going to start a new life. That's why I want a final talk with you—before I go.

BARTLETT. (*dully*) I've naught to say to ye.

NAT. You will have. Listen. I've absolute proof the "Sarah Allen" is lost.

BARTLETT. (*fiercely*) Ye lie!

NAT. (*curiously*) Why do you say that? You know it's true. It's just that you *won't believe*.

BARTLETT. (*wanderingly—the word heading his mind into another channel*) Believe? Aye, he wouldn't believe. Brass and junk, he said, not worth a damn—but in the end I made him own up 'twas gold.

NAT. (*repeating the word fascinatedly*) Gold?

BARTLETT. A year ago today she sailed. Ye lie! Ye don't believe either, do ye?—like him. But I'll show ye! I'll make ye own up as I made him! (*With mad exultation*) She's comin' home tonight as I ordered Horne she must! I kin feel her makin' for home, I tell ye! A red an' a green at the mainm'st head if ye make port o' night, I ordered Horne. Ye'll see! (*He goes to look out of a porthole.* NAT, *as if under a spell, goes to another.*)

NAT. (*turning away disappointedly—making an effort to throw off his thoughts—without conviction*) Nonsense. There's nothing there—no lights—and I don't believe there ever will be.

BARTLETT. (*his wild eyes fixed on his son's with an intense effort of will as if he were trying to break down his resistance*) Ye'll see, I tell ye—a red and a green! It ain't time yet, boy, but when it be they'll be plain in the night afore your eyes. (*He goes and sits down by the table.* NAT *follows him and sits down in the other chair. He sees the map and stares at it fascinatedly.*)

NAT. What is this—the map of the island? (*He reaches out his hand for it.*)

BARTLETT. (*snatching it up—with a momentary return to reason—frightenedly*) Not for ye, boy. Keep clear o' this for your own good. (*Then with a crazed triumph*) Aye! Ye'd believe this soon enough, wouldn't ye?

NAT. (*intensely*) I've always believed there was something—and a moment ago you mentioned gold. (*Triumphant in his turn*) So you needn't try to hide the secret any longer. I know now. It's gold—gold you found on that island—gold you fitted out the "Sarah Allen" to sail back for—gold you buried where I saw that cross marked on the map! (*Passionately*) Why have you been afraid to confide in me, your own son? Did you think I wouldn't believe—?

BARTLETT. (*with a mad chuckle*) Aye, ye believe now, right enough.

NAT. I always believed, I tell you. (*Pleadingly*) And now that I know so much why can't you tell me the rest? I must know! I have a right to be heir to the secret. Why don't you confess—

BARTLETT. (*interrupting—his brain catching at the word*) Confess! Confess, did ye say, Sarah? To Nat, did ye mean? Aye, Sarah, I'll tell him all and leave it to him to say if I did wrong. (*His gleaming eyes fixed on his son's*) I'll tell ye, boy, from start to finish of it. I been eatin' my heart to tell someone—someone who'd believe—someone that 'd say I did no wrong. Listen, boy, ye know o' our four days in an open boat after the "Triton" went down. I told ye o' that when I come home. But what I didn't tell ye was they was six o' us in that boat, not four.

NAT. Six? There were you and Horne and Cates and Jimmy—

BARTLETT. The cook o' the "Triton" and the ship's boy. We'd been on the island two days—an island barren as hell, mind—without food or drink. We was roasted by the sun and nigh mad with thirst. Then, on the second day, I seed a Malay canoe—a proper war canoe such as the pirates use—sunk down inside the reef. I sent Jimmy down to go over her thinkin' they might be some cask o' water in her the sea'd not got to. (*With impressive emphasis*) He found no water, boy, but he did find—d'ye know what, boy?

NAT. (*exultantly*) The gold, of course!

BARTLETT. (*laughing harshly*) Ha-ha! Ye do believe right enough, don't ye! Aye, the gold—in a chest. We hauled her up ashore and forced the lid open. (*Gloatingly*) And there it was afore our eyes in the sun—gold bracelets and rings and ornaments o' all sorts fixed up fancy with diamonds and emeralds and rubies and sech—red and green—shinin' in the sun! (*He stops impressively.*)

NAT. (*fascinatedly*) Diamonds and— But how did they get there?

BARTLETT. Looted treasure o' some Chinese junk, likely. What matter how it come about? There it was afore our eyes. And then, mind ye, that thief o' a cook came runnin' up from where he'd been shirkin' to look at what we'd found. "No share for ye, ye swab," I yelled at him; and then he says: "It ain't gold—brass and junk," he says and run off for fear o' me. Aye, he run off to the boy and told him to jine with his sneakin' plan to steal the gold from us!

NAT. (*savagely*) But why didn't you stop him? Why didn't you—?

BARTLETT. I be comin' to that, boy, and ye'll see if I did wrong. We carried the chest to the shade o' a palm and there was that thief o' a cook an' the boy waitin'. I collared 'em both and made 'em look at the gold. "Look and tell me if it's gold or no," I says. (*Triumphantly*) They was afeered to lie. Even that thief o' a cook owned up 'twas gold. Then when I turned 'em loose, because he knowed he'd git no share, he shouted again: "Brass and junk. Not worth a damn."

NAT. (*furiously*) But why did you allow— Why didn't you—

BARTLETT. (*with mad satisfaction*) Aye, ye be seein' the way o' it, boy. It was just then we sighted the schooner that picked us up after. We made a map and was buryin' the gold when we noticed them two thieves sneakin' about to see where we'd hide it. I saw 'em plain, the scum! That thief o' a cook was thinkin' he'd tell the folks on the schooner and go shares with them—and leave us on the island to rot; or he was thinkin' he and the boy'd be able to come back and dig it up afore I could. We had to do somethin' quick to spile their plan afore the schooner come. (*In a tone of savage satisfaction*) And so—though I spoke no word to him—Jimmy knifed 'em both and covered 'em up with sand. But I spoke no word, d'ye hear? Their deaths be on Jimmy's head alone.

NAT. (*passionately*) And what if you had? They deserved what they got.

BARTLETT. Then ye think I did no wrong?

NAT. No! Any man—I'd have done the same myself.

BARTLETT. (*gripping his son's hand tensely*) Ye be true son o' mine, Nat. I ought to told ye before. (*Exultantly*) Ye hear, Sarah? Nat says I done no wrong.

NAT. The map! Can I see it?

BARTLETT. Aye. (*He hands it to* NAT *who spreads it out on the table and pores over it.*)

NAT. (*excitedly*) Why, with this I—we—can go back—even if the "Sarah Allen" is lost.

BARTLETT. She ain't lost, boy—not her. Don't heed them lies ye been hearin'. She's due now. I'll go up and look. (*He goes up the companionway stairs.* NAT *does not seem to notice his going, absorbed in the map. Then there is a loud muffled hail in* BARTLETT's *voice*) " 'Sarah Allen,' ahoy!" (NAT *starts, transfixed—then rushes to one of the portholes to look. He turns back, passing his hand over his eyes, frowning bewilderedly. The door above is flung open and slammed shut and* BARTLETT *stamps down the stairs.*)

BARTLETT. (*fixing* NAT *hypnotically with his eyes—triumphantly*) What did I tell ye? D'ye believe now she'll come back? D'ye credit your own eyes?

NAT. (*vaguely*) Eyes? I looked. I didn't see—

BARTLETT. Ye lie! The "Sarah Allen," ye blind fool, come back from the Southern Seas as I swore she must! Loaded with gold as I swore she would be!—makin' port!—droppin' her anchor just when I hailed her.

NAT. (*feebly, his will crumbling*) But—how do you know?—some other schooner—

BARTLETT. Not know my own ship—and the signal I'd ordered Horne to make!

NAT. (*mechanically*) I know—a red and a green at the mainm'st head.

BARTLETT. Then look out if ye dare! (*He goes to a porthole*) Ye kin see it plain from here. (*Commandingly*) Will ye believe your eyes? Look! (NAT *comes to him slowly—looks through the porthole—and starts back, a possessed expression coming over his face.*)

NAT. (*slowly*) A red and a green—clear as day!

BARTLETT. (*his face is now transfigured by the ecstasy of a dream come true*) They've lowered a boat—the three—Horne an' Cates and Jimmy Kanaka. They're rowin' ashore. Listen. I hear the oars in the locks. Listen!

NAT. (*staring into his father's eyes—after a pause during which he appears to be straining his hearing to the breaking point—excitedly*) I hear!

BARTLETT. Listen! They've landed. They'll be comin' up the path now. (*In a crooning, monotonous tone*) They move slowly—slowly. It be heavy, I know—that chest. (*After a pause*) Hark! They're below at the door in front.

NAT. I hear!

BARTLETT. Ye'll see it now in a moment, boy—the gold. Up with it, bullies! Up ye come! Up, bullies! It's heavy, heavy!

NAT. (*madly*) I hear them! They're on the floor below! They're coming! I'll open the door. (*He springs to the door and flings it open, shouting*) Welcome home, boys! (SUE *is discovered outside just climbing up the stairs from below. She steps inside, then stops, looking with amazement and horror from father to brother.* NAT *pushes her roughly aside to look behind her down the stairs.*)

SUE. Nat!

NAT. (*Turning to his father*) I'll go down to the wharf. They must

189

be there or— (*The rest of his words are lost as he hurries down the stairs.* BARTLETT *steps back, shrinking away from his daughter, and sinks on a chair by the table with a groan, his hands over his eyes.*)

SUE. (*comes to him and shakes him by the shoulder—alarmed*) Pa! What has happened? What is the matter with Nat? What have you told him? (*With bitter despair*) Oh, can't you see you're driving him mad, too?

BARTLETT. (*letting his hands fall and staring at her haggardly—falteringly, as if reason were slowly filtering back into his brain*) Sue— ye said—drivin' him mad, *too!* Then ye think I be—? (*He staggers to his feet.* SUE *breaks down, sobbing.* BARTLETT *falters on*) But I seen her—the "Sarah Allen"—the signal lights—

SUE. Oh, Pa, there's nothing there! You know it! She was lost months ago.

BARTLETT. Lost? (*He stumbles over to a porthole and looks out. His body sags as if he were going to fall. He turns away and cries hopelessly in a tone of heart-rending grief*) Lost! Aye, they be no "Sarah Allen" there—no lights—nothin'!

SUE. (*pleading fiercely*) Pa, you've got to save Nat! He won't heed anyone else. Can't you tell him the truth—the whole truth whatever it is—now when I'm here and you're yourself again—and set him free from this crazy dream!

BARTLETT. (*with wild grief*) Confess, ye mean? Sue, ye be houndin' me like your Ma did to her dyin' hour! Confess—that I spoke the word to Jimmy—in my mind! Confess—brass and junk—not worth a damn! (*In frenzied protest*) No! Ye lie!

SUE. Oh, Pa, I don't know what you mean. Tell Nat the truth! Save him!

BARTLETT. The truth? It's a lie! (*As* SUE *tries to bar his way to the companionway—sternly*) Out o' my way, girl! (*He pulls himself feebly up the stairs. The door is heard slamming above.* SUE *sits down in a chair in a hopeless, exhausted attitude. After a pause* NAT *re-enters.*

He is panting heavily from his exertions. His pale face is set in an expression of despair.)

NAT. (*looking about the room wildly*) Where is he? Sue! (*He comes forward and falls on his knees beside her chair, hiding his face in her lap like a frightened child. He sobs hoarsely*) Sue! What does it all mean? I looked. There was nothing there—no schooner—nothing.

SUE. (*soothing him as if he were a little boy*) Of course there wasn't. Did you expect there would be, you foolish boy? Come, you know better than that. Why, Nat, you told the doctor and me that you were absolutely convinced the "Sarah Allen" was lost.

NAT. (*dully*) Yes, I know—but I don't believe—like him—

SUE. Sshhhh! You know the state Pa is in. He doesn't realize what he's saying half the time. You ought to have better sense than to pay any attention—

NAT. (*excitedly*) But he told me all he's been hiding from us—all about the gold!

SUE. (*looking at him with alarm—mystified*) Gold? (*Then forcing a smile*) Don't be silly, Nat. It doesn't exist except in his poor, deranged mind.

NAT. (*fiercely*) That's a lie, Sue! I saw the map, I tell you—the map of the island with a cross marked on it where they buried the gold.

SUE. He showed a map to you—a real map? (*Gently*) Are you sure you're not just imagining that, too?

NAT. I had it in my hands, you fool, you! There—on the table. (*He springs to his feet, sees the map on the table, and snatches it up with an exclamation of joy—showing it to* SUE) See! Now will you believe me? (*She examines the map perplexedly.* NAT *paces up and down—excitedly*) I tell you it's all true. You can't deny it now. It's lucky for us I forced him to confess. He might have died keeping the secret and then we'd have lost—I'll tell you what I'm going to do now, Sue. I'm going to raise the money somewhere, somehow, and fit out another schooner and this time I'll sail on her myself. No trusting to Danny or anyone else! Yes, Sue, we'll come into our own yet, even if the

"Sarah Allen" is lost— (*He stops—then in accents of bewildered fear*) But—she can't be lost—I saw the lights, Sue—as plain as I see you now— (*He goes to one of the portholes again.*)

SUE. (*who has been watching him worriedly, puts the map back on the table, gets up and, assuming a brisk, matter-of-fact tone, she goes over and takes him by the arm*) Come downstairs, Nat. Don't think any more about it tonight. It's late and you're worn out. You need rest and a good sleep.

NAT. (*following her toward the door—confusedly*) But Sue—I saw them— (*From above in the night comes the muffled hail in* BARTLETT'S *voice*) "Sarah Allen," ahoy! (NAT *stops, tortured, his hands instinctively raised up to cover his ears.* SUE *gives a startled cry. The door above is slammed and* BARTLETT *comes down the stairs, his face revealing that the delusion has again full possession of his mind.*)

BARTLETT. (*pointing his finger at his son and fixing him with his eyes—in ringing, triumphant tones*) The "Sarah Allen," boy—in the harbor below! Come back from the Southern Seas as I swore she must! Loaded with gold as I swore she would be! (NAT *again seems to crumble—to give way to the stronger will. He takes a step toward his father, his eyes lighting up.* SUE *looks at his face—then rushes to her father.*)

SUE. (*putting her hands to her father's head and forcing him to look down into her face—intensely*) Pa! Stop, do you hear me! It's all mad! You're driving Nat mad, too! (*As she sees her father hesitate, the wild light dying out of his eyes, she summons all her power to a fierce pleading*) For my sake, Pa! For Ma's sake! Think of how she would feel if she were alive and saw you acting this way with Nat! Tell him! Tell him now—before me—tell him it's all a lie!

BARTLETT. (*trying in an agony of conflict to get hold of his reason—incoherently*) Yes, Sue—I hear ye—confess—aye, Sarah, your dyin' words—keep Nat clear o' this—but—red and green—I seen 'em plain— (*Then suddenly after a tremendous struggle, lifting his tortured face to* NAT'S—*in tones of despair*) Nothin' there, boy! Don't ye believe! No red and green! She'll never come! Derelict and lost, boy, the "Sarah Allen." (*After another struggle with himself*) And I lied to ye, boy. I gave the word—in my mind—to kill them two. I murdered 'em in cold blood.

SUE. (*shrinking from him in horror*) Pa! You don't know what you're saying.

BARTLETT. The truth, girl. Ye said—confess—

NAT. (*bewilderedly*) But—it was right. They were trying to steal—

BARTLETT. (*overcome by the old obsession for a moment—savagely*) Aye, that's it! The thievin' scum! They was tryin'— (*He stops short, throwing his head back, his whole body tense and quivering with the effort he makes to force this sustaining lie out of his brain—then, broken but self-conquering, he looks again at NAT—gently*) No, Nat. That be the lie I been tellin' myself ever since. That cook—he said 'twas brass— But I'd been lookin' for ambergris—gold—the whole o' my life—and when we found that chest—I *had* to believe, I tell ye! I'd been dreamin' o' it all my days! But he said brass and junk, and told the boy—and I give the word to murder 'em both and cover 'em up with sand.

NAT. (*very pale—despairingly*) But he lied, didn't he? It is gold—real gold—isn't it?

BARTLETT. (*slowly takes the studded anklet from his pocket and holds it out to NAT. The latter brings it to the light of the lantern. BARTLETT sits on a chair, covering his face with his hands—in a tone of terrible suffering*) Ye'll tell me, boy—if it's gold or no. I've had it by me all this time—but I've been afeerd to show—

NAT. (*in a tone of wild scorn*) Why, it's brass, of course! The cheapest kind of junk—not worth a damn! (*He flings it savagely into a corner of the room. BARTLETT groans and seems to shrink up and turn into a figure of pitiable feebleness.*)

SUE. (*pityingly*) Don't, Nat. (*She puts her arms around her father's shoulders protectingly.*)

193

NAT. (*in a stifled voice*) What a damned fool I've been! (*He flings himself down on the cot, his shoulders heaving.*)

BARTLETT. (*uncovers his gray face on which there is now settling an expression of strange peace—stroking his daughter's hand*) Sue— don't think hard o' me. (*He takes the map*) An end to this! (*He slowly tears it into small pieces, seeming to grow weaker and weaker as he does so. Finally as he lets the fragments filter through his fingers, his whole frame suddenly relaxes. He sighs, his eyes shut, and sags back in his chair, his head bent forward limply on his chest.*)

SUE. (*alarmed*) Pa! (*She sinks to her knees beside him and looks up into his face*) Pa! Speak to me! It's Sue! (*Then turning toward her brother—terrifiedly*) Nat! Run—get the doctor— (NAT *starts to a sitting position.* SUE *tries with trembling hands to feel of her father's pulse, his heart—then begins to sob hysterically*) Oh, Nat—he's dead. I think—he's dead!

CURTAIN

DIFF'RENT

A Play in Two Acts

1920

CHARACTERS

CAPTAIN CALEB WILLIAMS
EMMA CROSBY
CAPTAIN JOHN CROSBY, *her father*
MRS. CROSBY, *her mother*
JACK CROSBY, *her brother*
HARRIET WILLIAMS, *Caleb's sister* (*later* MRS. ROGERS)
ALFRED ROGERS
BENNY ROGERS, *their son*

SCENES

ACT ONE

Parlor of the Crosby home on a side street of a seaport village in New England—mid-afternoon of a day in late spring in the year 1890.

ACT TWO

The same. Late afternoon of a day in the early spring of the year 1920.

DIFF'RENT

ACT ONE

SCENE—*Parlor of the* CROSBY *home. The room is small and low-ceilinged. Everything has an aspect of scrupulous neatness. On the left, forward, a stiff plush-covered chair. Farther back, in order, a window looking out on a vegetable garden, a black horsehair sofa, and another window. In the far left corner, an old mahogany chest of drawers. To the right of it, in rear, a window looking out on the front yard. To the right of this window is the front door, reached by a dirt path through the small lawn which separates the house from the street. To the right of door, another window. In the far right corner, a diminutive, old-fashioned piano with a stool in front of it. Near the piano on the right, a door leading to the next room. On this side of the room are also a small bookcase half filled with old volumes, a big open fireplace, and another plush-covered chair. Over the fireplace a mantel with a marble clock and a Rogers group. The walls are papered a brown color. The floor is covered with a dark carpet. In the center of the room there is a clumsy, marble-topped table. On the table, a large china lamp, a bulky Bible with a brass clasp, and several books that look suspiciously like cheap novels. Near the table, three plush-covered chairs, two of which are rockers. Several enlarged photos of strained, stern-looking people in uncomfortable poses are hung on the walls.*

It is mid-afternoon of a fine day in late spring of the year 1890. Bright sunlight streams through the windows on the left. Through the window and the screen door in the rear the fresh green of the lawn and of the elm trees that line the street can be seen. Stiff, white curtains are at all the windows.

As the curtain rises, EMMA CROSBY *and* CALEB WILLIAMS *are discovered.* EMMA *is a slender girl of twenty, rather under the medium height. Her face, in spite of its plain features, gives an impression of prettiness, due to her large, soft blue eyes which have an incongruous quality of absent-minded romantic dreaminess about them. Her mouth and chin are heavy, full of a self-willed stubbornness. Although her body is slight and thin, there is a quick, nervous vitality about all her movements that reveals an underlying constitution of reserve power and health. She has light brown hair, thick and heavy. She is dressed soberly and neatly in her black Sunday best, style of the period.*

CALEB WILLIAMS *is tall and powerfully built, about thirty. Black hair, keen, dark eyes, face rugged and bronzed, mouth obstinate but good-natured. He, also, is got up in black Sunday best and is uncomfortably self-conscious and stiff therein.*

They are sitting on the horsehair sofa, side by side. His arm is about her waist. She holds one of his big hands in both of hers, her head leaning back against his shoulder, her eyes half closed in a dreamy contentedness. He stares before him rigidly, his whole attitude wooden and fixed as if he were posing for a photograph; yet his eyes are expressively tender and protecting when he glances down at her diffidently out of the corners without moving his head.

EMMA. (*sighing happily*) Gosh, I wish we could sit this way forever! (*Then after a pause, as he makes no comment except a concurring squeeze*) Don't you, Caleb?

CALEB. (*with another squeeze—emphatically*) Hell, yes! I'd like it, Emmer.

EMMA. (*softly*) I do wish you wouldn't swear so awful much, Caleb.

CALEB. S'cuse me, Emmer, it jumped out o' my mouth afore I thought. (*Then with a grin*) You'd ought to be used to that part o' men's wickedness—with your Pa and Jack cussin' about the house all the time.

EMMA. (*with a smile*) Oh, I haven't no strict religious notions about it. I'm hardened in sin so far's they're concerned. Goodness me, how would Ma and me ever have lived in the same house with them two if we wasn't used to it? I don't even notice their cussing no more. And I don't mind hearing it from the other men, either. Being seafaring men, away from their women folks most of the time, I know it just gets to be part of their natures and they ain't responsible. (*Decisively*) But you're diff'rent. You just got to be diff'rent from the rest.

CALEB. (*amused by her seriousness*) Diff'rent? Ain't I a sea-farin' man, too?

EMMA. You're diff'rent just the same. That's what made me fall in love with you 'stead of any of them. And you've got to stay diff'rent. Promise me, Caleb, that you'll always stay diff'rent from them—even after we're married years and years.

CALEB. (*embarrassed*) Why—I promise to do my best by you, Emmer. You know that, don't ye? On'y don't git the notion in your head I'm any better'n the rest. They're all good men—most of 'em, anyway. Don't tell me, for instance, you think I'm better'n your Pa or Jack—'cause I ain't. And I don't know as I'd want to be, neither.

EMMA. (*excitedly*) But you got to want to be—when I ask it.

CALEB. (*surprised*) Better'n your Pa?

EMMA. (*struggling to convey her meaning*) Why, Pa's all right. He's a fine man—and Jack's all right, too. I wouldn't hear a bad word about them for anything. And the others are all right in their way, too, I s'pose. Only—don't you see what I mean?—I look on you as diff'rent from all of them. I mean there's things that's all right for them to do that wouldn't be for you—in my mind, anyway.

CALEB. (*puzzled and a bit uneasy*) Sailors ain't plaster saints, Emmer,—not a darn one of 'em ain't!

EMMA. (*hurt and disappointed*) Then you won't promise me to stay diff'rent for my sake?

CALEB. (*with rough tenderness*) Oh, hell, Emmer, I'll do any cussed thing in the world you want me to, and you know it!

EMMA. (*lovingly*) Thank you, Caleb. It means a lot to me—more'n you think. And don't you think I'm diff'rent, too—not just the same as all the other girls hereabouts?

CALEB. 'Course you be! Ain't I always said that? You're wo'th the whole pack of 'em put together.

EMMA. Oh, I don't mean I'm any better. I mean I just look at things diff'rent from what they do—getting married, for example, and other things, too. And so I've got it fixed in my head that you and me ought to make a married couple—diff'rent from the rest—not that they ain't all right in their way.

CALEB. (*puzzled—uncertainly*) Waal—it's bound to be from your end of it, you bein' like you are. But I ain't so sure o' mine.

EMMA. Well, I am!

CALEB. (*with a grin*) You got me scared, Emmer. I'm scared you'll want me to live up to one of them high-fangled heroes you been readin' about in them books. (*He indicates the novels on the table.*)

EMMA. No, I don't. I want you to be just like yourself, that's all.

CALEB. That's easy. It ain't hard bein' a plain, ordinary cuss.

EMMA. You are not!

CALEB. (*with a laugh*) Remember, I'm warnin' you, Emmer; and after we're married and you find me out, you can't say I got you under no false pretenses.

EMMA. (*laughing*) I won't. I won't ever need to. (*Then after a pause*) Just think, it's only two days more before you and me'll be man and wife.

CALEB. (*squeezing her*) Waal, it's about time, ain't it?—after waitin' three years for me to git enough money saved—and us not seein' hide or hair of each other the last two of 'em. (*With a laugh*) Shows ye what trust I put in you, Emmer, when I kin go off on a two-year whalin' vige and leave you all 'lone for all the young fellers in town to make eyes at.

200

EMMA. But lots and lots of the others does the same thing without thinking nothing about it.

CALEB. (*with a laugh*) Yes, but I'm diff'rent, like you says.

EMMA. (*laughing*) Oh, you're poking fun now.

CALEB. (*with a wink*) And you know as well's me that some o' the others finds out some funny things that's been done when they was away.

EMMA. (*laughing at first*) Yes, but you know I'm diff'rent, too. (*Then frowning*) But don't let's talk about that sort o' ructions. I hate to think of such things—even joking. I ain't like that sort.

CALEB. Thunder, I know you ain't, Emmer. I was on'y jokin'.

EMMA. And I never doubted you them two years; and I won't when you sail away again, neither.

CALEB. (*with a twinkle in his eye*) No, even a woman'd find it hard to git jealous of a whale!

EMMA. (*laughing*) I wasn't thinking of whales, silly! But there's plenty of diversion going on in the ports you touched, if you'd a mind for it.

CALEB. Waal, I didn't have no mind for it, that's sartin. My fust vige as skipper, you don't s'pose I had time for no monkey-shinin', do ye? Why, I was that anxious to bring back your Pa's ship with a fine vige that'd make him piles o' money, I didn't even think of nothin' else.

EMMA. 'Cepting me, I hope?

CALEB. O' course! What was my big aim in doin' it if it wasn't so's wed git married when I come to home? And then, s'far as ports go, we didn't tech at one the last year—'ceptin' when that durn tempest blowed us south and we put in at one o' the Islands for water.

EMMA. What island? You never told me nothing about that.

CALEB. (*growing suddenly very embarrassed as if some memory occurred to him*) Ain't nothin' to tell, that's why. Just an island near the Line, that's all. O'ny naked heathen livin' there—brown colored savages that ain't even Christians. (*He gets to his feet abruptly and pulls out his watch*) Gittin' late, must be. I got to go down to the store and git some things for Harriet afore I forgets 'em.

EMMA. (*rising also and putting her hands on his shoulders*) But you did think of me and miss me all the time you was gone, didn't you?—same as I did you.

CALEB. 'Course I did. Every minute.

EMMA. (*nestling closer to him—softly*) I'm glad of that, Caleb. Well, good-by for a little while.

CALEB. I'll step in again for a spell afore supper—that is, if you want me to.

EMMA. Yes, of course I do, Caleb. Good-by. (*She lifts her face to his.*)

CALEB. Good-by, Emmer. (*He kisses her and holds her in his arms for a moment. JACK comes up the walk to the screen door. They do not notice his approach.*)

JACK. (*peering in and seeing them—in a joking bellow*) Belay, there! (*They separate with startled exclamations. JACK comes in grinning. He is a hulking, stocky-built young fellow of 25. His heavy face is sunburned, handsome in a coarse, good-natured animal fashion. His small blue eyes twinkle with the unconsciously malicious humor of the born practical joker. He wears high seaboots turned down from the knee, dirty cotton shirt and pants, and a yellow sou'wester pushed jauntily on the back of his head, revealing his disheveled, curly blond hair. He carries a string of cod heads.*)

JACK. (*laughing at the embarrassed expression on their faces*) Caught ye that time, by gum! Go ahead! Kiss her again, Caleb. Don't mind me.

EMMA. (*with flurried annoyance*) You got a head on you just like one of them cod heads you're carrying—that stupid! I should think you'd be ashamed at your age—shouting to scare folks as if you was a little boy.

JACK. (*putting his arm about her waist*) There, kitty, don't git to spittin'. (*Stroking her hair*) Puss, puss, puss! Nice kitty! (*He laughs.*)

EMMA. (*forced to smile—pushing him away*) Get away! You'll never get sense. Land sakes, what a brother to have!

JACK. Oh, I dunno. I ain't so bad, as brothers go—eh, Caleb?

CALEB. (*smiling*) I reckon you'll do, Jack.

JACK. See there! Listen to Caleb. You got to take his word—love, honor, and *obey,* ye know, Emmer.

EMMA. (*laughing*) Leave it to men folks to stick up for each other, right or wrong.

JACK. (*cockily*) Waal, I'm willin' to leave it to the girls, too. Ask any of 'em you knows if I ain't a jim-dandy to have for a brother. (*He winks at* CALEB *who grins back at him.*)

EMMA. (*with a sniff*) I reckon you don't play much brother with them—the kind you knows. You may fool 'em into believing you're some pumpkins but they'd change their minds if they had to live in the same house with you playing silly jokes all the time.

JACK. (*provokingly*) A good lot on 'em 'd be on'y too damn glad to git me in the same house—if I was fool enough to git married.

EMMA. "Pride goeth before a fall." But shucks, what's the good paying any attention to you. (*She smiles at him affectionately.*)

JACK. (*exaggeratedly*) You see, Caleb? See how she misuses me—her lovin' brother. Now you know what you'll be up against for the rest o' your natural days.

CALEB. Don't see no way but what I got to bear it, Jack.

EMMA. Caleb needn't fear. He's diff'rent.

JACK. (*with a sudden guffaw*) Oh, hell, yes! I was forgittin'. Caleb's a Sunday go-to-meetin' Saint, ain't he? Yes, he is!

EMMA. (*with real resentment*) He's better'n what you are, if that's what you mean.

JACK. (*with a still louder laugh*) Ho-ho! Caleb's one o' them goody-goody heroes out o' them story books you're always readin', ain't he?

CALEB. (*soberly—a bit disturbed*) I was tellin' Emmer not to take me that high.

JACK. No use, Caleb. She won't hear of it. She's got her head sot t'other way. You ought to heard her argyin' when you was gone about what a parson's pet you was. Butter won't melt in your mouth, no siree! Waal, love is blind—and deaf, too, as the feller says—and I can't argy no more 'cause I got to give Ma these heads. (*He goes to the door on right—then glances back at his sister maliciously and says meaningly*) You ought to have a talk with Jim Benson, Emmer. Oughtn't she, Caleb? (*He winks ponderously and goes off laughing uproariously.*)

CALEB. (*his face worried and angry*) Jack's a durn fool at times, Emmer—even if he is your brother. He needs a good lickin'.

EMMA. (*staring at him—uneasily*) What'd he mean about Jim Benson, Caleb?

CALEB. (*frowning*) I don't know—ezactly. Makin' up foolishness for a joke, I reckon.

EMMA. You don't know—*exactly?* Then there is—something?

CALEB. (*quickly*) Not as I know on. On'y Jim Benson's one o' them slick jokers, same's Jack; can't keep their mouths shet or mind their own business.

EMMA. Jim Benson was mate with you this last trip, wasn't he?

CALEB. Yes.

EMMA. Didn't him and you get along?

CALEB. (*a trifle impatiently*) 'Course we did. Jim's all right. We got along fust rate. He just can't keep his tongue from waggin', that's all's the matter with him.

EMMA. (*uneasily*) What's it got to wag about? You ain't done nothing wrong, have you?

CALEB. Wrong? No, nothin' a man'd rightly call wrong.

EMMA. Nothing you'd be ashamed to tell me?

CALEB. (*awkwardly*) Why—no, Emmer.

EMMA. (*pleadingly*) You'd swear that, Caleb?

CALEB. (*hesitating for a second—then firmly*) Yes, I'd swear. I'd own up to everything fair and square I'd ever done, if it comes to that p'int. I ain't ashamed o' anything I ever done, Emmer. On'y—women folks ain't got to know everything, have they?

EMMA. (*turning away from him—frightenedly*) Oh, Caleb!

CALEB. (*preoccupied with his own thoughts—going to the door in rear*) I'll see you later, Emmer. I got to go up street now more'n ever. I want to give that Jim Benson a talkin' to he won't forgit in a hurry— that is, if he's been tellin' tales. Good-by, Emmer.

EMMA. (*faintly*) Good-by, Caleb. (*He goes out. She sits in one of the rockers by the table, her face greatly troubled, her manner nervous and uneasy. Finally she makes a decision, goes quickly to the door on the right and calls*) Jack! Jack!

JACK. (*from the kitchen*) What you want?

EMMA. Come here a minute, will you?

JACK. Jest a second. (*She comes back by the table, fighting to conceal her agitation. After a moment, JACK comes in from the right. He has evidently been washing up, for his face is red and shiny, his hair wet and slicked in a part. He looks around for CALEB*) Where's Caleb?

EMMA. He had to go up street. (*Then coming to the point abruptly with feigned indifference*) What's that joke about Jim Benson, Jack? It seemed to get Caleb all riled up.

JACK. (*with a chuckle*) You got to ask Caleb about that, Emmer.

EMMA. I did. He didn't seem to want to own up it was anything.

JACK. (*with a laugh*) 'Course he wouldn't. He don't 'preciate a joke when it's on him.

EMMA. How'd you come to hear of it?

JACK. From Jim. Met him this afternoon and me and him had a long talk. He was tellin' me all 'bout their vige.

EMMA. Then it was on the vige this joke happened?

JACK. Yes. It was when they put in to git water at them South Sea Islands where the tempest blowed 'em.

EMMA. Oh. (*Suspiciously*) Caleb didn't seem willing to tell me much about their touching there.

JACK. (*chuckling*) 'Course he didn't. Wasn't I sayin' the joke's on him? (*Coming closer to her—in a low, confidential tone, chucklingly*) We'll fix up a joke on Caleb, Emmer, what d'ye say?

EMMA. (*tortured by foreboding—resolved to find out what is back of all this by hook or crook—forcing a smile*) All right, Jack. I'm willing.

JACK. Then I'll tell you what Jim told me. And you put it up to Caleb, see, and pertend you're madder'n hell. (*Unable to restrain his mirth*) Ho-ho! It'll git him wild if you do that. On'y I didn't tell ye, mind. You heard it from someone else. I don't want to git Caleb down on me. And you'd hear about it from someone sooner or later 'cause Jim and the rest o' the boys has been tellin' the hull town.

EMMA. (*taken aback—frowning*) So all the town knows about it?

JACK. Yes, and they're all laffin' at Caleb. Oh, it ain't nothin' so out o' the ordinary. Most o' the whalin' men hereabout have run up against it in their time. I've heard Pa and all the others tellin' stories like it out o' their experience. On'y with Caleb it ended up so damn funny! (*He laughs*) Ho-ho! Jimminy!

EMMA. (*in a strained voice*) Well, ain't you going to tell me?

JACK. I'm comin' to it. Waal, seems like they all went ashore on them islands to git water and the native brown women, all naked a'most, come round to meet 'em same as they always does—wantin' to swap for terbaccer and other tradin' stuff with straw mats and whatever other junk they got. Them brown gals was purty as the devil, Jim says—that is, in their heathen, outlandish way—and the boys got makin' up to 'em; and then, o' course, everything happened like it always does, and even after they'd got all the water they needed aboard, it took 'em a week to round up all hands from where they was foolin' about with them nigger women.

EMMA. (*in anguish*) Yes—but Caleb—he ain't like them others. He's diff'rent.

JACK. (*with a sly wink*) Oho, is he? I'm comin' to Caleb. Waal, seems 's if he kept aboard mindin' his own business and winkin' at what the boys was doin'. And one o' them gals—the purtiest on 'em,

Jim says—she kept askin', where's the captain? She wouldn't have nothin' to do with any o' the others. She thought on'y the skipper was good enough for her, I reckon. So one night jest afore they sailed some o' the boys, bein' drunk on native rum they'd stole, planned to put up a joke on Caleb and on that brown gal, too. So they tells her the captain had sent for her and she was to swim right out and git aboard the ship where he was waitin' for her alone. That part of it was true enough 'cause Caleb was alone, all hands havin' deserted, you might say.

EMMA. (*letting an involuntary exclamation escape her*) Oh!

JACK. Waal, that fool brown gal b'lieved 'em and she swum right off, tickled to death. What happened between 'em when she got aboard, nobody knows. Some thinks one thing and some another. And I ain't sayin' nothin' 'bout it—(*With a wink*) but I know damn well what I'd 'a done in Caleb's boots, and I guess he ain't the cussed old woman you makes him out. But that part of it's got nothin' to do with the joke nohow. The joke's this: that brown gal took an awful shine to Caleb and when she saw the ship was gittin' ready to sail she raised ructions, standin' on the beach howlin' and screamin', and beatin' her chest with her fists. And when they ups anchors, she dives in the water and swims out after 'em. There's no wind hardly and she kin swim like a fish and catches up to 'em and tries to climb aboard. At fust, Caleb tries to treat her gentle and argy with her to go back. But she won't listen, she gits wilder and wilder, and finally he gits sick of it and has the boys push her off with oars while he goes and hides in the cabin. Even this don't work. She keeps swimmin' round and yellin' for Caleb. And finally they has to p'int a gun at her and shoot in the water near her afore the crazy cuss gives up and swims back to home, howlin' all the time. (*With a chuckle*) And Caleb lyin' low in the cabin skeered to move out, and all hands splittin' their sides! Gosh, I wish I'd been there! It must have been funnier'n hell! (*He laughs loudly—then noticing his sister's stony expression,*

207

stops abruptly) What're you pullin' that long face for, Emmer? (*Offendedly*) Hell, you're a nice one to tell a joke to!

EMMA. (*after a pause—forcing the words out slowly*) Caleb's comin' back here, Jack. I want you to see him for me. I want you to tell him—

JACK. Not me! You got to play this joke on him yourself or it won't work.

EMMA. (*tensely*) This ain't a joke, Jack—what I mean. I want you to tell him I've changed my mind and I ain't going to marry him.

JACK. What!

EMMA. I been thinking things over, tell him—and I take back my promise—and he can have back his ring—and I ain't going to marry him.

JACK. (*flabbergasted—peering into her face anxiously*) Say—what the hell—? Are you tryin' to josh me, Emmer? Or are you gone crazy all of a sudden?

EMMA. I ain't joking nor crazy neither. You tell him what I said.

JACK. (*vehemently*) I will like— Say, what's come over you, anyhow?

EMMA. My eyes are opened, that's all, and I ain't going to marry him.

JACK. Is it—'count of that joke about Caleb I was tellin' you?

EMMA. (*her voice trembling*) It's 'count of something I got in my own head. What you told only goes to prove I was wrong about it.

JACK. (*greatly perturbed now*) Say, what's the matter? Can't you take a joke? Are you mad at him 'count o' that brown gal?

EMMA. Yes, I am—and I ain't going to marry him and that's all there is to it.

JACK. (*argumentatively*) Jealous of a brown, heathen woman that ain't no better'n a nigger? God sakes, Emmer, I didn't think you was that big a fool. Why, them kind o' women ain't women like you. They don't count like folks. They ain't Christians—nor nothin'!

EMMA. That ain't it. I don't care what they are.

JACK. And it wasn't Caleb anyhow. It was all her fixin'. And how'd you know he had anything to do with her—like that? I ain't said he did. Jim couldn't swear he did neither. And even if he did—what difference does it make? It ain't rightly none o' your business what he does on a vige. He didn't ask her to marry him, did he?

EMMA. I don't care. He'd ought to have acted diff'rent.

JACK. Oh golly, there you go agen makin' a durned creepin'-Jesus out of him! What d'you want to marry, anyhow—a man or a sky-pilot? Caleb's a man, ain't he?—and a damn good man and as smart a skipper as there be in these parts! What more d'you want, anyhow?

EMMA. (*violently*) I want you to shet up! You're too dumb stupid and bad yourself to ever know what I'm thinking.

JACK. (*resentfully*) Go to the devil, then! I'm goin' to tell Ma and sic her onto you. You'll maybe listen to her and git some sense. (*He stamps out, right, while he is speaking.* EMMA *bursts into sobs and throws herself on a chair, covering her face with her hands.* HARRIET WILLIAMS *and* ALFRED ROGERS *come up the path to the door in rear. Peering through the screen and catching sight of* EMMA, HARRIET *calls*) Emmer! (EMMA *leaps to her feet and dabs at her eyes with a handkerchief in a vain effort to conceal traces of her tears.* HARRIET *has come in, followed by* ROGERS. CALEB'S *sister is a tall, dark girl of twenty. Her face is plainly homely and yet attracts the eye by a certain boldly-appealing vitality of self-confident youth. She wears an apron and has evidently just come out of the kitchen.* ROGERS *is a husky young fisherman of twenty-four, washed and slicked up in his ill-fitting best.*)

ROGERS. Hello, Emmer.

EMMA. (*huskily, trying to force a smile*) Hello, Harriet. Hello, Alfred. Won't you set?

HARRIET. No, I jest run over from the house a second to see if— Where's Caleb, Emmer?

EMMA. He's gone up street.

HARRIET. And here I be waitin' in the kitchen for him to bring back the things so's I can start his supper. (*With a laugh and a roguish*

209

look at ROGERS) Dearie me, it ain't no use dependin' on a man to re-member nothin' when he's in love.

ROGERS. (*putting his arm about her waist and giving her a squeeze—grinning*) How 'bout me? Ain't I in love and ain't I as reliable as an old hoss?

HARRIET. Oh, you! You're the worst of 'em all.

ROGERS. You don't think so. (*He tries to kiss her.*)

HARRIET. Stop it. Ain't you got no manners? What'll Emmer think?

ROGERS. Emmer can't throw stones. Her and Caleb is worser at spoonin' than what we are. (HARRIET *breaks away from him laughingly and goes to* EMMA.)

HARRIET. (*suddenly noticing the expression of misery on* EMMA's *face—astonished*) Why, Emmer Crosby, what's the matter? You look as if you'd lost your last friend.

EMMA. (*trying to smile*) Nothing. It's nothing.

HARRIET. It is, too! Why, I do believe you've been crying!

EMMA. No, I ain't.

HARRIET. You have, too! (*Putting her arms about* EMMA) Goodness, what's happened? You and Caleb ain't had a spat, have you, with your weddin' only two days off?

EMMA. (*with quick resentful resolution*) There ain't going to be any wedding.

HARRIET. What!

ROGERS. (*pricking up his ears—inquisitively*) Huh?

EMMA. Not in two days nor no time.

HARRIET. (*dumbfounded*) Why, Emmer Crosby! Whatever's got into you? You and Caleb must have had an awful spat!

ROGERS. (*with a man-of-the-world attitude of cynicism*) Don't take her so dead serious, Harriet. Emmer'll git over it like you all does.

EMMA. (*angrily*) You shet up, Alf Rogers! (MRS. CROSBY *enters bustlingly from the right. She is a large, fat, florid woman of fifty. In spite of her two hundred and more pounds she is surprisingly active, and the passive, lazy expression of her round moon face is belied by her quick, efficient movements. She exudes an atmosphere of motherly good nature. She wears an apron on which she is drying her hands as she enters.* JACK *follows her into the room. He has changed to a dark suit, is ready for "up street.")*

MRS. CROSBY. (*smiling at* HARRIET *and* ROGERS) Afternoon, Harriet— and Alf.

HARRIET. Afternoon, Ma.

ROGERS. Afternoon.

JACK. (*grinning*) There she be, Ma. (*Points to* EMMA) Don't she look like she'd scratch a feller's eyes out! Phew! Look at her back curve! Meow? Sptt-sptt! Nice puss! (*He gives a vivid imitation of a cat fight at this last. Then he and* ROGERS *roar with laughter and* HARRIET *cannot restrain a giggle and* MRS. CROSBY *smiles.* EMMA *stares stonily before her as if she didn't hear.*)

MRS. CROSBY. (*good-naturedly*) Shet up your foolin', Jack.

JACK. (*pretending to be hurt*) Nobody in this house kin take a joke. (*He grins and beckons to* ROGERS) Come along, Alf. You kin 'preciate a joke. Come on in here till I tell you. (*The grinning* ROGERS *follows him into the next room where they can be heard talking and laughing during the following scene.*)

MRS. CROSBY. (*smiling, puts her arms around* EMMA) Waal, Emmer, what's this foolishness Jack's been tellin' about—

EMMA. (*resentfully*) It ain't foolishness, Ma. I've made up my mind, I tell you that right here and now.

MRS. CROSBY. (*after a quick glance at her face—soothingly*) There, there! Let's set down and be comfortable. Me, I don't relish roostin' on my feet. (*She pushes* EMMA *gently into a rocker—then points to a chair on the other side of the table*) Set down, Harriet.

HARRIET. (*torn between curiosity and a sense of being one too many*) Maybe I'd best go to home and leave you two alone?

MRS. CROSBY. Shucks! Ain't you like one o' the family—Caleb's sister and livin' right next door ever since you was all children playin' together. We ain't got no secrets from you. Set down. (HARRIET *does so*

211

with an uncertain glance at the frozen EMMA. MRS. CROSBY *has efficiently bustled another rocker beside her daughter's and sits down with a comfortable sigh*) There. (*She reaches over and takes one of her daughter's hands in hers*) And now, Emmer, what's all this fuss over? (*As* EMMA *makes no reply*) Jack says as you've sworn you was breakin' with Caleb. Is that true?

EMMA. Yes.

MRS. CROSBY. Hmm. Caleb don't know this yet, does he?

EMMA. No. I asked Jack to tell him when he comes back.

MRS. CROSBY. Jack says he won't.

EMMA. Then I'll tell him myself. Maybe that's better, anyhow. Caleb'll know what I'm driving at and see my reason—(*Bitterly*) which nobody else seems to.

MRS. CROSBY. Hmm. You ain't tried me yet. (*After a pause*) Jack was a dumb fool to tell you 'bout them goin's-on at them islands they teched. Ain't no good repeatin' sech things.

EMMA. (*surprised*) Did you know about it before Jack—

MRS. CROSBY. Mercy, yes. Your Pa heard it from Jim Benson fust thing they landed here, and Pa told me that night.

EMMA. (*resentfully*) And you never told me!

MRS. CROSBY. Mercy, no. 'Course I didn't. They's trouble enough in the world without makin' more. If you was like most folks I'd told it to you. Me, I thought it was a good joke on Caleb.

EMMA. (*with a shudder*) It ain't a joke to me.

MRS. CROSBY. That's why I kept my mouth shet. I knowed you was touchy and diff'rent from most.

EMMA. (*proudly*) Yes, I am diff'rent—and that's just what I thought Caleb was, too—and he ain't.

HARRIET. (*breaking in excitedly*) Is it that story about Caleb and that heathen brown woman you're talking about? Is that what you're mad at Caleb for, Emmer?

MRS. CROSBY. (*as* EMMA *remains silent*) Yes, Harriet, that's it.

HARRIET. (*astonished*) Why, Emmer Crosby, how can you be so silly? You don't s'pose Caleb took it serious, do you, and him makin' them fire shots round her to scare her back to land and get rid of her? Good gracious! (*A bit resentfully*) I hope you ain't got it in your head my brother Caleb would sink so low as to fall in love serious with one of them critters?

EMMA. (*harshly*) He might just as well.

HARRIET. (*bridling*) How can you say sech a thing! (*Sarcastically*) I ain't heard that Caleb offered to marry her, have you? Then you might have some cause— But d'you s'pose he's ever give her another thought? Not Caleb! I know him better'n that. He'd forgot all about the hull thing before they was out o' sight of land, I'll bet, and if them fools hadn't started this story going, he'd never remembered it again.

MRS. CROSBY. (*nodding*) That's jest it. Harriet's right, Emmer.

EMMA. Ma!

MRS. CROSBY. Besides, you don't know they was nothin' wrong happened. Nobody kin swear that for sartin. Ain't that so, Harriet?

HARRIET. (*hesitating—then frankly*) I don't know. Caleb ain't no plaster saint and I reckon he's as likely to sin that way as any other man. He wasn't married then and I s'pose he thought he was free to do as he'd a mind to 'til he was hitched up. Goodness sakes, Emmer, all the men thinks that—and a lot of 'em after they're married, too.

MRS. CROSBY. Harriet's right, Emmer. If you've been wide awake to all that's happened in this town since you was old enough to know, you'd ought to realize what men be.

HARRIET. (*scornfully*) Emma'd ought to have fallen in love with a minister, not a sailor. As for me, I wouldn't give a durn about a man that was too goody-goody to raise Cain once in a while—before he married me, I mean. Why, look at Alf Rogers, Emmer. I'm going to marry him some day, ain't I? But I know right well all the foolin' he's done—and still is doing, I expect. I ain't sayin' I like it but I do like him and I got to take him the way he is, that's all. If you're looking for saints, you got to die first and go to heaven. A girl'd never git married hereabouts if she expected too much.

213

MRS. CROSBY. Harriet's right, Emmer.

EMMA. (*resentfully*) Maybe she is, Ma, from her side. I ain't claiming she's wrong. Her and me just looks at things diff'rent, that's all. And she can't understand the way I feel about Caleb.

HARRIET. Well, there's one thing certain, Emmer. You won't find a man in a day's walk is any better'n Caleb—or as good.

EMMA. (*wearily*) I know that, Harriet.

HARRIET. Then it's all right. You'll make up with him, and I s'pose I'm a fool to be takin' it so serious. (*As* EMMA *shakes her head*) Oh, yes, you will. You wouldn't want to get him all broke up, would you? (*As* EMMA *keeps silent—irritably*) Story-book notions, that's the trouble with you, Emmer. You're gettin' to think you're better'n the rest of us.

EMMA. (*vehemently*) No, I don't! Can't you see—

MRS. CROSBY. Thar, now! Don't you two git to fightin'—to make things worse.

HARRIET. (*repentantly, coming and putting her arms around* EMMA *and kissing her*) I'm sorry, Emmer. You know I wouldn't fall out with you for nothing or nobody, don't you? Only it gits me riled to think of how awful broke up Caleb'd be if— But you'll make it all up with him when he comes, won't you? (EMMA *stares stubbornly before her. Before she has a chance to reply a roar of laughter comes from the next room as* JACK *winds up his tale.*)

ROGERS. (*from the next room*) Gosh, I wished I'd been there! (*He follows* JACK *into the room. Both are grinning broadly.* ROGERS *says teasingly*) Reckon I'll take to whalin' 'stead o' fishin' after this. You won't mind, Harriet? From what I hears o' them brown women, I'm missin' a hull lot by stayin' to home.

HARRIET. (*in a joking tone—with a meaning glance at* EMMA) Go on, then! There's plenty of fish in the sea. Anyhow, I'd never git jealous of your foolin' with one o' them heathen critters. They ain't worth notice from a Christian.

JACK. Oho, ain't they! They're purty as pictures, Benson says. (*With*

214

a wink) And mighty accommodatin' in their ways. (*He and* ROGERS *roar delightedly.* EMMA *shudders with revulsion.*)

MRS. CROSBY. (*aware of her daughter's feelings—smilingly but firmly*) Get out o' this, Jack. You, too, Alf. Go on up street if you want to joke. You're in my way.

JACK. Aw right, Ma. Come on up street, Alf.

HARRIET. Wait. I'll go with you a step. I got to see if Caleb's got back with them supper things. (*They all go to the door in rear.* JACK *and* ROGERS *pass out, talking and laughing.* HARRIET *turns in the doorway— sympathetically*) I'll give Caleb a talking-to before he comes over. Then it'll be easy for you to finish him. Treat him firm but gentle and you'll see he won't never do it again in a hurry. After all, he wasn't married, Emmer—and he's a man—and what can you expect? Good-by. (*She goes.*)

EMMA. (*inaudibly*) Good-by.

MRS. CROSBY. (*after a pause in which she rocks back and forth study- ing her daughter's face—placidly*) Harriet's right, Emmer. You give him a good talkin'-to and he won't do it again.

EMMA. (*coldly*) I don't care whether he does or not. I ain't going to marry him.

MRS. CROSBY. (*uneasy—persuasively*) Mercy, you can't act like that, Emmer. Here's the weddin' on'y two days off, and everythin' fixed up with the minister, and your Pa and Jack has bought new clothes speshul for it, and I got a new dress—

EMMA. (*turning to her mother—pleadingly*) You wouldn't want me to keep my promise to Caleb if you knew I'd be unhappy, would you, Ma?

MRS. CROSBY. (*hesitatingly*) N-no, Emmer. (*Then decisively*) 'Course I wouldn't. It's because I know he'll make you happy. (*As* EMMA *shakes her head*) Pshaw, Emmer, you can't tell me you've got over all likin' for him jest 'count o' this one foolishness o' hisn.

EMMA. I don't love him—what he is now. I loved—what I thought he was.

MRS. CROSBY. (*more and more uneasy*) That's all your queer notions, and I don't know where you gits them from. Caleb ain't changed, neither have you. Why, Emmer, it'd be jest like goin' agen an act of Nature for you not to marry him. Ever since you was children you been livin' side by side, goin' round together, and neither you nor him ever did seem to care for no one else. Shucks, Emmer, you'll git me to lose patience with you if you act that stubborn. You'd ought to remember all he's been to you and forget this one little wrong he's done.

EMMA. I can't, Ma. It makes him another person—not Caleb, but someone just like all the others.

MRS. CROSBY. Waal, is the others so bad? Men is men the world over, I reckon.

EMMA. No, they ain't bad. I ain't saying that. Don't I like 'em all? If it was one of the rest—like Jim Benson or Jack, even—had done this I'd thought it was a joke, too. I ain't strict in judging 'em and you know it. But—can't you see, Ma?—Caleb always seemed diff'rent— and I thought he was.

MRS. CROSBY. (*somewhat impatiently*) Wall, if he ain't, he's a good man jest the same, as good as any sensible girl'd want to marry.

EMMA. (*slowly*) I don't want to marry nobody no more. I'll stay single.

MRS. CROSBY. (*tauntingly*) An old maid! (*Then resentfully*) Emmer, d'you s'pose if I'd had your high-fangled notions o' what men ought to be when I was your age, d'you s'pose you'd ever be settin' there now?

EMMA. (*slowly*) No. I know from what I can guess from his own stories Pa never was no saint.

MRS. CROSBY. (*in a tone of finality as if this settled the matter*) There, now! And ain't he been as good a husband to me as ever lived, and a good father to you and Jack? You'll find out Caleb'll turn out the same. You think it over. (*She gets up—bustlingly*) And now I got to git back in the kitchen.

EMMA. (*wringing her hands—desperately*) Oh, Ma, why can't you see what I feel? Of course, Pa's good—as good as good can be—

CAPTAIN CROSBY. (*from outside the door which he has approached without their noticing him—in a jovial bellow*) What's that 'bout Pa bein' good? (*He comes in laughing. He is a squat, bow-legged, powerful man, almost as broad as he is long—sixty years old but still in the prime of health and strength, with a great, red, weather-beaten face seamed by sun wrinkles. His sandy hair is thick and disheveled. He is dressed in an old baggy suit much the worse for wear—striped cotton shirt open at the neck. He pats* EMMA *on the back with a playful touch that almost jars her off her feet*) Thunderin' Moses, that's the fust time ever I heerd good o' myself by listenin'! Most times it's: "Crosby? D'you mean that drunken, good-for-nothin', mangy old cuss?" That's what I hears usual. Thank ye, Emmer. (*Turning to his wife*) What ye got to say now, Ma? Here's Emmer tellin' you the truth after you hair-pullin' me all these years 'cause you thought it wa'n't. I always told ye I was good, ain't I—good as hell I be! (*He shakes with laughter and kisses his wife a resounding smack.*)

MRS. CROSBY. (*teasing lovingly*) Emmer don't know you like I do.

CROSBY. (*turning back to* EMMA *again*) Look-a-here, Emmer, I jest seen Jack. He told me some fool story 'bout you fallin' out with Caleb. Reckon he was joshin', wa'nt he?

MRS. CROSBY. (*quickly*) Oh, that's all settled, John. Don't you go stirrin' it up again. (EMMA *seems about to speak but stops helplessly after one glance at her father.*)

CROSBY. An' all 'count o' that joke they're tellin' 'bout him and that brown female critter, Jack says. Hell, Emmer, you ain't a real Crosby if you takes a joke like that serious. Thunderin' Moses, what the hell d'you want Caleb to be—a durned, he-virgin, sky-pilot? Caleb's a man wo'th ten o' most and, spite o' his bein' on'y a boy yit, he's the smartest skipper out o' this port and you'd ought to be proud you'd got him. And as for them islands, all whalin' men knows 'em. I've teched thar for water more'n once myself, and I know them brown females like a

217

book. And I tells you, after a year or more aboard ship, a man'd have to be a goll-durned geldin' if he don't—

MRS. CROSBY. (*glancing uneasily at* EMMA) Ssshh! You come out in the kitchen with me, Pa, and leave Emmer be.

CROSBY. God A'mighty, Ma, I ain't sayin' nothin' agen Emmer, be I? I knows Emmer ain't that crazy. If she ever got religion that bad, I'd ship her off as female missionary to the damned yellow Chinks. (*He laughs.*)

MRS. CROSBY. (*taking his arm*) You come with me. I want to talk with you 'bout somethin'.

CROSBY. (*going*) Aye-aye, skipper! You're boss aboard here. (*He goes out right with her, laughing.* EMMA *stands for a while, staring stonily before her. She sighs hopelessly, clasping and unclasping her hands, looking around the room as if she longed to escape from it. Finally she sits down helplessly and remains fixed in a strained attitude, her face betraying the conflict that is tormenting her. Slow steps sound from the path in front of the house.* EMMA *recognizes them and her face freezes into an expression of obstinate intolerance.* CALEB *appears outside the screen door. He looks in, coughs—then asks uncertainly*) It's me, Emmer. Kin I come in?

EMMA. (*coldly*) Yes.

CALEB. (*comes in and walks down beside her chair. His face is set emotionlessly but his eyes cannot conceal a worried bewilderment, a look of uncomprehending hurt. He stands uncomfortably, fumbling with his hat, waiting for her to speak or look up. As she does neither, he finally blurts out*) Kin I set a spell?

EMMA. (*in the same cold tone*) Yes. (*He lowers himself carefully to a wooden posture on the edge of a rocker near hers.*)

CALEB. (*after a pause*) I seen Jim Benson. I give him hell. He won't tell no more tales, I reckon. (*Another pause*) I stopped to home on the way back from the store. I seen Harriet. She says Jack'd told you that story they're all tellin' as a joke on me. (*Clenching his fists—angrily*) Jack's a durn fool. He needs a good lickin' from someone.

EMMA. (*resentfully*) Don't try to put the blame on Jack. He only told me the truth, didn't he? (*Her voice shows that she hopes against hope for a denial.*)

CALEB. (*after a long pause—regretfully*) Waal, I guess what he told is true enough.

EMMA. (*wounded*) Oh!

CALEB. But that ain't no good reason for tellin' it. Them sort o' things ought to be kept among men. (*After a pause—gropingly*) I didn't want nothin' like that to happen, Emmer. I didn't mean it to. I was thinkin' o' how you might feel—even down there. That's why I stayed aboard all the time when the boys was ashore. I wouldn't have b'lieved it could happen—not to me. (*A pause*) I wish you could see them Islands, Emmer, and be there for a time. Then you might see— It's hard 's hell to explain, and you havin' never seen 'em. Everything is diff'rent down there—the weather—and the trees and water. You git lookin' at it all, and you git to feel diff'rent from what you do to home here. It's purty hereabouts sometimes—like now, in spring—but it's purty there all the time—and down there you notice it and you git feelin'—diff'rent. And them native women—they're diff'rent. A man don't think of 'em as women—like you. But they're purty—in their fashion—and at night they sings—and it's all diff'rent like something you'd see in a painted picture. (*A pause*) That night when she swum out and got aboard when I was alone, she caught me by s'prise. I wasn't expectin' nothin' o' that sort. I tried to make her git back to land at fust—but she wouldn't go. She couldn't understand enough English for me to tell her how I felt—and I reckon she wouldn't have seed my p'int anyhow, her bein' a native. (*A pause*) And then I was afeerd she'd catch cold goin' round all naked and wet in the moonlight—though it was warm—and I wanted to wrap a blanket round her. (*He stops as if he had finished.*)

EMMA. (*after a long, tense pause—dully*) Then you own up—there really was something happened?

219

CALEB. (*after a pause*) I was sorry for it, after. I locked myself in the cabin and left her to sleep out on deck.

EMMA. (*after a pause—fixedly*) I ain't going to marry you, Caleb.

CALEB. Harriet said you'd said that; but I didn't b'lieve you'd let a slip like that make—such a diff'rence.

EMMA. (*with finality*) Then you can believe it now, Caleb.

CALEB. (*after a pause*) You got queer, strict notions, Emmer. A man'll never live up to 'em—with never one slip. But you got to act accordin' to your lights, I expect. It sort o' busts everythin' to bits for me— (*His voice betrays his anguish for a second but he instantly regains his iron control*) But o' course, if you ain't willin' to take me the way I be, there's nothin' to do. And whatever you think is best, suits me.

EMMA. (*after a pause—gropingly*) I wish I could explain my side of it—so's you'd understand. I ain't got any hard feelings against you, Caleb—not now. It ain't plain jealousy—what I feel. It ain't even that I think you've done nothing terrible wrong. I think I can understand —how it happened—and make allowances. I know that most any man would do the same, and I guess all of 'em I ever met has done it.

CALEB. (*with a glimmer of eager hope*) Then—you'll forgive it, Emmer?

EMMA. Yes, I forgive it. But don't think that my forgiving is going to make any diff'rence—'cause I ain't going to marry you, Caleb. That's final. (*After a pause—intensely*) Oh, I wish I could make you see—my reason. You don't. You never will, I expect. What you done is just what any other man would have done—and being like them is exactly what'll keep you from ever seeing my meaning. (*After a pause—in a last effort to make him understand*) Maybe it's my fault more'n your'n. It's like this, Caleb. Ever since we was little I guess I've always had the idea that you was—diff'rent. And when we growed up and got engaged I thought that more and more. And you was diff'rent, too! And that was why I loved you. And now you've proved you ain't. And so how can I love you any more? I don't, Caleb, and that's all there is to it. You've busted something way down inside me —and I can't love you no more.

CALEB. (*gloomily*) I've warned you often, ain't I, you was settin' me up where I'd no business to be. I'm human like the rest and always was. I ain't diff'rent. (*After a pause—uncertainly*) I reckon there ain't no use sayin' nothin' more. I'll go home. (*He starts to rise.*)

EMMA. Wait. I don't want you to go out of here with no hard feelings. You 'n' me, Caleb, we've been too close all our lives to ever get to be enemies. I like you, Caleb, same's I always did. I want us to stay friends. I want you to be like one of the family same's you've always been. There's no reason you can't. I don't blame you—as a man—for what I wouldn't hold against any other man. If I find I can't love you —that way—no more or be your wife, it's just that I've decided— things being what they be and me being what I am—I won't marry no man. I'll stay single. (*Forcing a smile*) I guess there's worse things than being an old maid.

CALEB. I can't picture you that, Emmer. It's natural in some, but it ain't in you. (*Then with a renewal of hope*) And o' course I want to stay friends with you, Emmer. There's no hard feelin's on my side. You got a right to your own way—even if— (*hopefully*) And maybe if I show you what I done wasn't natural to me—by never doin' it again—maybe the time'll come when you'll be willin' to forget—

EMMA. (*shaking her head—slowly*) It ain't a question of time, Caleb. It's a question of something being dead. And when a thing's died, time can't make no diff'rence.

CALEB. (*sturdily*) You don't know that for sure, Emmer. You're human, too, and as liable to make mistakes as any other. Maybe you on'y think it's dead, and when I come back from the next vige and you've had two years to think it over, you'll see diff'rent and know I ain't as bad as I seem to ye now.

EMMA. (*helplessly*) But you don't seem bad, Caleb. And two years can't make no change in me—that way.

CALEB. (*feeling himself somehow more and more heartened by*

221

hope) I ain't givin' up hope, Emmer, and you can't make me. Not by a hell of a sight. (*With emphasis*) I ain't never goin' to marry no woman but you, Emmer. You can trust my word for that. And I'll wait for ye to change your mind, I don't give a durn how long it'll take—till I'm sixty years old—thirty years if it's needful! (*He rises to his feet as he is speaking this last.*)

EMMA. (*with a mournful smile*) You might just as well say for life, Caleb. In thirty years we'll both be dead and gone, probably. And I don't want you to think it's needful for you to stay single 'cause I—

CALEB. I ain't goin' to stay single. I'm goin' to wait for you. And some day when you realize men was never cut out for angels you'll—

EMMA. (*helplessly*) Me 'n' you'll never understand each other, Caleb, so long as we live. (*Getting up and holding out her hand*) Good-by, Caleb. I'm going up and lie down for a spell.

CALEB. (*made hopeless again by her tone—clasps her hand mechanically—dully*) Good-by, Emmer. (*He goes to the door in the rear, opens it, then hesitates and looks back at her as she goes out the door on the right without turning around. Suddenly he blurts out despairingly*) You'll remember what I told ye 'bout waitin', Emmer? (*She is gone, makes no reply. His face sets in its concealment mask of emotionlessness and he turns slowly and goes out the door as the curtain falls.*)

ACT TWO

SCENE—*Thirty years after—the scene is the same but not the same. The room has a grotesque aspect of old age turned flighty and masquerading as the most empty-headed youth. There is an obstreperous newness about everything. Orange curtains are at the windows. The carpet has given way to a varnished hardwood floor, its glassy surface set off by three small, garish-colored rugs, placed with precision in front of the two doors and under the table. The wallpaper is now a cream color sprayed with pink flowers. Seascapes, of the painted-to-order quality, four in number, in gilded frames, are hung on the walls at mathematically-spaced intervals. The plush-covered chairs are gone, replaced by a set of varnished oak. The horsehair sofa has been relegated to the attic. A cane-bottomed affair with fancy cushions serves in its stead. A Victrola is where the old mahogany chest had been. A brand new piano shines resplendently in the far right corner by the door, and a bookcase with glass doors that pull up and slide in flanks the fireplace. This bookcase is full of installment-plan sets of uncut volumes. The table at center is of varnished oak. On it are piles of fashion magazines and an electric reading lamp. Only the old Bible, which still preserves its place of honor on the table, and the marble clock on the mantel, have survived the renovation and serve to emphasize it all the more by contrast.*

It is late afternoon of a day in the early spring of the year 1920.

As the curtain rises, EMMA *and* BENNY ROGERS *are discovered. She is seated in a rocker by the table. He is standing by the Victrola on which a jazz band record is playing. He whistles, goes through the motions of dancing to the music. He is a young fellow of twenty-three, a replica of his father in Act One, but coarser, more hardened and cocksure. He is dressed in the khaki uniform of a private in the United States Army. The thirty years have transformed* EMMA *into a with-*

223

ered, scrawny woman. But there is something revoltingly incongruous about her, a pitiable sham, a too-apparent effort to cheat the years by appearances. The white dress she wears is too frilly, too youthful for her; so are the high-heeled pumps and clocked silk stockings. There is an absurd suggestion of rouge on her tight cheeks and thin lips, of penciled make-up about her eyes. The black of her hair is brazenly untruthful. Above all there is shown in her simpering, self-consciously coquettish manner that laughable—and at the same time irritating and disgusting—mockery of undignified age snatching greedily at the empty simulacra of youth. She resembles some passé stock actress of fifty made up for a heroine of twenty.

BENNY. (*as the record stops—switches off the machine*) Oh, baby! Some jazz, I'll tell the world!

EMMA. (*smiling lovingly at his back*) I'm glad you like it. It's one of them you picked out on the list.

BENNY. Oh, I'm a swell little picker, aw right. (*Turning to her*) Say, you're a regular feller—gettin' them records for me.

EMMA. (*coquettishly*) Well, if that ain't just like a man! Who told you I got them just for you?

BENNY. Well, didn't you?

EMMA. No indeedy! I only took your advice on what to get. I knew you'd know, being growed to a man of the world now since you was overseas. But I got 'em because I like them jazz tunes myself. They put life and ginger in an old lady like me—not like them slow, old-timey tunes.

BENNY. (*bends over chair—kiddingly*) You ain't old. That's all bunk.

EMMA. (*flattered*) Now, now, Benny!

BENNY. You ain't. You're a regular, up-to-date sport—the only live one in this dead dump. (*With a grin*) And if you fall for that jazz stuff, all you got to do now is learn to dance to it.

EMMA. (*giggling*) I will—if you'll teach me.

BENNY. (*struggling with a guffaw*) Oh, oui! Sure I will! We'll have a circus, me an' you. Say, you're sure one of the girls aw right, Aunt Emmer.

EMMA. Oh, you needn't think we're *all* so behind the times to home here just because you've been to France and all over.

BENNY. *You* ain't, I'll say, Aunt Emmer.

EMMA. And how often have I got to tell you not to call me Aunt Emmer?

BENNY. (*with a grin*) Oh, oui! My foot slipped. 'Scuse me, Emmer.

EMMA. (*delighted by his coarse familiarity*) That's better. Why, you know well enough I ain't your aunt anyway.

BENNY. I got to get used to the plain Emmer. They taught me to call you "aunt" when I was a kid. (EMMA *looks displeased at this remark and* BENNY *hastens to add cajolingly*) And you almost was my aunt-in-law one time from what I've heard. (*Winks at her cunningly.*)

EMMA. (*flustered*) That was ages ago. (*Catching herself quickly*) Not so awful long really, but it's all so dead and gone it seems a long while.

BENNY. (*unthinkingly*) It was before I was born, wasn't it? (*Seeing her expression he hurries on*) Well, that ain't so darned long. Say, here's something I never could make out—how did you ever come to fall for Uncle Caleb?

EMMA. (*bridling quickly*) I never did. That's all talk, Benny. We was good friends and still are. I was young and foolish and got engaged to him—and then discovered I didn't like him that way. That's all there ever was to it.

BENNY. (*resentfully*) I can't figure how anybody'd ever like him anyway. He's a darn stingy, ugly old cuss, if you want my dope on him. I can't see him at all. I've hated him ever since Pa died and Ma and me had to go live next door with him.

EMMA. You oughtn't to say that. He's kind at bottom, spite of his rough ways, and he's brought you up.

BENNY. (*grumpily*) Dragged me up, you mean. (*With a calculat-*

ing look at her out of the corners of his eyes) He's a tight-wad and I hate folks that're tight with their coin. Spend and be a good sport, that's my motto. (*Flattering*) He'd ought to be more like you that way, Emmer.

EMMA. (*pleased—condescendingly*) Your Uncle Caleb's an old man, remember. He's sot in his ways and believes in being strict with you— too strict, I've told him.

BENNY. He's got piles of money hoarded in the bank but he's too mean even to retire from whalin' himself—goes right on makin' vige after vige to grab more and never spends a nickel less'n he has to. It was always like pryin' open a safe for me to separate him from a cent. (*With extreme disgust*) Aw, he's a piker. I hate him and I always did!

EMMA. (*looking toward the door apprehensively*) Ssshh!

BENNY. What you scared of? He don't get in from New Bedford till the night train and even if he's got to the house by this he'll be busy as a bird dog for an hour getting himself dolled up to pay you a call.

EMMA. (*perfunctorily*) I hope he's had a good vige and is in good health.

BENNY. (*roughly*) You needn't worry. He's too mean ever to get real sick. Gosh, I wish Pa'd lived—or Uncle Jack. They wasn't like him. I was only a kid when they got drowned, but I remember enough about 'em to know they was good sports. Wasn't they?

EMMA. (*rather primly*) They was too sporty for their own good.

BENNY. Don't you hand me that. That don't sound like you. You're a sport yourself. (*After a pause*) Say, it's nutty when you come to think of it—Uncle Caleb livin' next door all these years and comin' to call all the time when he ain't at sea.

EMMA. What's funny about that? We've always been good friends.

BENNY. (*with a grin*) It's just as if the old guy was still mashin' you. And I'll bet anything he's as stuck on you as he ever was—the old fool!

EMMA. (*with a coquettish titter*) Land sakes, Benny, a body'd think you were actually jealous of your uncle the way you go on.

BENNY. (*with a mocking laugh*) Jealous! Oh, oui! Sure I am! Kin

226

you blame me? (*Then seriously, with a calculating look at her*) No, all kiddin' aside, I know he'll run me down first second he sees you. Ma'll tell him all her tales, and he'll be sore at me right off. He's always hated me anyway. He was glad when I enlisted, 'cause that got him rid of me. All he was hopin' was that some German'd get me for keeps. Then when I come back he wouldn't do nothin' for me so I enlisted again.

EMMA. (*chiding—playfully*) Now, Benny! Didn't you tell me you enlisted again 'cause you were sick o' this small place and wanted to be out where there was more fun?

BENNY. Well, o' course it was that, too. But I could have a swell time even in this dump if he'd loosen up and give me some kale. (*Again with the calculating look at her*) Why, look here, right now there's a buddy of mine wants me to meet him in Boston and he'll show me a good time, and if I had a hundred dollars—

EMMA. A hundred dollars! That's an awful pile to spend, Benny.

BENNY. (*disgustedly*) Now you're talkin' tight like him.

EMMA. (*hastily*) Oh, no, Benny. You know better'n that. What was you sayin'—if you had a hundred dollars—?

BENNY. That ain't such a much these days with everything gone up so. If I went to Boston I'd have to get dolled up and everything. And this buddy of mine is a sport and a spender. Easy come, easy go is his motto. His folks ain't tight-wads like mine. And I couldn't show myself up as a cheap skate by travelin' 'round with him without a nickel in my jeans and just spongin' on him. (*With the calculating glance to see what effect his words are having—pretending to dismiss the subject*) But what's the good of talkin'? I got a swell chance tellin' that to Uncle Caleb. He'd give me one look and then put a double padlock on his roll. But it ain't fair just the same. Here I'm sweatin' blood in the army after riskin' my life in France and when I get a leave to home, everyone treats me like a wet dog.

EMMA. (*softly*) Do you mean me, too, Benny?

BENNY. No, not you. You're diff'rent from the rest. You're regular

227

—and you ain't any of my real folks, either, and ain't got any reason.

EMMA. (*coquettishly*) Oh, yes, I have a reason. I like you very, very much, Benny—better than anyone in the town—especially since you've been to home these last few times and come to call so often and I feel I've growed to know you. When you first came back from France I never would have recognized you as Harriet's Benny, you was so big and strong and handsome.

BENNY. (*uncomfortably*) Aw, you're kiddin'. But you can tell how good I think you are from me bein' over here so much—so you know I ain't lyin'. (*Made more and more uncomfortable by the ardent looks* EMMA *is casting at him*) Well, guess I'll be movin' along.

EMMA. (*pleadingly*) Oh, you mustn't go yet! Just when we're gettin' so friendly!

BENNY. Uncle Caleb'll be over soon and I don't want him to catch me here—nor nowhere else till he gets calmed down after hearin' Ma's kicks about me. So I guess I better beat it up street.

EMMA. He won't come for a long time yet. I know when to expect him. (*Pleading ardently and kittenishly*) Do set down a spell, Benny! Land sakes, I hardly get a sight of you before you want to run away again. I'll begin to think you're only pretending to like me.

BENNY. (*seeing his calculations demand it*) Aw right—jest for a second. (*He looks about him, seeking a neutral subject for conversation*) Gee, you've had this old place fixed up swell since I was to home last.

EMMA. (*coquettishly*) Guess who I had it all done for, mostly?

BENNY. For yourself, of course.

EMMA. (*shaking her head roguishly*) No, not for me, not for me! Not that I don't like it but I'd never have gone to the trouble and expense for myself. (*With a sigh*) I s'pose poor Ma and Pa turned over in their graves when I ordered it done.

BENNY. (*with a sly grin*) Who d'you have it done for, then?

EMMA. For you! Yes, for you, Benny—so's you'd have a nice, up-to-date place to come to when you was on vacation from the horrid old army.

BENNY. (*embarrassed*) Well, it's great aw right. And it sure looks swell—nothing cheap about it.

EMMA. (*delighted*) As long as you like it, I'm satisfied. (*Then suddenly, wagging an admonishing finger at him and hiding beneath a joking manner an undercurrent of uneasiness*) I was forgetting I got a bone to pick with you, young man! I heard them sayin' to the store that you'd been up callin' on that Tilly Small evenin' before last.

BENNY. (*with a lady-killer's carelessness*) Aw, I was passin' by and she called me in, that's all.

EMMA. (*frowning*) They said you had the piano goin' and was singing and no end of high jinks.

BENNY. Aw, these small town boobs think you're raising hell if you're up after eleven.

EMMA. (*excitedly*) I ain't blamin' you. But her—she ought to have better sense—at her age, too, when she's old enough to be your mother.

BENNY. Aw, say, she ain't half as old— (*Catching himself*) Oh, she's an old fool, you're right there, Emmer.

EMMA. (*severely*) And I hope you know the kind of woman she is and has been since she was a girl.

BENNY. (*with a wink*) I wasn't born yesterday. I got her number long ago. I ain't in my cradle, get me! I'm in the army! Oui! (*Chuckles.*)

EMMA. (*fidgeting nervously*) What'd you—what'd you do when you was there?

BENNY. Why, nothin'. I told her to cut the rough work and behave—and a nice time was had by all. (*He grins provokingly.*)

EMMA. (*springs to her feet nervously*) I don't know what to think—when you act so queer about it.

BENNY. (*carelessly*) Well, don't think nothing wrong—'cause there wasn't. Bill Tinker was with me and we was both wishin' we had a drink. And Bill says, "Let's go see Tilly Small. She always has some buried and if we hand her a line of talk maybe she'll drag out the old bottle." So we did—and she did. We kidded her for a couple of drinks. (*He snickers.*)

EMMA. (*standing in front of him—fidgeting*) I want you to promise you won't go to see her no more. If you—if you want liquor now and again maybe I—maybe I can fix it so's I can get some to keep here for you.

BENNY. (*eagerly*) Say, that'd be great! Will you? (*She nods. He goes on carelessly*) And sure I'll promise not to see Tilly no more. Gosh, what do you think I care about her? Or about any dame in this town, for that matter—'ceptin' you. These small town skirts don't hand me nothin'. (*With a grin*) You forgot I was in France— and after the dames over there these birds here look some punk.

EMMA. (*sits down—wetting her lips*) And what—what are those French critters like?

BENNY. (*with a wink*) Oh, boy! They're some pippins! It ain't so much that they're better lookin' as that they've got a way with 'em— lots of ways. (*He laughs with a lascivious smirk.*)

EMMA. (*unconsciously hitches her chair nearer his. The turn the conversation has taken seems to have aroused a hectic, morbid intensity in her. She continually wets her lips and pushes back her hair from her flushed face as if it were stifling her*) What do you mean, Benny? What kind of ways have they got—them French girls?

BENNY. (*smirking mysteriously*) Oh, ways of dressin' and doin' their hair—and lots of ways.

EMMA. (*eagerly*) Tell me! Tell me all about 'em. You needn't be scared—to talk open with me. I ain't as strict as I seem—about hearin' things. Tell me! I've heard French girls was awful wicked.

BENNY. I don't know about wicked, but they're darned good sports. They'd do anything a guy'd ask 'em. Oui, tooty sweet! (*Laughs foolishly.*)

EMMA. And what—what'd you ask 'em, for instance?

BENNY. (*with a wink*) Curiosity killed a cat! Ask me no questions and I'll tell you no lies.

EMMA. (*with queer, stupid insistence*) But won't you tell me? Go on!

BENNY. Can't be did, Aunt Emmer, can't be did! (*With a silly laugh*) You're too young. No, all I'll say is, that to the boys who've knocked around over there the girls in town here are just rank amatoors. They don't know how to love and that's a fact. (*He gets to his feet*) And as for an old bum like Tilly—not me! Well, I guess I'll hike along—

EMMA. (*getting up and putting a hand on his arm—feverishly*) No, don't go. Not yet—not yet. No, don't go.

BENNY. (*stepping away with an expression of repulsion*) Why not? What's the matter with you, Aunt Emmer? You look 's if you was gettin' sick. (*Before she can reply,* HARRIET's *voice is heard calling.*)

HARRIET. Benny! Benny! (*This acts like a pail of cold water on* EMMA *who moves away from* BENNY *quickly.*)

EMMA. That's Harriet. It's your Ma calling, Benny.

BENNY. (*impatiently*) I know. That means Uncle Caleb has come and she's told him her stories and it's up to me to catch hell. (*Stopping* EMMA *as she goes toward the door as if to answer* HARRIET's *hail*) Don't answer, Aunt Emmer. Let her come over here to look. I want to speak to her and find out how I stand before he sees me.

EMMA. (*doubtfully*) I don't know as she'll come. She's been actin' funny to me lately, Harriet has, and she ain't put her foot in my door the last month.

BENNY. (*as his mother's voice is heard much nearer, calling* "Benny!") There! Sure she's comin'.

EMMA. (*flustered*) Land sakes, I can't let her see me this way. I got to run upstairs and tidy myself a little. (*She starts for the door at right.*)

BENNY. (*flatteringly*) Aw, you look swell. Them new duds you got looks great.

EMMA. (*turning in the doorway—coquettishly*) Oh, them French girls ain't the only ones knows how to fix up. (*She flounces out.* BENNY *stands looking after her with a derisive grin of contempt. There is a sharp knock on the door in the rear.* BENNY *goes to open it, his expression turning surly and sullen.* HARRIET *enters. She wears an apron over her old-fashioned black dress with a brooch at the neck. Her hair is gray, her face thin, lined and careworn, with a fretful, continuously irritated expression. Her shoulders stoop, and her figure is flabby and ugly. She stares at her son with resentful annoyance.*)

HARRIET. Ain't you got sense enough, you big lump, to answer me when I call, and not have me shouting my lungs out?

BENNY. I never heard you callin'.

HARRIET. You're lyin' and you know it. (*Then severely*) Your uncle's to home. He's waitin' to talk to you.

BENNY. Let him wait. (*In a snarling tone*) I s'pose you've been givin' him an earful of lies about me?

HARRIET. I told him the truth, if that's what you mean. How you stole the money out of the bureau drawer—

BENNY. (*alarmed but pretending scorn*) Aw, you don't know it was me. You don't know nothin' about it.

HARRIET. (*ignoring this*) And about your disgracin' him and me with your drunken carryin's-on with that harlot, Tilly Small, night after night.

BENNY. Aw, wha'd you know about that?

HARRIET. And last but not least, the sneakin' way you're makin' a silly fool out of poor Emmer Crosby.

BENNY. (*with a grin*) You don't notice her kickin' about it, do you? (*Brusquely*) Why don't you mind your own business, Ma?

HARRIET. (*violently*) It's a shame, that's what it is! That I should live to see the day when a son of mine'd descend so low he'd tease an old woman to get money out of her, and her alone in the world. Oh, you're low, you're low all through like your Pa was—and since you been in the army you got bold so you ain't even ashamed of your dirtiness no more!

BENNY. (*in a snarling whisper*) That's right! Blame it all on me. I s'pose she ain't got nothin' to do with it. (*With a wink*) You oughter see her perform sometimes. You'd get wise to something then.

HARRIET. Shut up! You've got the same filthy mind your Pa had. As for Emmer, I don't hold her responsible. She's been gettin' flighty the past two years. She couldn't help it, livin' alone the way she does, shut up in this house all her life. You ought to be 'shamed to take advantage of her condition—but shame ain't in you.

BENNY. Aw, give us a rest!

HARRIET. (*angrily*) Your Uncle Caleb'll give you a rest when he sees you! Him and me's agreed not to give you another single penny if you was to get down on your knees for it. So there! You can git along on your army pay from this out.

BENNY. (*worried by the finality in her tone—placatingly*) Aw, say, Ma, what's eatin' you? What've I done that's so bad? Gosh, you oughta know some of the gang I know in the army. You'd think I was a saint if you did. (*Trying a confidential tone*) Honest, Ma, this here thing with Aunt Emmer ain't my fault. How can I help it if she goes bugs in her old age and gets nutty about me? (*With a sly grin— in a whisper*) Gee, Ma, you oughta see her today. She's a scream, honest! She's upstairs now gettin' calmed down. She was gettin' crazy when your callin' stopped her. Wait till she comes down and you git a look! She'll put your eye out—all dolled up like a kid of sixteen and enough paint on her mush for a Buffalo Bill Indian—

HARRIET. (*staring at him with stern condemnation*) You're a worthless loafer, Benny Rogers, same as your Pa was.

BENNY. (*frustrated and furious*) Aw, g'wan with that bunk! (*He turns away from her.*)

HARRIET. And I'm goin' to tell Emma about you and try to put some sense back into her head.

BENNY. Go ahead. You'll get fat runnin' me down to her!

HARRIET. And if my word don't have no influence, I'll tell your Uncle Caleb everything, and get him to talk to her. She'll mind him.

BENNY. (*defiantly*) You just try it, that's all!

HARRIET. I've been scared to do more'n hint about it to him. I'm hopin' any day Emma'll come out of this foolishness, and he'll never know.

BENNY. Aw!

HARRIET. If shame was in you, you'd remember your Uncle Caleb's been in love with Emma all his life and waited for her year after year hopin' in the end she'd change her mind and marry him. And she will, too, I believe, if she comes out of this fit in her sane mind—which she won't if you keep fussin' with her.

BENNY. (*with revengeful triumph*) She'll never marry the old cuss— I'll fix that!

HARRIET. Now you're showin' yourself up for what you are! And I kin see it's come to the p'int where I got to tell your Uncle Caleb everythin' no matter how it breaks him up. I got to do it for Emmer's sake as well as his'n. We got to get her cured of your bad influence once and for all. It's the only hope for the two of 'em.

BENNY. You just try it!

HARRIET. And as for you, you get back to the army where you b'long! And don't never expect another cent from me or Caleb 'cause you won't get it! And don't never come to see us again till you've got rid of the meanness and filth that's the Rogers part of you and found the honesty and decency that's the Williams part—if you got any of me in you at all, which I begin to doubt. (*Goes to the door in rear*) And now I'm goin' back to Caleb—and you better not let him find you here when he comes less'n you want a good hidin' for once in your life. (*She goes out.*)

BENNY. (*stammering between fear and rage—shouting after her*) G'wan! Tell him! What the hell do I care? I'll fix him! I'll spill the beans for both of you, if you try to gum me! (*He stands in the middle of the room hesitating whether to run away or stay, concentrating his*

234

thoughts on finding some way to make good his bluff. Suddenly his face lights up with a cruel grin and he mutters to himself with savage satisfaction) By God, that's it! I'll bet I kin work it, too! By God, that'll fix 'em! (*He chuckles and goes quickly to the door on right and calls up to the floor above*) Emmer! Emmer!

EMMA. (*her voice faintly heard answering*) Yes, Benny, I'm coming.

BENNY. (*he calls quickly*) Come down! Come down quick! (*He comes back to the center of the room where he stands waiting, planning his course of action.*)

EMMA. (*appears in the doorway. Her face is profusely powdered—with nervous excitement*) Benny! What's the matter? You sounded so— Why, where's your Ma?

BENNY. Gone. Gone back to home.

EMMA. (*offendedly*) Without waiting to see me? Why, I only sat down for a minute to give you a chance to talk to her. I was coming right down. Didn't she want to see me? Whatever's got into Harriet lately?

BENNY. She's mad as thunder at you 'cause I come over here so much 'stead of stayin' to home with her.

EMMA. (*pleased*) Oh, is that why? Well, if she ain't peculiar! (*She sits in a rocker by the table.*)

BENNY. (*with a great pretense of grief, taking one of her hands in his*) Say, Emmer—what I called you down for was—I want to say good-by and thank you for all you've done—

EMMA. (*frightenedly*) Good-by? How you say that! What—?

BENNY. Good-by for good this time.

EMMA. For good?

BENNY. Yep. I've got to beat it. I ain't got no home here no more. Ma and Uncle Caleb, they've chucked me out.

EMMA. Good gracious, what're you saying?

BENNY. That's what Ma come over to tell me—that Uncle Caleb'd said I'd never get another cent from him, alive or after he's dead, and she said for me to git back to the army and never come home again.

235

EMMA. (*gaspingly*) She was only joking. She—they couldn't mean it.

BENNY. If you'd heard her you wouldn't think she was joking.

EMMA. (*as he makes a movement as if to go away*) Benny! You can't go! Go, and me never see you again, maybe! You can't! I won't have it!

BENNY. I got to, Emmer. What else is there for me to do when they've throwed me out? I don't give a damn about leaving them—but I hate to leave you and never see you again.

EMMA. (*excitedly—grabbing his arm*) You can't! I won't let you go!

BENNY. I don't want to—but what can I do?

EMMA. You can stay here with me.

BENNY. (*his eyes gleaming with satisfaction*) No, I couldn't. You know this dump of a town. Folks would be sayin' all sorts of bad things in no time. I don't care for myself. They're all down on me anyway because I'm diff'rent from small-town boobs like them and they hate me for it.

EMMA. Yes, you are diff'rent. And I'll show 'em I'm diff'rent, too. You can stay with me—and let 'em gossip all they've a mind to!

BENNY. No, it wouldn't be actin' square with you. I got to go. And I'll try to save up my pay and send you back what I've borrowed now and again.

EMMA. (*more and more wrought up*) I won't hear of no such thing. Oh, I can't understand your Ma and your Uncle Caleb bein' so cruel!

BENNY. Folks have been lyin' to her about me, like I told you, and she's told him. He's only too glad to believe it, too, long as it's bad.

EMMA. I can talk to your Uncle Caleb. He's always minded me more'n her.

BENNY. (*hastily*) Don't do that, for God's sake! You'd only make it worse and get yourself in Dutch with him, too!

EMMA. (*bewilderedly*) But—I—don't see—

BENNY. (*roughly*) Well, he's still stuck on you, ain't he?

EMMA. (*with a flash of coquetry*) Now, Benny!

BENNY. I ain't kiddin'. This is dead serious. He's stuck on you and you know it.

EMMA. (*coyly*) I haven't given him the slightest reason to hope in thirty years.

BENNY. Well, he hopes just the same. Sure he does! Why Ma said when she was here just now she'd bet you and him'd be married some day yet.

EMMA. No such thing! Why, she must be crazy!

BENNY. Oh, she ain't so crazy. Ain't he spent every durn evenin' of the time he's to home between trips over here with you—for the last thirty years?

EMMA. When I broke my engagement I said I wanted to stay friends like we'd been before, and we always have; but every time he'd even hint at bein' engaged again I'd always tell him we was friends only and he'd better leave it be that way. There's never been nothing else between us. (*With a coy smile*) And besides, Benny, you know how little time he's had to home between viges.

BENNY. I kin remember the old cuss marchin' over here every evenin' he was to home since I was a kid.

EMMA. (*with a titter of delight*) D'you know, Benny, I do actually believe you're jealous!

BENNY. (*loudly—to lend conviction*) Sure I'm jealous! But that ain't the point just now. The point is *he's* jealous of me—and you can see what a swell chance you've got of talkin' him over now, can't you! You'd on'y make him madder.

EMMA. (*embarrassedly*) He's getting foolish. What cause has he got—

BENNY. When Ma tells him the lies about us—

EMMA. (*excitedly*) What lies?

BENNY. I ain't goin' to repeat 'em to you but you kin guess, can't you, me being so much over here?

EMMA. (*springing to her feet—shocked but pleased*) Oh!

237

BENNY. (*turning away from her*) And now I'm going to blow. I'll stay at Bill Grainger's tonight and get the morning train.

EMMA. (*grabbing his arm*) No such thing! You'll stay right here!

BENNY. I can't—Emmer. If you was really my aunt, things'd be diff'rent and I'd tell 'em all to go to hell.

EMMA. (*smiling at him coquettishly*) But I'm glad I ain't your aunt.

BENNY. Well, I mean if you was related to me in some way. (*At some noise he hears from without, he starts frightenedly*) Gosh, that sounded like our front door slamming. It's him and he's coming over. I got to beat it out the back way. (*He starts for the door on the right.*)

EMMA. (*clinging to him*) Benny! Don't go! You mustn't go!

BENNY. (*inspired by alarm and desire for revenge suddenly blurts out*) Say, let's me 'n' you git married, Emmer—tomorrow, eh? Then I kin stay! That'll stop 'em, damn 'em, and make 'em leave me alone.

EMMA. (*dazed with joy*) Married? You 'n' me? Oh, Benny, I'm too old. (*She hides her head on his shoulder.*)

BENNY. (*hurriedly, with one anxious eye on the door*) No, you ain't! Honest, you ain't! You're the best guy in this town! (*Shaking her in his anxiety*) Say yes, Emmer! Say you will—first thing tomorrow.

EMMA. (*choking with emotion*) Yes—I will—if I'm not too old for you.

BENNY. (*jubilantly*) Tell him. Then he'll see where he gets off! Listen! I'm goin' to beat it to the kitchen and wait. You come tell me when he's gone. (*A knock comes at the door. He whispers*) That's him. I'm goin'.

EMMA. (*embracing him fiercely*) Oh, Benny! (*She kisses him on the lips. He ducks away from her and disappears off right. The knock is repeated.* EMMA *dabs tremblingly at her cheeks with a handkerchief. Her face is beaming with happiness and looks indescribably silly. She trips lightly to the door and opens it—forcing a light, careless tone*) Oh, it's you, Caleb. Come right in and set. I was kind of expecting you. Benny—I'd heard you was due to home tonight. (*He comes in and shakes the hand she holds out to him in a limp, vague, absent-minded manner. In appearance, he has changed but little in the thirty years save that his hair is now nearly white and his face more deeply lined and wrinkled. His body is still erect, strong and vigorous. He wears dark clothes, much the same as he was dressed in Act One.)*

CALEB. *(mechanically)* Hello, Emmer. *(Once inside the door, he stands staring about the room, frowning. The garish strangeness of everything evidently repels and puzzles him. His face wears its set expression of an emotionless mask but his eyes cannot conceal an inward struggle, a baffled and painful attempt to comprehend, a wounded look of bewildered hurt.)*

EMMA. *(blithely indifferent to this—pleasantly)* Are you looking at the changes I've made? You ain't seen this room since, have you? Of course not. What am I thinking of? They only got through with the work two weeks ago. Well, what d' you think of it?

CALEB. *(frowning—hesitatingly)* Why—it's—all right, I reckon.

EMMA. It was so gloomy and old-timey before, I just couldn't bear it. Now it's light and airy and young-looking, don't you think? *(With a sigh)* I suppose Pa and Ma turned over in their graves.

CALEB. *(grimly)* I reckon they did, too.

EMMA. Why, you don't mean to tell me you don't like it neither, Caleb? *(Then as he doesn't reply,—resentfully)* Well, you always was a sot, old-fashioned critter, Caleb Williams, same as they was. *(She plumps herself into a rocker by the table—then, noticing the lost way in which he is looking about him)* Gracious sakes, why don't you set, Caleb? You give me the fidgets standing that way! You ain't a stranger that's got to be invited, are you? *(Then suddenly realizing the cause of his discomfiture, she smiles pityingly, not without a trace of malice)* Are you looking for your old chair you used to set in? Is that it? Well, I had it put up in the attic. It didn't fit in with them new things.

CALEB. *(dully)* No, I s'pose it wouldn't.

EMMA. *(indicating a chair next to hers)* Do set down and make

239

yourself to home. (*He does so gingerly. After a pause she asks perfunctorily*) Did you have good luck this voyage?

CALEB. (*again dully*) Oh, purty fair. (*He begins to look at her as if he were seeing her for the first time, noting every detail with a numb, stunned astonishment.*)

EMMA. You're looking as well as ever.

CALEB. (*dully*) Oh, I ain't got nothin' to complain of.

EMMA. You're the same as me, I reckon. (*Happily*) Why I seem to get feelin' younger and more chipper every day, I declare I do. (*She becomes uncomfortably aware of his examination—nervously*) Land sakes, what you starin' at so?

CALEB. (*brusquely blurting out his disapproval*) You've changed, Emmer—changed so I wouldn't know you, hardly.

EMMA. (*resentfully*) Well, I hope you think it's for the best.

CALEB. (*evasively*) I ain't enough used to it yet—to tell.

EMMA. (*offended*) I ain't old-timey and old-maidy like I was, I guess that's what you mean. Well, I just got tired of mopin' alone in this house, waiting for death to take me and not enjoyin' anything. I was gettin' old before my time. And all at once, I saw what was happenin' and I made up my mind I was going to get some fun out of what Pa'd left me while I was still in the prime of life, as you might say.

CALEB. (*severely*) Be that paint and powder you got on your face, Emmer?

EMMA. (*embarrassed by this direct question*) Why, yes—I got a little mite—it's awful good for your complexion, they say—and in the cities now all the women wears it.

CALEB. (*sternly*) The kind of women I've seed in cities wearin' it— (*He checks himself and asks abruptly*) Wa'n't your hair turnin' gray last time I was to home?

EMMA. (*flustered*) Yes—yes—so it was—but then it started to come in again black as black all of a sudden.

CALEB. (*glancing at her shoes, stockings, and dress*) You're got up in them things like a young girl goin' to a dance.

EMMA. (*forcing a defiant laugh*) Maybe I will go soon's I learn—and Benny's goin' to teach me.

CALEB. (*keeping his rage in control—heavily*) Benny—

EMMA. (*suddenly bursting into hysterical tears*) And I think it's real mean of you, Caleb—nasty mean to come here on your first night to home—and—make—fun—of—my—clothes—and everything. (*She hides her face in her hands and sobs.*)

CALEB. (*overcome by remorse—forgetting his rage instantly—gets up and pats her on the shoulder—with rough tenderness*) Thar, thar, Emmer! Don't cry, now! I didn' mean nothin'. Don't pay no 'tention to what I said. I'm a durned old fool! What the hell do I know o' women's fixin's anyhow? And I reckon I be old-fashioned and sot in my ideas.

EMMA. (*reassured—pressing one of his hands gratefully*) It hurts—hearing you say—me 'n' you such old friends and—

CALEB. Forgit it, Emmer. I won't say no more about it. (*She dries her eyes and regains her composure. He goes back to his seat, his face greatly softened, looking at her with the blind eyes of love. There is a pause. Finally, he ventures in a gentle tone*) D'you know what time this be, Emmer?

EMMA. (*puzzled*) I don't know exactly, but there's a clock in the next room.

CALEB. (*quickly*) Hell, I don't mean that kind o' time. I mean—it was thirty years ago this spring.

EMMA. (*hastily*) Land sakes, don't let's talk of that. It only gets me thinking how old I am.

CALEB. (*with an affectionate smile*) We both got to realize now and then that we're gettin' old.

EMMA. (*bridling*) That's all right for you to say. You're twelve years older 'n me, don't forget, Caleb.

241

CALEB. (*smiling*) Waal, even that don't make you out no spring chicken, Emmer.

EMMA. (*stiffly*) A body's as old as they feels—and I feel right young.

CALEB. Waal, so do I as far as health goes. I'm as able and sound as ever. (*After a pause*) But, what I meant was, d'you remember what happened thirty years back?

EMMA. I suppose I do.

CALEB. D'you remember what I said that day?

EMMA. (*primly*) You said a lot that it's better to forget, if you ask me.

CALEB. I don't mean—that part of it. I mean when I was sayin' good-by, I said— (*He gasps—then blurts it out*) I said I'd wait thirty years—if need be. (*After a pause*) I know you told me time and again not to go back to that. On'y—I was thinkin' all this last vige—that maybe—now when the thirty years are past—I was thinkin' that maybe— (*He looks at her humbly, imploring some encouragement. She stares straight before her, her mouth set thinly. He sighs forlornly and blunders on*) Thirty years—that's a hell of a long time to wait, Emmer—makin' vige after vige always alone—and feelin' even more alone in between times when I was to home livin' right next door to you and callin' on you every evenin'. (*A pause*) I've made money enough, I know—but what the hell good's that to me—long as you're out of it? (*A pause*) Seems to me, Emmer, thirty o' the best years of a man's life ought to be proof enough to you to make you forget—that one slip o' mine.

EMMA. (*rousing herself—forcing a careless tone*) Land sakes, I forgot all about that long ago. And here you go remindin' me of it!

CALEB. (*doggedly*) You ain't answered what I was drivin' at, Emmer. (*A pause; then, as if suddenly afraid of what her answer will be, he breaks out quickly*) And I don't want you to answer right now, neither. I want you to take time to think it all over.

EMMA. (*feebly evasive*) All right, Caleb, I'll think it over.

CALEB. (*after a pause*) Somehow—seems to me 's if—you might really *need* me now. You never did before.

EMMA. (*suspiciously*) Why should I need you now any more'n any other time?

CALEB. (*embarrassedly*) Oh, I just feel that way.

EMMA. It ain't count o' nothin' Harriet's been tellin' you, is it? (*Stiffly*) Her 'n' me ain't such good friends no more, if you must know.

CALEB. (*frowning*) Her 'n' me nearly had a fight right before I came over here. (EMMA *starts*) Harriet lets her tongue run away with her and says dumb fool things she don't really mean. I didn't pay much 'tention to what she was sayin'—but it riled me jest the same. She won't repeat such foolishness after the piece o' my mind I gave her.

EMMA. What did she say?

CALEB. Oh, nothin' worth tellin'. (*A pause*) But neither you nor me ought to get mad at Harriet serious. We'd ought, by all rights, to make allowances for her. You know 's well as me what a hard time she's had. Bein' married to Alf Rogers for five years'd pizin' any woman's life.

EMMA. No, he wasn't much good, there's no denyin'.

CALEB. And now there's Benny drivin' her crazy.

EMMA. (*instantly defensive*) Benny's all right!

CALEB. (*staring at her sharply—after a pause*) No, that's jest it. He ain't all right, Emmer.

EMMA. He is, too! He's as good as gold!

CALEB. (*frowning—with a trace of resentment*) You kin say so, Emmer, but the facts won't bear you out.

EMMA. (*excitedly*) What facts, Caleb Williams? If you mean the nasty lies the folks in this town are mean enough to gossip about him, I don't believe any of 'em. I ain't such a fool.

CALEB. (*bitterly*) Then you've changed, Emmer. You didn't stop about believin' the fool stories they gossiped about me that time.

EMMA. You owned up yourself that was true!

CALEB. And Benny'd own up if he was half the man I was! (*Angrily*) But he ain't a man noways. He's a mean skunk from truck to keelson!

EMMA. (*springing to her feet*) Oh!

CALEB. (*vehemently*) I ain't judged him by what folks have told me. But I've watched him grow up from a boy and every time I've come to home I've seed he was gittin' more 'n' more like his Pa—and you know what a low dog Alf Rogers turned out to be, and what a hell he made for Harriet. Waal, I'm sayin' this boy Benny is just Alf all over again—on'y worse!

EMMA. Oh!

CALEB. They ain't no Williams' blood left in Benny. He's a mongrel Rogers! (*Trying to calm himself a little and be convincing*) Listen, Emmer. You don't suppose I'd be sayin' it, do you, if it wasn't so? Ain't he Harriet's boy? Ain't I brought him up in my own house since he was knee-high? Don't you know I got some feelin's 'bout it and I wouldn't hold nothing agen him less'n I knowed it was true?

EMMA. (*harshly*) Yes, you would! You're only too anxious to believe all the bad you can about him. You've always hated him, he says—and I can see it's so.

CALEB. (*roughly*) You know damned well it ain't, you mean! Ain't I talked him over with you and asked your advice about him whenever I come to home? Ain't I always aimed to do all I could to help him git on right? You know damned well I never hated him! It's him that's always hated me! (*Vengefully*) But I'm beginning to hate him now—and I've good cause for it!

EMMA. (*frightenedly*) What cause?

CALEB. (*ignoring her question*) I seed what he was comin' to years back. Then I thought when the war come, and he was drafted into it, that the army and strict discipline'd maybe make a man o' him. But it ain't! It's made him worse! It's killed whatever mite of decency was left in him. And I reckon now that if you put a coward in one of them there uniforms, he thinks it gives him the privilege to be a

bully! Put a sneak in one and it gives him the courage to be a thief!
That's why when the war was over Benny enlisted again 'stead o'
goin' whalin' with me. He thinks he's found a good shield to cover
up his natural-born laziness—and crookedness!

EMMA. (*outraged*) You can talk that way about him that went way
over to France to shed his blood for you and me!

CALEB. I don't need no one to do my fightin' for me—against German or devil. And you know durned well he was only in the Quar-
termaster's Department unloadin' and truckin' groceries, as safe from
a gun as you and me be this minute. (*With heavy scorn*) If he shed
any blood, he must have got a nose bleed.

EMMA. Oh, you do hate him, I can see it! And you're just as mean
as mean, Caleb Williams! All you've said is a wicked lie and you've
got no cause—

CALEB. I ain't, eh? I got damned good cause, I tell ye! I ain't minded
his meanness to me. I ain't even give as much heed to his meanness
to Harriet as I'd ought to have, maybe. But when he starts in his
sneakin' thievery with you, Emmer, I put my foot down on him for
good and all!

EMMA. What sneakin' thievery with me? How dare you say such
things?

CALEB. I got proof it's true. Why, he's even bragged all over town
about bein' able to borrow all the money from you he'd a mind to—
boastin' of what an old fool he was makin' of you, with you fixin' up
your house all new to git him to comin' over.

EMMA. (*scarlet—blazing*) It's a lie! He never said it! You're makin'
it all up—'cause you're—'cause you're—

CALEB. 'Cause I'm what, Emmer?

EMMA. (*flinging it at him like a savage taunt*) 'Cause you're jealous
of him, that's what! Any fool can see that!

CALEB. (*getting to his feet and facing her—slowly*) Jealous? Of
Benny? How—I don't see your meanin' rightly.

EMMA. (*with triumphant malice*) Yes, you do! Don't pretend you don't! You're jealous 'cause you know I care a lot about him.

CALEB. (*slowly*) Why would I be jealous 'count o' that? What kind o' man d'you take me for? Don't I know you must care for him when you've been a'most as much a mother to him for years as Harriet was?

EMMA. (*wounded to the quick—furiously*) No such thing! You're a mean liar! I ain't never played a mother to him. He's never looked at me that way—never! And I don't care for him that way at all. Just because I'm a mite older 'n him—can't them things happen just as well as any other—what d'you suppose—can't I care for him same as any woman cares for a man? And I do! I care more'n I ever did for you! And that's why you're lying about him! You're jealous of that!

CALEB. (*staring at her with stunned eyes—in a hoarse whisper*) Emmer! Ye don't know what you're sayin', do ye?

EMMA. I do too!

CALEB. Harriet said you'd been actin' out o' your right senses.

EMMA. Harriet's mad because she knows Benny loves me better 'n her. And he does love me! He don't mind my bein' older. He's said so! And I love him, too!

CALEB. (*stepping back from her in horror*) Emmer!

EMMA. And he's asked me to marry him tomorrow. And I'm going to! Then you can all lie all you've a mind to!

CALEB. You're—going to—marry Benny?

EMMA. First thing tomorrow. And since you've throwed him out of his house in your mad jealousness, I've told him he can stay here with me tonight. And he's going to!

CALEB. (*his fists clenching—tensely*) Where—where is the skunk now?

EMMA. (*hastily*) Oh, he ain't here. He's gone up street.

CALEB. (*starting for the door in rear*) I'm goin' to find the skunk.

EMMA. (*seizing his arms—frightenedly*) What're you going to do?

CALEB. (*between his clenched teeth*) I don't know, Emmer—I don't know— On'y he ain't goin' to marry you, by God!

EMMA. Caleb! (*She tries to throw her arms about him to stop his going. He pushes her firmly but gently aside. She shrieks*) Caleb! (*She flings herself on her knees and wraps her arms around his legs in supplicating terror*) Caleb! You ain't going to kill him, Caleb? You ain't going to hurt him, be you? Say you ain't! Tell me you won't hurt him! (*As she thinks she sees a relenting softness come into his face as he looks down at her*) Oh, Caleb, you used to say you loved me! Don't hurt him then, Caleb,—for my sake! I love him, Caleb! Don't hurt him—just because you think I'm an old woman ain't no reason—and I won't marry you, Caleb. I won't—not even if you have waited thirty years. I don't love you. I love him! And I'm going to marry him—tomorrow. So you won't hurt him, will you, Caleb— not when I ask you on my knees!

CALEB. (*breaking away from her with a shudder of disgust*) No, I won't touch him. If I was wantin' to git even with ye, I wouldn't dirty my hands on him. I'd let you marry the skunk and set and watch what happened—or else I'd offer him money not to marry ye—more money than the little mite you kin bring him—and let ye see how quick he'd turn his back on ye!

EMMA. (*getting to her feet—frenziedly*) It's a lie! He never would!

CALEB. (*unheeding—with a sudden ominous calm*) But I ain't goin' to do neither. You ain't worth it—and he ain't—and no one ain't, nor nothin'. Folks be all crazy and rotten to the core and I'm done with the whole kit and caboodle of 'em. I kin only see one course out for me and I'm goin' to take it. "A dead whale or a stove boat!" we says in whalin'—and my boat is stove! (*He strides away from her, stops, and turns back—savagely*) Thirty o' the best years of my life flung for a yeller dog like him to feed on. God! You used to say you was diff'rent from the rest o' folks. By God, if you are, it's just you're a mite madder'n they be! By God, that's all! (*He goes, letting the door slam to behind him.*)

EMMA. (*in a pitiful whimper*) Caleb! (*She sinks into a chair by*

247

the table sobbing hysterically. Benny sneaks through the door on right, hesitates for a while, afraid that his uncle may be coming back.)

BENNY. *(finally, in a shrill whisper)* Aunt Emmer!

EMMA. *(raising her face to look at him for a second)* Oh, Benny! *(She falls to weeping again.)*

BENNY. Say, you don't think he's liable to come back, do you?

EMMA. No—he'll—never come back here—no more. *(Sobs bitterly.)*

BENNY. *(his courage returning, comes forward into the room)* Say, he's way up in the air, ain't he? *(With a grin)* Say, that was some bawlin' out he give you!

EMMA. You—you heard what he said?

BENNY. Sure thing. When you got to shoutin' I sneaked out o' the kitchen into there to hear what was goin' on. *(With a complacent grin)* Say, you certainly stood up for me all right. You're a good old scout at that, d'you know it?

EMMA. *(raising her absurd, besmeared face to his, as if expecting him to kiss her)* Oh, Benny, I'm giving up everything I've held dear all my life for your sake.

BENNY. *(turning away from her with a look of aversion)* Well, what about it? Ain't I worth it? Ain't I worth a million played-out old cranks like him? *(She stares at him bewilderedly. He takes a handful of almonds from his pocket and begins cracking and eating them, throwing the shells on the floor with an impudent carelessness)* Hope you don't mind my havin' a feed? I found them out in the kitchen and helped myself.

EMMA. *(pitifully)* You're welcome to anything that's here, Benny.

BENNY. *(insolently)* Sure, I know you're a good scout. Don't rub it in. *(After a pause—boastfully)* Where did you get that stuff about askin' him not to hurt me? He'd have a swell chance! There's a lot of hard guys in the army have tried to get funny with me till I put one over on 'em. I'd like to see him start something! I could lick him with my hands handcuffed.

EMMA. *(revolted)* Oh!

248

BENNY. (*resentfully*) Think I'm bluffin'? I'll show you sometime. (*He swaggers about the room—finally stopping beside her. With a cunning leer*) Say, I been thinkin' it over and I guess I'll call his bluff.

EMMA. (*confusedly*) What—do you mean?

BENNY. I mean what he said just before he beat it—that he could get me not to marry you if he offered me more coin than you got. (*Very interestedly*) Say, d'you s'pose the old miser really was serious about that?

EMMA. (*dazedly—as if she could not realize the significance of his words*) I—I—don't know, Benny.

BENNY. (*swaggering about again*) If I was only sure he wasn't stallin'! If I could get the old cuss to shell out that way! (*With a tickled chuckle*) Gosh, that'd be the real stunt aw right, aw right. Oui, oui! Maybe he wasn't kiddin' at that, the old simp! It's worth takin' a stab at, damned if it ain't. I ain't got nothin' to lose.

EMMA. (*frightenedly*) What—what're you talkin' about, Benny?

BENNY. Say, I think I'll go over and talk to Ma after a while. You can go over first to make sure he ain't there. I'll get her to put it up to him straight. If he's willin' to dig in his jeans for some real coin—real dough, this time!—I'll agree to beat it and not spill the beans for him with you. (*Threateningly*) And if he's too tight, I'll go right through with what I said I would, if only to spite him! That's me!

EMMA. You mean—if he's willing to bribe you with money, you won't marry me tomorrow?

BENNY. Sure! If he'll put up enough money. I won't stand for no pikin'.

EMMA. (*whimpering*) Oh, Benny, you're only jokin', ain't you? You can't—you can't mean it!

BENNY. (*with careless effrontery*) Why can't I? Sure I mean it!

EMMA. (*hiding her face in her hands—with a tortured moan*) Oh, Benny!

BENNY. (*disgustedly*) Aw, don't go bawlin'! (*After a pause—a bit *embarrassedly*) Aw, say, what d'you think, anyway? What're you takin' it so damned serious for—me askin' you to marry me, I mean? I was on'y sort of kiddin' anyway—just so you'd tell him and get his goat right. (*As she looks up at him with agonized despair. With a trace of something like pity showing in his tone*) Say, honest, Aunt Emmer, you didn't believe—you didn't think I was really stuck on you, did you? Ah, say, how could I? Have a heart! Why, you're as old as Ma is, ain't you, Aunt Emmer? (*He adds ruthlessly*) And I'll say you look it, too!

EMMA. (*cowering—as if he had struck her*) Oh! Oh!

BENNY. (*a bit irritated*) What's the use of blubberin', for God's sake? Can't you take it like a sport? Hell, I ain't lookin' to marry no one, if I can help it. What do I want a wife for? There's too many others. (*After a pause—as she still sobs—calculatingly*) Aw, come on, be a sport—and say, listen, if he ain't willin' to come across, I'll marry you all right, honest I will. (*More and more calculatingly*) Sure! If they mean that stuff about kickin' me out of home—sure I'll stay here with you! I'll do anything you want. If you want me to marry you, all you've got to do is say so—anytime! Only not tomorrow, we'd better wait and see—

EMMA. (*hysterically*) Oh, go away! Go away!

BENNY. (*looking down at her disgustedly*) Aw, come up for air, can't you? (*He slaps her on the back*) Buck up! Be a pal! Tell me what your dope is. This thing's got me so balled up I don't know how I stand. (*With sudden fury*) Damn his hide! I'll bet he'll go and leave all he's got to some lousy orphan asylum now.

EMMA. Oh, go away! Go away!

BENNY. (*viciously*) So you're givin' me the gate, too, eh? I'd like to see you try it! You asked me to stay and I'll stick. It's all your fool fault that's got me in wrong. And now you want to shake me! This is what I get for foolin' around with an old hen like you that oughta been planted in the cemetery long ago! Paintin' your old mush and dressin' like a kid! Christ A'mighty!

EMMA. (*in a cry of despair*) Don't! Stop! Go away.

BENNY. (*suddenly alert—sharply*) Sh! I hear someone coming. (*Shaking her*) Stop—now, Emmer! Damn it, you gotta go to the door. Maybe it's him. (*He scurries into the room on right. There is a faint knock at the door.* EMMA *lifts her head. She looks horribly old and worn out. Her face is frozen into an expressionless mask, her eyes are red-rimmed, dull and lifeless. The knock is repeated more sharply.* EMMA *rises like a weary automaton and goes to the door and opens it.* HARRIET *is revealed standing outside.*)

HARRIET. (*making no movement to come in—coldly*) I want to speak to Caleb.

EMMA. (*dully*) He ain't here. He left a while back—said he was goin' up street—I think.

HARRIET. (*worriedly*) Oh, land sakes! (*Then hostilely*) Do you know where Benny is?

EMMA. (*dully*) Yes, he's here.

HARRIET. (*contemptuously*) I might have guessed that! (*Icily formal*) Would you mind tellin' him I want to see him?

EMMA. (*turns and calls*) Benny! Here's your Ma!

BENNY. (*comes from the next room*) Aw right. (*In a fierce whisper as he passes* EMMA) What d'you tell her I was here for, you old fool?

EMMA. (*gives no sign of having heard him but comes back to her chair and sits down.* BENNY *slouches to the door—sullenly*) What d'you want, Ma?

HARRIET. (*coldly*) I wanted your Uncle Caleb, not you, but you'll have to do, bein' the only man about.

BENNY. (*suspiciously*) What is it?

HARRIET. (*a bit frightenedly*) I just heard a lot of queer noises down to the barn. Someone's in there, Benny, sure as I'm alive. They're stealin' the chickens, must be.

BENNY. (*carelessly*) It's only the rats.

HARRIET. (*angrily*) Don't play the idiot! This was a big thumpin' noise no rat'd make.

251

BENNY. What'd any guy go stealin' this early— (*As* HARRIET *turns away angrily—placatingly*) Aw right, I'm coming. I'll have a look if that'll satisfy you. Don't go gettin' sore at me again. (*While he is speaking he goes out and disappears after his mother.* EMMA *sits straight and stiff in her chair for a while, staring before her with waxy eyes. Then she gets to her feet and goes from window to window taking down all the curtains with quick mechanical movements. She throws them on a pile in the middle of the floor. She lifts down the framed pictures from the walls and piles them on the curtains. She takes the cushions and throws them on; pushes the rugs to the pile with her feet; sweeps everything off the table onto the floor. She does all this without a trace of change in her expression—rapidly, but with no apparent effort. There is the noise of running footsteps from outside and* BENNY *bursts into the room panting for breath. He is terribly excited and badly frightened.*)

BENNY. (*stops short as he sees the pile on the floor*) What the hell—

EMMA. (*dully*) The junk man's coming for them in the morning.

BENNY. (*too excited to be surprised*) To hell with that! Say, listen, Aunt Emmer, he's hung himself—Uncle Caleb—in the barn—he's dead!

EMMA. (*slowly letting the words fall—like a beginner on the typewriter touching two new letters*) Caleb—dead!

BENNY. (*voluble now*) Dead as a door nail! Neck's busted. I just cut him down and carried him to home. Say, you've got to come over and help look after Ma. She's goin' bugs. I can't do nothin' with her.

EMMA. (*as before*) Caleb hanged himself—in the barn?

BENNY. Yes—and made a sure job of it. (*With morbid interest in the details*) He got a halter and made a noose of the rope for his neck and climbed up in the loft and hitched the leather end to a beam and then let himself drop. He must have kicked in that quick! (*He snaps his fingers—then urgently*) Say, come on. Come on over 'n' help me with Ma, can't you? She's goin' wild. I can't do nothin'!

EMMA. (*vaguely*) I'll be over—in a minute. (*Then with a sudden air of having decided something irrevocably*) I got to go down to the barn.

BENNY. Barn? Say, are you crazy? He ain't there now. I told you I carried him home.

EMMA. I mean—my barn. I got to go down—

BENNY. (*exasperated*) Oh hell! You're as bad as Ma! Everyone's lost their heads but me. Well, I got to get someone else, that's all. (*He rushes out rear, slamming the door behind him.*)

EMMA. (*after a tense pause—with a sudden outburst of wild grief*) Caleb! (*Then in a strange whisper*) Wait, Caleb, I'm going down to the barn. (*She moves like a sleepwalker toward the door in the rear as the curtain falls.*)

WELDED

A Play in Three Acts

1922-1923

CHARACTERS

MICHAEL CAPE

ELEANOR

JOHN

A WOMAN

SCENES

ACT ONE
Scene: Studio apartment.

ACT TWO
Scene i: Library.
Scene ii: Bedroom.

ACT THREE
Scene: Same as Act I.

WELDED

ACT ONE

Scene—*Studio apartment. In the rear, a balcony with a stairway at center leading down to the studio floor.*

The room is in darkness. Then a circle of light reveals ELEANOR *lying back on a chaise longue. She is a woman of thirty. Her figure is tall. Her face, with its high, prominent cheek-bones, lacks harmony. It is dominated by passionate, blue-gray eyes, restrained by a high forehead from which the mass of her dark brown hair is combed straight back. The first impression of her whole personality is one of charm, partly innate, partly imposed by years of self-discipline.*

She picks up a letter from the table, which she opens and reads, an expression of delight and love coming over her face. She kisses the letter impulsively—then gives a gay laugh at herself. She lets the letter fall on her lap and stares straight before her, lost in a sentimental reverie.

A door underneath the balcony is noiselessly opened and MICHAEL *comes in. (A circle of light appears with him, follows him into the room. These two circles of light, like auras of egoism, emphasize and intensify* ELEANOR *and* MICHAEL *throughout the play. There is no other lighting. The two other people and the rooms are distinguishable only by the light of* ELEANOR *and* MICHAEL.)*

MICHAEL *is thirty-five, tall and dark. His unusual face is a harrowed battlefield of supersensitiveness, the features at war with one another —the forehead of a thinker, the eyes of a dreamer, the nose and mouth of a sensualist. One feels a powerful imagination tinged with somber sadness—a driving force which can be sympathetic and cruel at the*

257

*same time. There is something tortured about him—a passionate ten-
sion, a self-protecting, arrogant defiance of life and his own weakness,
a deep need for love as a faith in which to relax.*

*He has a suitcase, hat, and overcoat which he sets inside on the floor,
glancing toward* ELEANOR, *trying not to make the slightest noise. But
she suddenly becomes aware of some presence in the room and turns
boldly to face it. She gives an exclamation of delighted astonishment
when she sees* MICHAEL *and jumps up to meet him as he strides toward
her.*

ELEANOR. Michael!

CAPE. (*with a boyish grin*) You've spoiled it, Nelly; I wanted a kiss
to announce me. (*They are in each other's arms. He kisses her tenderly.*)

ELEANOR. (*joyously*) This *is* a surprise!

CAPE. (*straining her in his arms and kissing her passionately*) Own
little wife!

ELEANOR. Dearest! (*They look into each other's eyes for a long moment.*)

CAPE. (*tenderly*) Happy?

ELEANOR. Yes, yes! Why do you always ask? You know. (*Suddenly
pushing him at arms' length—with a happy laugh*) It's positively
immoral for an old married couple to act this way. (*She leads him by
the hand to the chaise longue*) And you must explain. You wrote not
to expect you till the end of the week. (*She sits down*) Get a cushion.
Sit down here. (*He puts a cushion on the floor beside the chaise longue
and sits down*) Tell me all about it.

CAPE. (*notices the letter lying on the floor*) Were you reading my
letter? (*She nods. He gives a happy grin*) Do you mean to say you
still read them over—after five years of me?

ELEANOR. (*with a tender smile*) Oh—sometimes.

CAPE. Sweetheart! (*Smiling*) What were you dreaming about when
I intruded?

ELEANOR. Never mind. You're enough of an egotist already. (*Her hand caressing his face and hair*) I've been feeling so lonely—and it's only been a few weeks, hasn't it? (*She laughs*) How was everything in the country? (*Suddenly kissing him*) Oh, I'm so happy you're back. (*With mock severity*) But ought I? Have you finished the fourth act? You know you promised not to return until you did.

CAPE. This afernoon!

ELEANOR. You're sure you didn't force it—(*with a tender smile at him*)—because you were lonely, too?

CAPE. (*with a sudden change in manner that is almost stern*) No. I wouldn't. I couldn't. You know that.

ELEANOR. (*her face showing a trace of hurt in spite of herself*) I was only fooling. (*Then rousing herself as if conquering a growing depression*) I'm terribly anxious to hear what you've done.

CAPE. (*enthusiastically*) You'll see when I read you— And you're going to be marvelous! It's going to be the finest thing we've ever done!

ELEANOR. I love you for saying "we." But the "we" is you. I only— (*with a smile of ironical self-pity*)—act a part you've created.

CAPE. (*impetuously*) Nonsense! You're an artist. Each performance of yours has taught me something. Why, my women used to be— death masks. But now they're as alive as you are—(*with a sudden grin*)—at least, when you play them.

ELEANOR. (*her eyes shining with excited pleasure*) You don't know how much it means to have you talk like that! Oh, I'm going to work so hard, Michael! (*Impetuously*) You've simply got to read me that last act right now!

CAPE. (*jumping to his feet eagerly*) All right. (*He walks toward his bag—then stops when he is half-way and, hesitating, turns slowly and comes back. He bends down and lifts her face to his—with a smile*) No. I won't.

ELEANOR. (*disappointed*) Oh. Why not, dear?

CAPE. Because—

ELEANOR. Plagiarist!

CAPE. Because I've been hoping for this night as our own. Let's forget the actress and playwright. Let's just be—us—lovers.

ELEANOR. (*with a tender smile—musingly*) We *have* remained lovers, haven't we?

CAPE. (*with a grin*) Fights and all?

ELEANOR. (*with a little frown*) We don't fight so much.

CAPE. (*frowning himself*) Too much.

ELEANOR. (*forcing a smile*) Perhaps that's the price.

CAPE. Don't grow fatalistic—just when I was about to propose reform.

ELEANOR. (*smiling—quickly*) Oh, I'll promise to be good—if you will. (*Gently reproachful*) Do you think I enjoy fighting with you?

CAPE. (*with sudden passion*) It's wrong, Nelly. It's evil!

ELEANOR. Ssshh! We promised.

CAPE. (*hesitatingly*) We've been taking each other too much for granted. That may do very well with the common loves of the world —but ours—! (*He suddenly pulls her head down and kisses her impulsively*) But you understand! Oh, Nelly, I love you with all my soul!

ELEANOR. (*deeply moved*) And I love you, Michael—always and forever! (*They sit close, she staring dreamily before her, he watching her face.*)

CAPE. (*after a pause*) What are you thinking?

ELEANOR. (*with a tender smile*) Of the first time we met—at rehearsal, remember? I was thinking of how mistakenly I'd pictured you before that. (*She pauses—then frowning a little*) I'd heard such a lot of gossip about your love affairs.

CAPE. (*with a wry grin*) You must have been disappointed if you expected Don Juan. (*A pause—then forcing a short laugh*) I also had heard a lot of rumors about your previous— (*He stops abruptly with an expression of extreme bitterness.*)

ELEANOR. (*sharply*) Don't! (*A pause—then she goes on sadly*) It was only our past together I wanted to remember. (*A pause—then with a trace of scornful resentment*) I was forgetting your morbid obsession—

CAPE. (*with gloomy irritation*) Obsession? Why—? (*Then determinedly throwing off this mood—reproachfully forcing a joking tone*) We're not "starting something" now, are we—after our promise?

ELEANOR. (*impulsively pressing his hand*) No, no—of course not!

CAPE. (*after a pause—a bit awkwardly*) But you guessed my desire, at that. I wanted to dream with you in our past—to find there—a new faith—

ELEANOR. (*smiling*) Another Grand Ideal for our marriage?

CAPE. (*frowning*) Don't mock.

ELEANOR. (*teasingly*) But you're such a relentless idealist. You needn't frown. That was exactly what drew me to you in those first days. (*Earnestly*) I'd lost faith in everything. Your love saved me. Your work saved mine. I owe you myself, Michael! (*She kisses him*) Do you remember—our first night together?

CAPE. Do you imagine I could've forgotten?

ELEANOR. (*continuing as if she hadn't heard*) The play was such a marvelous success! I knew I had finally won—through your work! I loved myself! I loved you! You came to me— (*More and more intensely*) Oh, it was beautiful madness! I lost myself. I began living in you. I wanted to die and become you!

CAPE. (*passionately*) And I, you!

ELEANOR. (*softly*) And do you remember the dawn creeping in— and how we began to plan our future? (*She exclaims impulsively*) Oh, I'd give anything in the world to live those days over again!

CAPE. Why? Hasn't our marriage kept the spirit of that time—with a growth of something deeper—finer—

ELEANOR. Yes,—but— Oh, you know what I mean! It was revelation then—a miracle out of the sky!

CAPE. (*insistently*) But haven't we realized the ideal of our marriage— (*Smiling but with deep earnestness nevertheless*) Not for us

261

the ordinary family rite, you'll remember! We swore to have a true sacrament—or nothing! Our marriage must be a consummation demanding and combining the best in each of us! Hard, difficult, guarded from the commonplace, kept sacred as the outward form of our inner harmony! (*With an awkward sense of having become rhetorical he adds self-mockingly*) We'd tend our flame on an altar, not in a kitchen range! (*He forces a grin—then abruptly changing again, with a sudden fierce pleading*) It has been what we dreamed, hasn't it, Nelly?

ELEANOR. Our ideal was difficult. (*Sadly*) Sometimes I think we've demanded too much. Now there's nothing left but that something which can't give itself. And I blame you for this—because I can neither take more nor give more—and you blame me! (*She smiles tenderly*) And then we fight!

CAPE. Then let's be proud of our fight! It began with the splitting of a cell a hundred million years ago into you and me, leaving an eternal yearning to become one life again.

ELEANOR. At moments—we do.

CAPE. Yes! (*He kisses her—then intensely*) You and I—year after year—together—forms of our bodies merging into one form; rhythm of our lives beating against each other, forming slowly the one rhythm —the life of Us—created by us!—beyond us, above us! (*With sudden furious anger*) God, what I feel of the truth of this—the beauty!— but how can I express it?

ELEANOR. (*kissing him*) I understand.

CAPE. (*straining her to him with fierce passion*) Oh, my own, my own—and I your own—to the end of time!

ELEANOR. I love you!

CAPE. (*with passionate exultance*) Why do you regret our first days? Their fire still burns in us—deeper! Don't you feel that? (*Kissing her again and again*) I've become you! You've become me! One heart! One blood! Ours! (*He pulls her to her feet*) My wife! Come!

ELEANOR. (*almost swooning in his arms*) My lover—yes— My lover—

CAPE. Come! (*With his arms around her he leads her to the stairway. As they get to the foot, there is a noise from the hall. She hears it, starts, seems suddenly brought back to herself.* CAPE *is oblivious and continues up the stairs. She stands swaying, holding on to the bannister as if in a daze. At the top,* CAPE *turns in surprise at not finding her, as if he had felt her behind him. He looks down passionately, stretching out his arms, his eyes glowing*) Come!

ELEANOR. (*weakly*) Ssshh! A moment— Listen!

CAPE. (*bewilderedly*) What? What is it?

ELEANOR. Ssshh—Listen—Someone— (*She speaks in an unnatural, mechanical tone. A knock comes at the door. She gives a sort of gasp of relief*) There!

CAPE. (*still bewilderedly as if something mysterious were happening that he cannot grasp*) What—what—? (*Then as she takes a slow, mechanical step toward the door—with tense pleading*) Nelly! Come here! (*She turns to look at him and is held by his imploring eyes. She sways irresolutely toward him, again reaching to the bannister for support. Then a sharper knock comes at the door. It acts like a galvanic shock on her. Her eyes move in that direction, she takes another jerky step.* CAPE *stammers in a fierce whisper*) No! Don't go!

ELEANOR. (*without looking at him—mechanically*) I must.

CAPE. (*frantically*) They'll go away. Nelly, don't! Don't! (*Again she stops irresolutely like a hypnotized person torn by two conflicting suggestions. The knock is repeated, this time with authority, assurance. Her body reacts as if she were throwing off a load.*)

ELEANOR. (*with a return to her natural tone—but hysterical*) Please— don't be silly, Michael. It might be—something important. (*She hurries to the door.*)

CAPE. (*rushing down the stairs—frantically*) No! No! (*He just gets to the bottom as she opens the door. He stands there fixed, disorganized, trembling all over.*)

ELEANOR. (*as she sees who it is—in a relieved tone of surprise*) Why hello, John. Come in! Here's Michael. Michael, it's John. (JOHN *steps into the room. He is a man of about fifty, tall, loose-limbed, a bit stoop-shouldered, with iron-gray hair, and a gaunt, shrewd face. He is not handsome but his personality compels affection. His eyes are round and child-like. He has no nerves. His voice is low and calming.*)

JOHN. (*shaking* ELEANOR *by the hand*) Hello, Nelly. I was on my way home from the theater and I thought I'd drop in for a second. Hello, Michael. When'd you get in? Glad to see you back. (*He comes to him and shakes his hand which* CAPE *extends jerkily, as if in spite of himself, without a word.*)

ELEANOR. (*after a glance at her husband—in a forced tone*) We're so glad you've come. Sit down.

JOHN. (*he becomes aware of the disharmonious atmosphere his appearance has created*) I can't stay a second. (*To* CAPE) I wanted some news. I thought Nelly'd probably have heard from you. (*He slaps* CAPE *on the back with jovial familiarity*) Well, how's it coming?

CAPE. (*in a frozen tone*) Oh,—all right—all right.

ELEANOR. (*uneasily*) Won't you have a cigarette, John? (*She takes the box from the table and holds it out to him.*)

JOHN. (*taking one*) Thanks, Nelly. (*He half-sits on the arm of a chair. She holds out a light to him*) Thanks.

ELEANOR. (*nervously*) Why don't you sit down, Michael? (*He doesn't answer. She goes to him with the cigarettes*) Don't you want a cigarette? (CAPE *stares at her with a hot glance of scorn. She recoils from it, turning quickly away from him, visibly shaken. Without appearing to notice,* JOHN *scrutinizes their faces keenly, sizing up the situation.*)

JOHN. (*breaking in matter-of-fact*) You look done up, Michael.

CAPE. (*with a guilty start*) I—I'm tired out.

ELEANOR. (*with a forced air*) He's been working too hard. He finished the last act only this afternoon.

JOHN. (*with a grunt of satisfaction*) Glad to hear it. (*Abruptly*) When can I see it?

CAPE. In a day or so—I want to go over—

JOHN. All right. (*Getting to his feet*) Well, that's that. I'll run along.

ELEANOR. (*almost frightenedly*) Do stay. Why don't you read us the last act now, Michael?

CAPE. (*fiercely*) No! It's rotten! I hate the whole play!

JOHN. (*easily*) Reaction. This play's the finest thing you've done. (*He comes to* CAPE *and slaps him on the back reassuringly*) And it's the biggest chance the lady here has ever had. It'll be a triumph for you both, wait and see. So cheer up—and get a good night's rest. (CAPE *smiles with bitter irony*) Well, good-night. (CAPE *nods without speaking,* JOHN *goes to the door,* ELEANOR *accompanying him*) Good-night, Nelly. Better start on your part—only don't you overdo it, too. (*He pats her on the back*) Good-night.

ELEANOR. Good-night. (*She closes the door after him. She remains there for a moment staring at the closed door, afraid to turn and meet* CAPE's *fiercely accusing eyes which she feels fixed upon her. Finally, making an effort of will, she walks back to the table, avoiding his eyes, assuming a careless air.*)

CAPE. (*suddenly explodes in furious protest*) Why did you do that?

ELEANOR. (*with an assumed surprise but with a guilty air, turning over the pages of a magazine*) Do what?

CAPE. (*tensely, clutching her by the arm*) You know what I mean! (*Unconsciously he grips her tighter, almost shaking her.*)

ELEANOR. (*coldly*) You're hurting me. (*A bit shamefacedly,* CAPE *lets go of her arm. She glances quickly at his face, then speaks with a kind of dull remorse*) I suppose I can guess—my going to the door?

CAPE. He would've gone away— (*With anguish*) Nelly, why did you?

ELEANOR. (*defensively*) Wasn't it important you see John?

265

CAPE. (*with helpless anger*) Don't evade! (*With deep feeling*) I should think you'd be ashamed.

ELEANOR. (*after a pause—dully*) Perhaps—I am. (*A pause*) I couldn't help myself.

CAPE. (*intensely*) You should've been oblivious to everything! (*Miserably*) I—I can't understand!

ELEANOR. That's you, Michael. The other is me—or a part of me— I hardly understand myself.

CAPE. (*sinking down on a chair, his head in his hands*) After all we'd been to each other tonight—! (*With bitter despondency*) Ruined now—gone—a rare moment of beauty! It seems at times as if some jealous demon of the commonplace were mocking us. (*With a violent gesture of loathing*) Oh, how intolerably insulting life can be! (*Then brokenly*) Nelly, why, why did you?

ELEANOR. (*dully*) I—I don't know. (*Then after a pause she comes over and puts her hand on his shoulder*) Don't brood, dear. I'm sorry. I hate myself. (*A pause. She looks down at him, seeming to make up her mind to something—in a forced tone*) But—why is it gone—our beautiful moment? (*She strokes his hair*) We have the whole night— (*He stares up at her wonderingly. She forces a smile, half turning away.*)

CAPE. (*in wild protest*) Nelly, what are you offering me—a sacrifice? Please!

ELEANOR. (*revolted*) Michael! (*Then hysterically*) No, forgive me! I'm the disgusting one! Forgive me! (*She turns away from him and throws herself on a chair, staring straight before her. Their chairs are side by side, each facing front, so near that by a slight movement each could touch the other, but during the following scene they stare straight ahead and remain motionless. They speak, ostensibly to the other, but showing by their tone it is a thinking aloud to oneself, and neither appears to hear what the other has said.*)

CAPE. (*after a long pause*) More and more frequently. There's always some knock at the door, some reminder of the life outside which calls you away from me.

ELEANOR. It's so beautiful—and then—suddenly I'm being crushed. I feel a cruel presence in you paralyzing me, creeping over my body, possessing it so it's no longer my body—then grasping at some last inmost thing which makes me me—my soul—demanding to have that, too! I have to rebel with all my strength—seize any pretext! Just now at the foot of the stairs—the knock on the door was—liberation. (*In anguish*) And yet I love you! It's because I love you! If I'm destroyed, what is left to love you, what is left for you to love?

CAPE. I've grown inward into our life. But you keep trying to escape as if it were a prison. You feel the need of what is outside. I'm not enough for you.

ELEANOR. Why is it I can never know you? I try to know you and I can't. I desire to take all of you into my heart, but there's a great alien force— I hate that unknown power in you which would destroy me. (*Pleadingly*) Haven't I a right to myself as you have to yourself?

CAPE. You fight against me as if I were your enemy. Every word or action of mine which affects you, you resent. At every turn you feel your individuality invaded—while at the same time, you're jealous of any separateness in me. You demand more and more while you give less and less. And I have to acquiesce. Have to? Yes, because I can't live without you! You realize that! You take advantage of it while you despise me for my helplessness! (*This seems to goad him to desperation*) But look out! I still have the strength to—! (*He turns his head and stares at her challengingly.*)

ELEANOR. (*as before*) You insist that I have no life at all outside you. Even my work must exist only as an echo of yours. You hate my need of easy, casual associations. You think that weakness. You hate my friends. You're jealous of everything and everybody. (*Resentfully*) I have to fight. You're too severe. Your ideal is too inhuman. Why can't you understand and be generous—be just! (*She turns to meet his eyes, staring back with resentful accusation. They look at each other in this manner for a long moment.*)

CAPE. (*averting his eyes and addressing her directly in a cold, sarcastic tone*) Strange—that John should pop in on us suddenly like that.

ELEANOR. (*resentfully*) I don't see anything strange about it.

CAPE. It's past twelve—

ELEANOR. You're in New York now.

CAPE. (*sharply*) I'm quite aware of that. Nevertheless—

ELEANOR. (*shortly*) He explained. Didn't you hear him? He wanted news of the play and thought I might have a letter—

CAPE. That's just the point. He had no idea he would find me here.

ELEANOR. (*about to fly at him, checks herself after a pause, coldly*) Why shouldn't he come to see me? He's the oldest friend I've got. He gave me my first chance and he's always helped me since. I owe whatever success I've made to his advice and direction.

CAPE. (*stung—sarcastically*) Oh, undoubtedly!

ELEANOR. I suppose you think I ought to have said it's to you I owe everything?

CAPE. (*dryly*) I'd prefer to say it was to yourself, and no one else. (*After a pause—attempting a casual tone*) Has he been in the habit of calling here while I've been gone? (*Hurriedly*) Don't misunderstand me. I'm merely asking a question.

ELEANOR. (*scornfully*) Oh! (*A pause. She bites her lips—then coldly*) Yes, he's been here once before. (*Mockingly*) And after the theater, too! Think of that!

CAPE. (*sneeringly*) The same insatiable curiosity about my play?

ELEANOR. (*angrily*) Michael! (*A pause—then scornfully*) Don't tell me you're becoming jealous of John again!

CAPE. (*meaningly*) Again. That's just it.

ELEANOR. (*springing from her chair—excitedly*) This is insufferable! (*Then calming herself with an effort—with a forced laugh*) Please don't be so ridiculous, Michael. I'll only lose my temper if you keep on. (*Then suddenly she makes up her mind and comes to him*) Please stop, dear. We've made up our minds not to quarrel. Let's drop it. (*She pats his head with a friendly smile.*)

CAPE. (*impulsively takes her hand and kisses it*) All right. Forgive me. I'm all unstrung. His breaking in on us like that— (*He relapses into frowning brooding again. She sits down, this time facing him, and looks at him uneasily.*)

ELEANOR. (*after a pause—rather irritably*) It's too absolutely silly, your being jealous of John.

CAPE. I'm not jealous of him. I'm jealous of you—the something in you that repulses our love—the stranger in you.

ELEANOR. (*with a short laugh*) I should think after five years—

CAPE. (*unheeding*) And what makes me hate you at those times is that I know you like to make me jealous, that my suffering pleases you, that it satisfies some craving in you—for revenge!

ELEANOR. (*scornfully*) Can't you realize how absurd you are? (*Then with a forced placating laugh*) No, really, Michael, it'd be funny— if it weren't so exasperating.

CAPE. (*after a pause—somberly*) You mentioned our years together as proof. What of the years that preceded?

ELEANOR. (*challengingly*) Well, what of them?

CAPE. By their light, I have plausible grounds for jealousy in John's case. Or don't you acknowledge that?

ELEANOR. I deny it absolutely!

CAPE. Why, you've told me yourself he was in love with you for years, and that he once asked you to marry him!

ELEANOR. Well, did I marry him?

CAPE. But he still loves you.

ELEANOR. Don't be stupid!

CAPE. He does, I tell you!

ELEANOR. If you had any sense you'd know that his love has become purely that of an old friend. And I refuse to give up his friendship for your silly whims.

269

CAPE. (*after a pause in which they each brood resentfully—sarcastically*) You were a shining exception, it appears. The other women he helped could hardly claim he had remained—merely their friend.

ELEANOR. (*vehemently*) It's a lie! And even if it were true, you'd find it was they who offered themselves!

CAPE. (*significantly*) Ah! (*Then after a pause*) Perhaps because they felt it necessary for their careers.

ELEANOR. (*dryly*) Perhaps. (*Then after a pause*) But they discovered their mistake, then. John isn't that type.

CAPE. (*suddenly*) Why do you act so jealous—of those others?

ELEANOR. (*flushing angrily*) I don't. It's your imagination.

CAPE. Then why lose your temper?

ELEANOR. Because I resent your superior attitude that John had to bribe women to love him. Isn't he as worthy of love—as you are?

CAPE. (*sarcastically*) If I am to believe your story, you didn't think so.

ELEANOR. (*irritably*) Then let's stop arguing, for heaven's sake! Why do you always have to rake up the past? For the last year or so you've begun to act more and more as you did when we first lived together—jealous and suspicious of everything and everybody! (*Hysterically*) I can't bear it, Michael!

CAPE. (*ironically*) You used to love me for it then.

ELEANOR. (*calming herself*) Well, I can't endure it now. It's too degrading. I have a right to your complete faith. (*Reaching over and grasping his hands—earnestly*) You know I have in your heart of hearts. You know that there can never be anyone but you. Forget the past. It wasn't us. For your peace—and mine, Michael!

CAPE. (*moved—pressing her hands*) All right. Let's stop. It's only that I've thought I've felt you drawing away—! Perhaps it's all my supersensitiveness— (*Patting her hand and forcing a smile*) Let's talk of something else. (*Cheerfully—after a pause*) You can't imagine how wonderful it's been up in the country. There's just enough winter in the air to make one energetic. No summer fools about. Solitude and work. I was happy—that is, as happy as I ever can be without you.

ELEANOR. (*withdrawing her hands from his with a quick movement—sarcastically*) Thanks for that afterthought—but do you expect me to believe it? When you're working I might die and you'd never know it.

CAPE. (*amused but irritated*) There you go! You denounce my jealousy, but it seems to me your brand of it is much more ridiculous.

ELEANOR. (*sharply*) You imagine I'm jealous of your work? You— you flatter yourself!

CAPE. (*stung—bitingly*) It's an unnatural passion certainly—in your case. And an extremely ungrateful passion, I might add!

ELEANOR. (*losing her temper completely*) You mean I ought to be grateful for— I suppose you think that without your work I— (*Springing to her feet*) Your egotism is making a fool of you! You're becoming so exaggeratedly conceited no one can stand you! Everyone notices it!

CAPE. (*angrily*) You know that's untrue. You only say it to be mean. As for my work, you've acknowledged a million times—

ELEANOR. If I have—but please remember there are other playwrights in the world!

CAPE. (*bitingly*) You were on the stage seven years before I met you. Your appearance in the work of other playwrights—you must admit you were anything but successful!

ELEANOR. (*with a sneer of rage*) And I suppose you were?

CAPE. Yes! Not in your commercial sense, perhaps, but—

ELEANOR. You're contemptible! You know that's the very last thing you can say of me. It was exactly because I wasn't that kind—because I was an artist—that I found it so hard!

CAPE. (*unheeding*) My plays had been written. The one you played in first was written three years before. The work was done. That's the proof.

ELEANOR. (*scathingly*) That's absurd! You know very well if it hadn't been for John, you—

CAPE. (*violently*) Nonsense! There were other managers who—

ELEANOR. They didn't want your work, you know it!

CAPE. (*enraged*) I see what you're driving at! You'd like to pretend I was as much dependent on John as you were! (*Trembling all over with the violence of his passion*) I should think you'd be ashamed to boast so brazenly—to me!—of what he had done for you!

ELEANOR. Why should I be ashamed of my gratitude?

CAPE. To drag that relationship out of the past and throw it in my face!

ELEANOR. (*very pale—tensely*) What relationship?

CAPE. (*incoherently, strangled by his passion*) Ask anyone! (*Then suddenly with anguished remorse*) No, no! I don't mean that! (*Torturedly*) Wounds! Wounds! For God's sake!

ELEANOR. (*trembling with rage*) I'll never forget you said that!

CAPE. (*stung—in a passion again at once*) Because I resent that man's being here—late at night—when I was away? Oh, I don't mean I suspect you—now—

ELEANOR. (*viciously*) What noble faith! Maybe you're going to discover I don't deserve it!

CAPE. (*unheeding*) But there was scandal enough about you and him, and if you had any respect for me—

ELEANOR. I've lost it now!

CAPE. You wouldn't deliberately open the way—

ELEANOR. (*tensely*) So you believe—that gutter gossip? You think I—? Then all these years you've really believed—? Oh, you mean hypocrite!

CAPE. (*stung—bitingly*) Don't act moral indignation! What else could I have thought? When we first fell in love, you confessed frankly you had had lovers—not John but others—

ELEANOR. (*brokenly—with mingled grief and rage*) I was an idiot! I should have lied to you! But I thought you'd understand—that I'd been searching for something—that I needed love—something I found in you! I tried to make you see—the truth—that those experiences had only made me appreciate you all the more when I found you! I told you how little these men had meant to me, that in the state of mind I had been in they had no significance either one way or the other, and that such an attitude is possible for a woman without her being low. I thought you understood. But you didn't, you're not big enough for that! (*With a wild ironical laugh*) Now I know why the women in your plays are so wooden! You ought to thank me for breathing life into them!

CAPE. (*furiously*) Good God, how dare you criticize creative work, you actress!

ELEANOR. (*violently*) You deny that I create—? Perhaps if I'd have children and a home, take up knitting—! (*She laughs wildly*) I'd be safe then, wouldn't I—reliable, guaranteed not to— (*Her face seems suddenly to congeal*) So you think that I was John's mistress—that I loved him—or do you believe I just sold myself?

CAPE. (*in agony*) No, no! For God's sake, not that! I may have thought you once loved—

ELEANOR. (*frozenly*) Well, it was—that—just that! When he first engaged me—I'd heard the gossip—I thought he expected—and I agreed with myself—it meant nothing to me one way or the other— nothing meant anything then but a chance to do my work—yes, I agreed—but you see he didn't, he didn't agree. He loved me but he saw I didn't love him—that way—and he's a finer man than you think!

CAPE. (*hoarsely*) You're lying! (*Bewilderedly*) I can't believe—

ELEANOR. (*fiercely*) Oh yes, you can! You want to! You do! And you're glad! It makes me lower than you thought, but you're glad to know it just the same! You're glad because now you can really believe that—nothing ever happened between us! (*She stares into his eyes and seems to read some confirmation of her statement there, for she cries with triumphant bitterness*) You can't deny it!

CAPE. (*wildly*) No! You devil, you, you read thoughts into my mind!

ELEANOR. (*with wild hysterical scorn*) It's true! How could I ever love you?

CAPE. (*clutching her in his arms fiercely*) You do! (*He kisses her frantically. For a moment she submits, appears even to return his kisses in spite of herself.* CAPE *cries triumphantly*) You do! (*She suddenly pushes him away and glares at him at arms' length. Her features are working convulsively. Her whole tortured face expresses an abysmal self-loathing, a frightful hatred for him.*)

ELEANOR. (*as if to herself—in a strangled voice*) No! You can't crush—me! (*Her face becomes deadly calm. She speaks with intense, cold hatred*) Don't kiss me. I love him. He was—my lover—here—when you were away!

CAPE. (*stares dumbly into her eyes for a long moment—hoarsely, in agony*) You lie! You only want to torture—

ELEANOR. (*deathly calm*) It's true! (CAPE *stares at her another second—then, with a snarl of fury like an animal's he seizes her about the throat with both hands. He chokes her, forcing her down to her knees. She does not struggle but continues to look into his eyes with the same defiant hate. At last he comes to himself with a shudder and steps away from her. She remains where she is, only putting out her hand on the floor to support herself.*)

CAPE. (*in a terrible state, sobbing with rage and anguish*) Gone! All our beauty gone! And you don't love him! You lie! You did this out of hatred for me! You dragged our ideal in the gutter—with delight! (*Wildly*) And you pride yourself you've killed it, do you, you actress, you barren soul? (*With savage triumph*) But I tell you only a creator can really destroy! (*With a climax of frenzy*) And I will! I will! I won't give your hatred the satisfaction of seeing our love live on in me—to torture me! I'll drag it lower than you! I'll stamp it into the vilest depths! I'll leave it dead! I'll murder it—and be free! (*Again he threatens her, his hands twitching back toward her neck—then he rushes out of the door as if furies were pursuing him, slamming it shut behind him.*)

274

ELEANOR. (*with a cry of despair*) Michael! (*She stops as hatred and rage overpower her again—leaps up and runs to the door—opens it and screams after him violently*) Go! Go! I'm glad! I hate you. I'll go, too! I'm free! I'll go— (*She turns and runs up the stairs. She disappears for a moment, then comes back with a hat and coat on and, hurrying down the stairs again, rushes out leaving the door open behind her.*)

CURTAIN

ACT TWO—SCENE ONE

LIBRARY. *A door is in the rear, toward right. A large couch facing front. On the wall, a framed portrait study of* ELEANOR.

At first the room is in darkness. As the curtain rises, JOHN *can be dimly distinguished sitting, bent over wearily, his shoulders bowed, his long arms resting on his knees, his hands dangling. He sits on the extreme edge in the exact middle of the big couch, and this heightens the sense of loneliness about him.*

Suddenly he stares as the sound of a motor comes from the driveway. The car is heard driving up; it stops before the front door; its door is slammed, it drives off; a ringing of the doorbell sounds from somewhere back in the house. JOHN *has gotten up, gone toward the door in the rear, exclaiming irritably as the bell continues to ring—* All right, damn it! Who the devil—? (*He is heard opening the front door —in blank amazement*) Nelly! (*Then her voice in a strained, hysterical pitch*) John, I— (*The rest is lost incoherently. Then his voice soothingly*) Come in! Come in. (*He follows her into the room. Her face is pale, distraught, desperate. She comes quickly to the couch and flings herself down in one corner. He stands nearby uncertainly, watching her. His face holds a confused mixture of alarm, tenderness, perplexity, passionate hope.*)

JOHN. You're trembling.

ELEANOR. (*with a startled movement*) No—I—I'm— (*A pause. He waits for her to speak, not knowing what to think. She gradually collects herself. Memory crowds back on her and her face twitches with pain which turns to hatred and rage. She becomes conscious of* JOHN's *eyes, forces this back, her face growing mask-like and determined. She looks up at* JOHN *and forces the words out slowly*) John—you said, if ever— You once said I might always come—

276

JOHN. (*his face lights up for a second with a joy that is incongruously savage—at once controlling this—simply*) Yes, Nelly.

ELEANOR. (*a bit brokenly now*) I hope—you meant that.

JOHN. (*simply*) Yes, I meant it.

ELEANOR. I mean—that you still mean it—?

JOHN. (*forcing an awkward smile*) Then—now—forever after, amen—any old time at all, Nelly. (*Then overcome by a rush of bewildered joy—stammering*) Why—you ought to know—!

ELEANOR. (*smiling tensely*) Would I still be welcome if I'd come—to stay?

JOHN. (*his voice quivering*) Nelly! (*He stares toward her, then stops—in a low, uncertain voice*) And Michael?

ELEANOR. (*with an exclamation of pain*) Don't! (*Quickly recovering herself—in a cold, hard voice*) That's—dead! (JOHN *lets a held-back breath of suspense escape him.* ELEANOR *stammers a bit hysterically*) Don't talk of him! I've forgotten—as if he'd never lived! Do you still love me? Do you? Then tell me! I must know someone—

JOHN. (*still uncertain, but coming nearer to her—simply*) You knew once. Since then— My God, you've guessed, haven't you?

ELEANOR. I need to hear. You've never spoken—for years—

JOHN. There was—Michael.

ELEANOR. (*wildly, putting her hands up to her ears as if to shut out the name*) Don't! (*Then, driven by a desperate determination, forces a twisted smile*) Why do you stand there? Are you afraid? I'm beginning to suspect—perhaps, you've only imagined—

JOHN. Nelly! (*He seizes one of her hands awkwardly and covers it with kisses—confusedly, with deep emotion*) I— You know— You know—

ELEANOR. (*with the same fixed smile*) You must put your arms around me—and kiss me—on the lips—

JOHN. (*takes her in his arms awkwardly and kisses her on the lips—with passionate incoherence*) Nelly! I'd given up hoping—I—I can't believe— (*She submits to his kisses with closed eyes, her face like a*

277

mask, her body trembling with revulsion. Suddenly he seems to sense something disharmonious—confusedly) But you—you don't care for me.

ELEANOR. (*still with closed eyes—dully*) Yes. (*With a spurt of desperate energy she kisses him wildly several times, then sinks back again closing her eyes*) I'm so tired, John—so tired!

JOHN. (*immediately all concern*) You're trembling all over. I'm an idiot not to have seen— Forgive me. (*He puts his hand on her forehead*) You're feverish. You'd better go to bed, young lady, right away. Come. (*He raises her to her feet.*)

ELEANOR. (*wearily*) Yes, I'm tired. (*Bitterly*) Oh, it's good to be loved by someone who is unselfish and kind—

JOHN. Ssshh! (*Forcing a joking tone*) I'm cast for the Doctor now. Doctor's orders: don't talk, don't think, sleep. Come, I'll show you your room.

ELEANOR. (*dully*) Yes. (*As if she were not aware of what she is doing, she allows him to lead her to the door at right, rear. There she suddenly starts as if awakening—frightenedly.*) Where are we going?

JOHN. (*with gentle bullying*) You're going upstairs to bed.

ELEANOR. (*with a shudder—incoherently*) No, no! Not now—no—wait—you must wait— (*Then calming herself and trying to speak matter-of-factly*) I'd rather stay up and sit with you.

JOHN. (*worriedly, but giving in to her at once*) All right. Whatever suits you. (*They go back. She sits in a chair. He puts a cushion in back of her*) How's that?

ELEANOR. (*with a wan, grateful smile*) You're so kind, John. You've always been kind. You're so different— (*She checks herself, her face growing hard.* JOHN *watches her. There is a long pause.*)

JOHN. (*finally—in a gentle tone*) Nelly, don't you think it'd help if you told me—everything that's happened?

ELEANOR. (*with a shudder*) No! It was all horror and disgust! (*Wildly resentful*) Why do you make me remember? I've come to you. Why do you ask for reasons? (*With a harsh laugh*) Are you jealous—of him?

JOHN. (*quietly*) I've always envied Michael.

ELEANOR. If you'd seen him tonight, you wouldn't envy him. He's mean and contemptible! He makes everything as low as he is! He went away threatening, boasting he'd— (*Hysterically*) Why do you make me think of him? I want to be yours! (*She throws herself into his arms.*)

JOHN. (*straining her to him—with awkward passion*) Nelly! (*Under his kisses her face again becomes mask-like, her body rigid, her eyes closed.* JOHN *suddenly grows aware of this. He stares down at her face, his own growing bewildered and afraid. He stammers*) Nelly! What is it?

ELEANOR. (*opening her eyes—in alarm*) What—?

JOHN. (*with a sigh of relief*) You gave me a scare. You were like a corpse.

ELEANOR. (*breaks away from him*) I—I believe I do feel ill. I'll go to bed. (*She moves toward the door.*)

JOHN. (*uneasily—with a forced heartiness*) Now you're talking sense. Come on. (*He leads the way into the hall. She goes as far as the doorway—then stops. A queer struggle is apparent in her face, her whole body, as if she were fighting with all her will to overcome some invisible barrier which bars her way.* JOHN *is watching her keenly now, a sad foreboding coming into his eyes. He steps past her back into the room, saying kindly but with a faint trace of bitterness*) It's the first door upstairs on your right—if you'd rather go alone. (*He walks still further away, then turns to watch her, his face growing more and more aware and melancholy.*)

ELEANOR. (*vaguely*) No—you don't understand— (*She stands swaying, reaching out her hand to the side of the doorway for support—dully*) The first door to the right—upstairs?

JOHN. Yes.

ELEANOR. (*struggles with herself, confused and impotent, trying to will—finally turns to* JOHN *like a forlorn child*) John. Can't you help me?

JOHN. (*gravely*) No—not now when I do understand. You must do it alone.

ELEANOR. (*with a desperate cry*) I can! I'm as strong as he! (*This breaks the spell which has chained her. She grows erect and strong. She walks through the doorway.*)

JOHN. (*with a triumphant exclamation of joy*) Ah! (*He strides toward the doorway—then stops as he notices that she also has stopped at the bottom of the stairs, one foot on the first stair, looking up at the top. Then she wavers and suddenly bolts back ino the room, gropingly, her face strained and frightened.* JOHN *questions her with fierce disappointment*) What is it? Why did you stop?

ELEANOR. (*forcing a twisted smile—wildly*) You're right. I must be feverish. (*Trying to control herself—self-mockingly*) Seeing spooks, that's pretty far gone, isn't it? (*Laughing hysterically*) Yes—I swear I saw him—standing at the head of the stairs waiting for me—just as he was standing when you knocked at our door, remember? (*She laughs*) Really, it was too ridiculous—so plain—

JOHN. Ssshh! (*glancing at her worriedly*) Won't you lie down here? Try and rest.

ELEANOR. (*allowing him to make her comfortable on the couch before the fire*) Yes. (*Her eyes glance up into his bewilderedly.*)

JOHN. (*after a long pause—slowly*) You don't love me, Nelly.

ELEANOR. (*pitifully protesting*) But I do, John! I do! You're kind! You're unselfish and fine!

JOHN. (*with a wry smile*) That isn't me.

ELEANOR. (*desperately defiant, leaps to her feet*) I do! (*She takes his face between her hands and bringing her own close to it stares into his eyes. He looks back into hers. She mutters fiercely between her clenched teeth*) I do! (*For a long moment they remain there, as she brings her face nearer and nearer striving with all her will to kiss him on the lips. Finally, her eyes falter, her body grows limp, she turns away and throws herself on the couch in a fit of abandoned sobbing.*)

JOHN. (*with a sad smile*) You see?

ELEANOR. (*her voice muffled—between sobs*) But I—want to! And I will—I know—some day—I promise!

JOHN. (*forcing a light tone*) Well, I'll be resigned to wait and hope then—and trust in your good intentions. (*After a pause—in a calming, serious tone*) You're calmer now? Tell me what happened between you and Michael.

ELEANOR. No! Please!

JOHN. (*smiling but earnestly*) It'll relieve your mind, Nelly—and besides, how can I help you otherwise?

ELEANOR. (*after a pause—with resigned dullness*) We've quarreled, but never like this before. This was final. (*She shudders—then suddenly bursts out wildly*) Oh, John, for God's sake don't ask me! I want to forget! We tore each other to pieces. I realized I hated him! I couldn't restrain my hate! I had to crush him as he was crushing me! (*After a pause—dully again*) And so that was the end.

JOHN. (*tensely, hoping again now—pleadingly*) You're sure, Nelly?

ELEANOR. (*fiercely*) I hate him!

JOHN. (*after a pause—earnestly*) Then stay here. I think I can help you forget. Never mind what people say. Make this your home— and maybe—in time— (*He forces a smile*) You see, I'm already starting to nurse along that crumb of hope you gave. (*She is looking down, preoccupied with her own thoughts. He looks at her embarrassedly, then goes on gently, timidly persuasive*) I don't mind waiting. I'm used to it. And I've been hoping ever since I first met you. (*Forcing a half laugh*) I'll admit when you married him the waiting and hoping seemed excess labor. I tried to fire them—thought I had—but when you came tonight—they were right onto the job again! (*He laughs—then catching himself awkwardly*) But hell! I don't want to bother you now. Forget me.

ELEANOR. (*in a bland, absent-minded tone which wounds him*) You're so kind, John. (*Then following her own line of thought, she*

281

breaks out savagely) I told him I'd been your mistress while he was away!

JOHN. (*amazed*) Nelly!

ELEANOR. I had to tell that lie! He was degrading me! I had to revenge myself!

JOHN. But certainly he could never believe—

ELEANOR. (*with fierce triumph*) Oh, I made him believe! (*Then dully*) He went away. He said he'd kill our love as I had—worse— (*With a twisted smile*) That's what he's doing now. He's gone to one of those women he lived with before— (*Laughing harshly*) No! They wouldn't be vile enough—for his beautiful revenge on me! He has a wonderful imagination. Everyone acknowledges that! (*She laughs with wild bitterness*) My God, why do I think—? Help me, John! Help me to forget.

JOHN. (*after a pause—with a sad, bitter helplessness*) You mean— help you—to revenge yourself! But don't you realize I can't—you can't because you still love him!

ELEANOR. (*fiercely*) No! (*After a pause—brokenly*) Don't! I know! (*She sobs heartbrokenly.*)

JOHN. (*after a pause, as her sobbing grows quieter—sadly*) Go home.

ELEANOR. No! (*After a pause, brokenly*) He'll never come back now.

JOHN. (*with a bitter humor*) Oh, yes he will; take my word for it. I know—because I happen to love you, too.

ELEANOR. (*faintly*) And do you—hate me?

JOHN. (*after a pause—with melancholy self-disgust*) No. I'm too soft. (*Bitterly*) I ought to hate you! Twice now you've treated my love with the most humiliating contempt— Once when you were willing to endure it as the price of a career—again tonight, when you try to give yourself to me out of hate for him! (*In sudden furious revolt*) Christ! What am I, eh? (*Then checking his anger and forcing a wry smile*) I think your treatment has been rather hard to take, Nelly—

and even now I'm not cured, at that! (*He laughs harshly and turns away to conceal his real hurt.*)

ELEANOR. (*with a deep grief*) Forgive me.

JOHN. (*as if to himself—reassuringly*) Still—I'd have been the poorest slave. I couldn't have fought you like Michael. Perhaps, deep down, I'm glad— (*Then bluntly*) You'd better go home right away.

ELEANOR. (*dully*) Even if he—

JOHN. (*brusquely*) No matter what! Face the truth in yourself. Must you—or mustn't you?

ELEANOR. (*after a moment's defiant struggle with herself—forlornly*) Yes. (*After a pause, with a gesture toward the door and a weary, beaten smile*) Upstairs—if I could have gone—I might have been free. But he's trained me too well in his ideal. (*Then shrugging her shoulders, fatalistically*) It's broken me. I'm no longer anything. So what does it matter how weak I am? (*A slight pause*) I begin to know —something. (*With a sudden queer, exultant pride*) My love for him is my own, not his! That he can never possess! It's *my* own. It's *my* life! (*She turns to* JOHN *determinedly*) I must go home now.

JOHN. (*wonderingly*) Good. I'll drive you back. (*He starts for the door.*)

ELEANOR. (*suddenly grasping his arm*) Wait. (*Affectionately*) I was forgetting you—as usual. What can I do—?

JOHN. (*with a wry smile*) Study your part; help Michael; and we'll all three be enormously successful! (*He laughs mockingly.*)

ELEANOR. (*tenderly*) I'll always believe Fate should have let me love you, instead.

JOHN. (*with the same wry smile*) While I begin to suspect that in a way I'm lucky—to be heartbroken. (*With a laugh*) Curtain! You'll want to go upstairs and powder your nose. There's no angel with a flaming sword there now, is there? (*He points to the doorway.*)

ELEANOR. (*with a tired smile*) No. (*She goes to the doorway. He follows her. They both stop there for a moment instinctively and smile forlornly at each other.*)

JOHN. (*impulsively*) That time you stood here and called to me for help—if I could have given you a push, mental, moral, physical—?

ELEANOR. It wouldn't have helped. The angel was here. (*She touches her breast.*)

JOHN. (*with a sigh*) Thanks. That saves me a life-long regret.

ELEANOR. (*earnestly—gripping his right hand in hers and holding his eyes*). There must be no regrets—between old friends.

JOHN. (*gripping her hand in turn*) No, I promise, Nelly. (*Then letting her hand drop and turning away to conceal his emotion—forcing a joking tone*) After all, friendship is sounder, saner—more in the picture for my type, eh?

ELEANOR. (*absent-mindedly again now—vaguely*) I don't know. (*Then briskly*) We must hurry. I'll be right down. (*She goes out and up the stairway in the hall.*)

JOHN. (*Stares up after her for a second, then smiling grimly*) Well, business of living on as usual. (*He walks out, calling up the stairs*) I'm going to get the car, Nelly.

CURTAIN

ACT TWO—SCENE TWO

A BEDROOM. *In the rear, center, a door. A chair to left of door. In the left corner, a washstand. In the left wall, center, a small window with a torn dark shade pulled down. On the right, a bed. Ugly wall-paper, dirty, stained, criss-crossed with match-strokes.*

When the curtain rises, the room is in darkness except for a faint glow on the window shade from some street lamp. Then the door is opened and a woman's figure is silhouetted against the dim, yellow light of a hall. She turns and speaks to someone who is following her. Her voice is heavy and slow with the strong trace of a foreign intona-

*tion, although the words are clearly enough defined. A man's figure
appears behind hers. The* WOMAN *is fairly young. Her face, rouged,
powdered, penciled, is broad and stupid. Her small eyes have a glazed
look. Yet she is not ugly—rather pretty for her bovine, stolid type—
and her figure is still attractive although its movements just now are
those of a tired scrubwoman. She takes off her coat, hangs it on a
hook, and removes her hat.*

The man is MICHAEL. *He is bare-headed, his hair disheveled, his eyes
wild, his face has a feverish, mad expression. He stands in the doorway
watching each movement of the* WOMAN's *with an unnatural preoccupied concentration.*)

WOMAN. (*having removed her hat and put it on the washstand, turns
to him impatiently*) Ain't you comin' in? (*He starts and nods stupidly, moving his lips as if answering but not making a sound*) Come
in! Shut the door. (*He does so and locks it mechanically—then looks
from her around the room with a frightened, puzzled glance as if he
were aware of his surroundings for the first time.*)

WOMAN. (*forcing a trade smile—with an attempt at lightness*) Well,
here we are, dearie. (*Then with a sigh of physical weariness as she sits
on the side of the bed*) Gawd, I'm tired! My feet hurt fierce! I been
walkin' miles. I got corns, too. (*She sighs again, this time with a sort
of restful content*) It's good 'n' warm in this dump, I'll hand it that.
(*A pause*) I'd gave up hope and was beatin' it home when you come
along. (*A pause during which she takes him in calculatingly*) How'd
you lose your hat? (*He starts, passes a trembling hand through his
hair bewilderedly but does not answer. A pause—then the* WOMAN
sighs and yawns wearily—bored) Can't you say nothin'? You was
full enough of bull when you met me. Gawd, I thought you'd get us
both pinched. You acted like you was crazy. Remember kissing me
on the corner with a whole mob pipin' us off?

CAPE. (*with a start—evidently answering some train of thought in his mind—with a wild laugh*) Remember? (*He sinks on the chair with his head in his hands. There is a pause.*)

WOMAN. (*insinuatingly*) Goin' to stay all night? (*He glances up at her stupidly but doesn't answer. The* WOMAN *insists dully*) Say, you got ear-muffs on? I ast you, d'you wanta stay all night?

CAPE. (*after a moment's groping, nods emphatically again and again, swallowing hard several times as if he were striving to get control of his voice—finally blurts out in a tone of desperation*) Yes—yes—of course!— Where else would I go?

WOMAN. Home. (*Indifferently*) That's where most of 'em goes—afterwards.

CAPE. (*with a sudden burst of wild laughter*) Ha-ha-ha. Home! Is that your private brand of revenge—to go with men with homes? I congratulate you! (*He laughs to himself with bitter irony—then suddenly deadly calm*) Yes, I have a home, come to think of it—from now on Hell is my home! I suspect we're fellow-citizens. (*He laughs.*)

WOMAN. (*superstitiously*) You oughtn't to say them things.

CAPE. (*with dull surprise*) Why?

WOMAN. Somep'n might happen. (*A pause*) Don't you believe in no God?

CAPE. I believe in the devil!

WOMAN. (*frightened*) Say! (*Then after a pause, forcing a smile*) I'm wise to what's wrong with you. You been lappin' up some bum hooch.

CAPE. (*jerkily*) No. I'm not drunk. I thought of that—but it's evasion. (*Wildly*) And I must be conscious—fully conscious, do you understand? I will this as a symbol of release—of the end of all things! (*He stops, shuddering. She looks at him stolidly. A pause. He presses his hands to his forehead*) Stop thinking, damn you! (*Then after a pause—dully*) How long—? What time is it?

WOMAN. Little after two, I guess.

CAPE. (*amazed*) Only that? (*She nods*) Only two hours—? (*A pause*) I remember streets—lights—dead faces— Then you—your face

286

alone was alive for me, alive with my deliverance! That was why I kissed you.

WOMAN. (*looking up at him queerly*) Say, you talk nutty. Been dopin' up on coke, I bet you.

CAPE. (*with an abrupt exclamation*) Ha! (*He stares at her with unnatural intensity*) You seem to take it quite casually that men must be either drunk or doped—otherwise—! Marvelous! You,—you're the last depth— (*With a strange, wild exultance, leaps to his feet*) You're my salvation! You have the power—and the right—to murder love! You can satisfy hate! Will you let me kiss you again? (*He strides over to her.*)

WOMAN. (*in a stupid state of bewilderment, feeling she has been insulted but not exactly knowing by what or how to resent it—angrily, pushing him away*) No! Get away from me! (*Then afraid she may lose his trade by this rebuff*) Aw, all right. Sure you can. (*Making a tremendous visible effort he kisses her on the lips, then shrinks back with a shudder and forces a harsh laugh. She stares at him and mutters resentfully*) On'y don't get so fresh, see? I don't like your line of talk. (*He slumps down on the chair again, sunk in a somber stupor. She watches him. She yawns. Finally she asks insinuatingly*) Ain't you gettin' sleepy?

CAPE. (*starting—with wild scorn*) Do you think I—! (*Staring at her*) Oh—I see—you mean, what did I come here for?

WOMAN. (*in same tone*) It's gettin' late.

CAPE. (*dully, with no meaning to his question—like an automaton*) A little after two?

WOMAN. Yes. (*She yawns*) You better let me go to bed and come yourself.

CAPE. (*again staring at her with strange intensity—suddenly with a queer laugh*) How long have you and I been united in the unholy bonds of—bedlock? (*He chuckles sardonically at his own play on words.*)

WOMAN. (*with a puzzled grin*) Say!

CAPE. Ten thousand years—about—isn't it? Or twenty? Don't you remember?

WOMAN. (*keeping her forced grin*) Tryin' to kid me, ain't you?

CAPE. Don't lie about your age! You were beside the cradle of love, and you'll dance dead drunk on its grave!

WOMAN. I'm only twenty-six, honest.

CAPE. (*with a wild laugh*) A fact! You're right. Thoughts keep alive. Only facts kill—deeds! (*He starts to his feet*) Then hate will let me alone. Love will be dead. I'll be as ugly as the world. My dreams will be low dreams. I'll "lay me down among the swine." Will you promise me this, you?

WOMAN. (*vaguely offended—impatiently*) Sure, I'll promise anything. (*She gets up to start undressing. She has been pulling the pins out of her hair and, as she rises, it falls over her shoulders in a peroxided flood. She turns to him, smiling with childish pride*) D'you like my hair, kid? I got a lot of it, ain't I?

CAPE. (*laughing sardonically*) "O love of mine, let down your hair and I will make my shroud of it."

WOMAN. (*coquettishly pleased*) What's that—po'try? (*Then suddenly reminded of something she regards him calculatingly—after a pause, coldly*) Say, you ain't broke, are you? Is that what's troubling you?

CAPE. (*startled—then with bitter mockery*) Ha! I see you're a practical person. (*He takes a bill from his pocket and holds it out to her—contemptuously*) Here!

WOMAN. (*stares from the bill to him, flushing beneath her rouge*) Say! I don't like the way you act. (*Proudly*) I don't take nothin' for nothin'—not from you, see!

CAPE. (*surprised and ashamed*) I'll leave it here, then. (*He puts it on top of the washstand and turns to her—embarrassedly*) I didn't mean—to offend you.

WOMAN. (*her face clearing immediately*) Aw, never mind. It's all right.

CAPE. (*staring at her intently—suddenly deeply moved*) Poor woman!

WOMAN. (*stung—excitedly*) Hey, none of that! Nix! Cut it out! I don't stand for that from nobody! (*She sits down on the bed angrily.*)

CAPE. (*with unnatural intensity*) Do you know what you are? You're a symbol. You're all the tortures man inflicts on woman—and you're the revenge of woman! You're love revenging itself upon itself! You're the suicide of love—of my love—of all love since the world began! (*Wildly*) Listen to me! Two hours ago— (*Then he beats his head with both clenched hands—distractedly*) Leave me alone! Leave me alone, damn you! (*He flings himself on the chair in a violent outburst of dry sobbing.*)

WOMAN. (*bewilderedly*) Say! Say! (*Then touched, she comes to him and puts her arms around his shoulders, on the verge of tears herself*) Aw, come on, kid. Quit it. It's all right. Everything's all right, see. (*As his sobbing grows quieter—helpfully*) Say, maybe you ain't ate nothin', huh? Maybe soup'd fix you. S'posin' I go round the corner, huh? Sure, all I got to do is put up my hair—

CAPE. (*controlling hysterical laughter—huskily*) No—thanks. (*Then his bitter memories rush back agonizingly. He stammers wildly*) She confessed! She was proud of her hate! She was proud of my torture. She screamed: "I'll go too." Go where? Did she go? Yes, she must—! Oh, my God! Stop! Stop! (*He springs up, his face distorted, and clutches the* WOMAN *fiercely in his arms*) Save me, you! Help me to kill! Help me to gain peace! (*He kisses her again and again frenziedly. She submits stolidly. Finally with a groan he pushes her away, shuddering with loathing, and sinks back on the chair*) No! I can't—I can't!

WOMAN. (*wiping her lips with the back of her hand—a vague comprehension coming into her face—scornfully*) Huh! I got a hunch now what's eatin' you. (*Then with a queer sort of savage triumph*) Well, I'm glad one of youse guys got paid back like you oughter!

CAPE. (*with dull impotent rage*) I can't! I can't. I'm the weaker. Our love must live on in me. There's no death for it. There's no freedom—while I live. (*Struck by a sudden thought*) Then, why—? (*A pause*) An end of loathing—no wounds, no memories—sleep!

WOMAN. (*with a shudder*) Say, you're beginning to give me the creeps.

CAPE. (*startled—with a forced laugh*) Am I? (*He shakes his head as if to drive some thought from his mind and forces a trembling, mocking smile*) That's over. The great temptation, isn't it? I suppose you've known it. But also the great evasion. Too simple for the complicated,—too weak for the strong, too strong for the weak. One must go on, eh?—even wounded, on one's knees—if only out of curiosity to see what will happen—to oneself. (*He laughs harshly and turns with a quick movement toward the door*) Well, good-by, and forgive me. It isn't you, you know. You're the perfect death—but I'm too strong, or weak—and I can't, you understand—can't! So, good-by. (*He goes to the door.*)

WOMAN. (*frightenedly*) Say! What're you goin' to do?

CAPE. Go on in the dark.

WOMAN. You better beat it home, that's what.

CAPE. (*violently*) No!

WOMAN. (*wearily*) Aw, forget it. She's your wife, ain't she?

CAPE. How do you know? (*He comes back to her, curiously attracted.*)

WOMAN. (*cynically*) Aw, I'm wise. Stick to her, see? You'll get over it. You can get used to anything, take it from me!

CAPE. (*in anguish*) Don't! But it's true—it's the insult we all swallow as the price of life. (*Rebelliously*) But I—!

WOMAN. (*with a sort of forlorn chuckle*) Oh, you'll go back aw right! Don't kid yourself. You'll go back no matter what, and you'll loin to like it. Don't I know? You love her, don't you? Well, then! There's no use buckin' that game. Go home. Kiss and make up.

Ferget it! It's easy to ferget—when you got to! (*She finishes up with a cynical, weary scorn.*)

CAPE. (*very pale—stammering*) You—you make life despicable.

WOMAN. (*angrily*) Say! (*Then with groping, growing resentment*) I don't like your talk! You've pulled a lot of bum cracks about—about—never mind, I got you, anyhow! You ain't got no right—What'd you wanter pick me up for, anyway? Wanter just get me up here to say rotten things? Wanter use me to pay her back? Say! Where do I come in? Guys go with me 'cause they like my looks, see?—what I am, understand?—but you, you don't want nothin'. You ain't drunk, neither! You just don't like me. And you was beatin' it leavin' your money there—without nothin'. I was goin' to let you then. I ain't now. (*She suddenly gives him a furious push which sends him reeling back against the wall*) G'wan! Take your lousy coin and beat it! I wouldn't take nothin', nor have nothin' to do with you if you was to get down on your knees!

CAPE. (*stares at her—an expression comes as if he were seeing her for the first time—with great pity*) So—it still survives in you. They haven't killed it—that lonely life of one's own which suffers in solitude. (*Shame-facedly*) I should have known. Can you forgive me?

WOMAN. (*defensively*) No!

CAPE. Through separate ways love has brought us both to this room. As one lonely human being to another, won't you—?

WOMAN. (*struggling with herself—harshly*) No!

CAPE. (*gently*) Not even if I ask it on my knees? (*He kneels before her, looking up into her face.*)

WOMAN. (*bewildered, with hysterical fierceness*) No! Git up, you—! Don't do that, I tell you! Git up or I'll brain yuh! (*She raises her fist threateningly over his head.*)

CAPE. (*gently*) Not until you—

WOMAN. (*exhaustedly*) Aw right—aw right—I forgive—

CAPE. (*gets up and takes her face between his hands and stares into her eyes—then he kisses her on the forehead*) Sister.

WOMAN. (*with a half sob*) Nix! Lay off of me, can't you?

CAPE. But I learned that from you.

WOMAN. (*stammering*) What?—loined what? (*She goes away from him and sinks on the bed exhaustedly*) Say, you better beat it.

CAPE. I'm going. (*He points to the bill on the washstand*) You need this money. You'll accept it from me now, won't you?

WOMAN. (*dully*) Sure. Leave it there.

CAPE. (*in the same gentle tone*) You'll have to give it to him in the morning?

WOMAN. (*dully*) Sure.

CAPE. All of it?

WOMAN. Sure.

CAPE. Or he'd beat you?

WOMAN. Sure. (*Then suddenly grinning*) Maybe he'll beat me up, anyway—just for the fun of it.

CAPE. But you love him, don't you?

WOMAN. Sure. I'm lonesome.

CAPE. Yes. (*After a slight pause*) Why did you smile when you said he'd beat you, anyway?

WOMAN. I was thinkin' of the whole game. It's funny, ain't it?

CAPE. (*slowly*) You mean—life?

WOMAN. Sure. You got to laugh, ain't you? You got to loin to like it!

CAPE. (*this makes an intense impression on him. He nods his head several times*) Yes! That's it! That's exactly it! That goes deeper than wisdom. To learn to love life—to accept it and be exalted—that's the one faith left to us! (*Then with a tremulous smile*) Good-by. I've joined your church. I'm going home.

WOMAN. (*with a grin that is queerly affectionate*) Sure. That's the stuff. Close your eyes and your feet'll take you there.

CAPE. (*impressed again*) Yes! Yes! Of course they would! They've been walking there for thousands of years—blindly. However, now, I'll keep my eyes open—(*he smiles back at her affectionately*)—and learn to like it!

WOMAN. (*grinning*) Sure. Good luck.

CAPE. Good-by. (*He goes out, closing the door after him. She stares at the door listening to his footsteps as they die out down the stairs.*)

WOMAN. (*confusedly*) Say—?

CURTAIN

ACT THREE

SCENE—*Same as Act One.* ELEANOR *is standing by the table, leaning her back against it, facing the door, her whole attitude strained, expectant but frightened, tremblingly uncertain whether to run and hide from, or run forward and greet* CAPE, *who is standing in the doorway. For a long, tense moment they remain fixed, staring into each other's eyes with an apprehensive questioning. Then, as if unconsciously, falteringly, with trembling smiles, they come toward each other. Their lips move as if they were trying to speak. When they come close, they instinctively reach out their hands in a strange conflicting gesture of a protective warding off and at the same time a seeking possession. Their hands clasp and they again stop, searching each other's eyes. Finally their lips force out words.*

ELEANOR. (*penitently*) Michael!

CAPE. (*humbly*) Nelly! (*They smile with a queer understanding, their arms move about each other, their lips meet. They seem in a forgetful, happy trance at finding each other again. They touch each other testingly as if each cannot believe the other is really there. They act for the moment like two persons of different races, deeply in love but separated by a barrier of language.*)

ELEANOR. (*rambling tenderly*) Michael—I— I was afraid—

CAPE. (*stammeringly*) Nelly—it's no good!—I thought— (*They stare at each other—a pause.*)

ELEANOR. (*beginning to be aware—a bit bewilderedly, breaking away from him with a little shiver—stupidly*) I feel—there's a draught, isn't there?

CAPE. (*becoming aware in his turn—heavily*) I'll shut the door. (*He goes and does so. She walks to her chair and sits down. He comes and sits beside her. They are now side by side as in Act One. A pause.*

They stare ahead, each frowningly abstracted. Then each, at the same moment, steals a questioning side glance at the other. Their eyes meet, they look away, then back, they stare at each other with a peculiar dull amazement, recognition yet non-recognition. They seem about to speak, then turn away again. Their faces grow sad, their eyes begin to suffer, their bodies become nervous and purposeless. Finally CAPE *exclaims with a dull resentment directed not at her but at life*) What is—it? (*He makes a gesture of repulsing something before him.*)

ELEANOR. (*in his tone*) I don't know.

CAPE. (*harshly*) A moment ago—there— (*He indicates where they had stood in an embrace*) We knew everything. We understood!

ELEANOR. (*eagerly*) Oh, yes!

CAPE. (*bitterly*) Now—we must begin to think—to continue going on, getting lost—

ELEANOR. (*sadly*) It was happy to forget. Let's not think—yet.

CAPE. (*grimly*) We've begun. (*Then with a harsh laugh*) Thinking explains. It eliminates the unexplainable—by which we live.

ELEANOR. (*warningly*) By which we love. Sssh! (*A pause.*)

CAPE. (*wonderingly—not looking at her*) You have learned that, too?

ELEANOR. (*with a certain exultance*) Oh, yes, Michael—yes! (*She clasps his hand. A pause. Then she murmurs*) Now—we know peace. (*Their hands drop apart. She sighs.*)

CAPE. (*slowly*) Peace isn't our meaning.

ELEANOR. (*suddenly turns and addresses him directly in a sad, sympathetic tone*) You've something you want to ask me, Michael?

CAPE. (*turns to her with an immediate affirmative on his lips, checks it as he meets her eyes, turns away—a pause—then he turns back humbly*) No.

ELEANOR. (*her head has been averted since he turned away—without looking at him*) Yes.

CAPE. (*decisively*) No, Nelly. (*She still keeps her head averted.*

295

After a pause he asks simply) Why? Is there something you want to ask me?

ELEANOR. No. (*After a pause—with a trace of bitter humor*) I can't be less magnanimous than you, can I?

CAPE. Then there is something—?

ELEANOR. Haven't you something you want to tell?

CAPE. (*looks at her. Their eyes meet again*) Yes—the truth—if I can. And you?

ELEANOR. Yes, I wish to tell you the truth. (*They look into each other's eyes. Suddenly she laughs with a sad self-mockery*) Well, we've both been noble. I haven't asked you; you haven't asked me; and yet— (*She makes a helpless gesture with her hands. A pause. Then abruptly and mechanically*) I'll begin at the beginning. I left here right after you did.

CAPE. (*with an involuntary start*) Oh! (*He checks himself.*)

ELEANOR. (*her eyes reading his—after a pause—a bit dryly*) You thought I'd stayed here all the time? (*Mockingly*) Waiting for you?

CAPE. (*wounded*) Don't! (*After a pause—painfully*) When I found you—perhaps I hoped—

ELEANOR. (*dully*) I had only been back a few minutes. (*After a pause*) Was that why you seemed so happy—there—? (*She points to the spot where they had stood embraced.*)

CAPE. (*indignantly*) No, no! Don't think that! I'm not like that—not any more! (*Without looking at her he reaches out and clasps her hand.*)

ELEANOR. (*looks at him—after a pause, understandingly*) I'm sorry—

CAPE. (*self-defensively*) Of course, I knew you must have gone, you'd have been a fool to stay. (*Excitedly*) And it doesn't matter—not a damn! I've gotten beyond that.

ELEANOR. (*misunderstanding—coldly*) I'm glad. (*A pause. She asks coldly*) Shall I begin again?

CAPE. (*struggling with himself—disjointedly*) No—not unless—I don't need— I've changed. That doesn't matter. I— (*With a sudden twisted grin*) I'm learning to like it, you see.

ELEANOR. (*looks at him, strangely impressed—a pause—slowly*) I think I know what you mean. We're both learning.

CAPE. (*wonderingly*) You—? (*She has turned away from him. He turns to stare at her.*)

ELEANOR. (*after a pause, taking up her story matter-of-factly*) I went to John.

CAPE. (*trying with agony to take this stoically—mumbling stupidly*) Yes—of course—I supposed—

ELEANOR. (*in the same mechanical tone*) He drove me back here in his car. He predicted you'd be back any moment, so he went right home again.

CAPE. (*a wild, ironical laugh escapes his control*) Shrewd—Ha!

ELEANOR. (*after a pause—rebukingly*) John is a good man.

CAPE. (*startled, turns and stares at her averted face—then miserably humble, stammers*) Yes, yes—I know—I acknowledge—good— (*He breaks down, cursing pitiably at himself*) God damn you!

ELEANOR. Oh!

CAPE. Not you! Me! (*Then he turns to her—with fierce defiance*) I love John!

ELEANOR. (*moved, without looking at him, reaches and clasps his hand*) That—is fine, Michael. (*A pause.*)

CAPE. (*begins to frown somberly—lets go of her hand*) It's hard— after what you confessed—

ELEANOR. (*frightenedly*) Ssshh! (*Then calmly*) That was a lie. I lied to make you suffer more than you were making me suffer. (*A pause—then she turns to him*) Can you believe this?

CAPE. (*humbly*) I want to believe—

ELEANOR. (*immediately turning away—significantly*) Oh!

CAPE. (*fiercely as if to himself*) I will believe! But what difference does it make—believing or not believing? I've changed, I tell you! I accept!

ELEANOR. I can't be a lie you live with!

CAPE. (*turning to her resentfully*) Well, then— (*As if she were goading him to something against his will—threateningly*) Shall I tell you what happened to me?

ELEANOR. (*facing him defiantly*) Yes. (*He turns away. Immediately her brave attitude crumbles. She seems about to implore him not to speak.*)

CAPE. (*after a pause—hesitatingly*) You said that years ago you had offered yourself—to him— (*He turns suddenly—hopefully*) Was that a lie, too?

ELEANOR. No.

CAPE. (*turns away with a start of pain*) Ah. (*A pause. Suddenly his face grows convulsed. He turns back to her, overcome by a craving for revenge—viciously*) Then I may as well tell you I— (*He checks himself and turns away.*)

ELEANOR. (*defensively—with feigned indifference*) I don't doubt—you kept your threat.

CAPE. (*glares at her wildly*) Oho, you don't doubt that, do you? You saw I'd changed, eh?

ELEANOR. I saw—something.

CAPE. (*with bitter irony*) God! (*A pause.*)

ELEANOR. (*turning on him doggedly as if she were impersonally impelled to make the statement*) I want to tell you that tonight—John and I—nothing you may ever suspect— (*She falters, turns away with a bitter smile*) I only tell you this for my own satisfaction. I don't expect you to believe it.

CAPE. (*with a wry grin*) No. How could you? (*Then turning to her—determinedly—after a pause*) But it doesn't matter.

ELEANOR. I wanted revenge as much as you. I wanted to destroy—and be free of you forever! (*After a pause—simply*) I couldn't.

CAPE. (*turns and stares at her—a pause—then he asks wonderingly, eagerly*) Why couldn't you? Tell me that.

ELEANOR. (*simply*) Something stronger.

CAPE. (*with a passionate triumph*) Love! (*With intense pleading*) Nelly! Will you believe that I, too—? (*He tries to force her eyes to return to his.*)

ELEANOR. (*after a pause—looking before her—sadly*) You shouid have been generous sooner.

CAPE. It's the truth, Nelly! (*Desperately*) I swear to you—!

ELEANOR. (*after a pause—wearily*) We've sworn to so much.

CAPE. Everything is changed, I tell you! Something extraordinary happened to me—a revelation!

ELEANOR. (*with bitter cynicism*) A woman?

CAPE. (*wounded, turns away from her*) Don't. (*Then after a pause —with deep feeling*) Yes—she was a woman. And I had thought of her only as revenge—the lowest of the low!

ELEANOR. (*with a shudder*) Ah!

CAPE. Don't judge, Nelly. She was—good!

ELEANOR. Not her! You!

CAPE. (*desperately*) I tell you I—! (*He checks himself helplessly. She gives no sign. Then he asks sadly*) If you can think that, how could you come back?

ELEANOR. (*stammering hysterically*) How? How! (*Bursting into tears*) Because I love you!

CAPE. (*starting up from his chair and trying to take her in his arms— exultantly*) Nelly!

ELEANOR. (*pushing him away—violently*) No! I didn't come back to you! It conquered me, not you! Something in me—mine—not you! (*She stares him in the eyes defiantly, triumphantly.*)

CAPE. (*gently*) It doesn't matter. (*After a pause*) Did I come back to you?

ELEANOR. (*taken aback, turning away*) No, I suppose— (CAPE *stares at her uncertainly, then sits down in his chair again.*)

CAPE. (*after a pause, looking before him—assertively, as if taking a pledge*) But I have faith!

ELEANOR. (*wearily*) Now—for a moment.

CAPE. No!

ELEANOR. Yes. We'll believe—and disbelieve. We are—that.

CAPE. (*protesting*) Nelly! (*For a time they both sit staring bleakly before them. Suddenly he turns to her—desperately*) If there's nothing left but—resignation!—what use is there? How can we endure having our dream perish in this?

ELEANOR. Have we any choice?

CAPE. (*intensely—he seems to collect all his forces and turns on her with a fierce challenge*) We can choose—an end!

ELEANOR. (*shudders instinctively as she reads his meaning*) Michael! (*A pause—then looking into his eyes—as a calm counter-challenge*) Yes—if *you* wish.

CAPE. (*with passionate self-scorn*) We! We have become ignoble.

ELEANOR. As *you* wish. (*She again accents the you.*)

CAPE. I?

ELEANOR. I accept. (*A pause—gently*) You must not suffer too much. (*She reaches out her hand and clasps his comfortingly*) It's I who have changed most, Michael. (*Then she speaks sadly but firmly as if she had come to a decision*) There's only one way we can give life to each other.

CAPE. (*sharply*) How?

ELEANOR. By releasing each other.

CAPE. (*with a harsh laugh*) Are you forgetting we tried that once tonight?

ELEANOR. With hate. This would be because we loved.

CAPE. (*violently*) Don't be a fool! (*Controlling himself—forcing a smile*) Forgive me. (*Excitedly*) But, my God, what solution—?

ELEANOR. It will give you peace for your work—freedom—

CAPE. Nonsense!

ELEANOR. I'll still love you. I'll work for you! We'll no longer stand between one another. Then I can really give you my soul—

CAPE. (*controlling himself with difficulty*) You're talking rot!

ELEANOR. (*hurt*) Michael!

CAPE. (*suddenly glaring at her suspiciously*) Why did you come back? Why do you want to go? What are you hiding behind all·this?

ELEANOR. (*wounded*) Your faith? You see?

CAPE. (*brokenly*) I—I didn't mean— (*Then after a struggle—with desperate bitterness*) Well—I accept! Go—if you want to!

ELEANOR. (*hurt*) Michael! It isn't— (*Then determinedly*) But even if you misunderstand, I must be strong for you!

CAPE. (*almost tauntingly*) Then go now—if you're strong enough. (*Harshly*) Let me see you act nobility! (*Then suddenly remorseful, catching her hand and covering it with kisses*) No! Go now before— Be strong! Be free! I—I can't!

ELEANOR. (*brokenly*) We can try— (*She bends down swiftly and kisses his head, turns away quickly*) Good-by.

CAPE. (*in a strangled voice*) Good-by. (*He sits in anguish, in a tortured restraint. She grabs her cloak from the chair, goes quickly to the door, puts her hand on the knob—then stops as tense as he. Suddenly he can stand it no longer, he leaps to his feet and jumps toward the door with a pleading cry*) Nelly! (*He stands fixed as he sees her before the door as if he had expected to find her gone. She does not turn but remains staring at the door in front of her. Finally she raises her hand and knocks on the door softly—then stops to listen.*)

ELEANOR. (*in a queer far-away voice*) No. Never again "come out." (*She opens the door and turns to CAPE with a strange smile*) It opens inward, Michael. (*She closes it again, smiles to herself and walks back to the foot of the stairway. Then she turns to face CAPE. She looks full of some happy certitude. She smiles at him and speaks with a tender weariness*) It must be nearly dawn. I'll say good-night instead of good-by. (*They stare into each other's eyes. It is as if now by a sudden flash from within they recognized themselves, shorn of all the ideas, attitudes, cheating gestures which constitute the vanity of personality. Everything, for this second, becomes simple for them—*

301

serenely unquestionable. It becomes impossible that they should ever deny life, through each other, again.)

ELEANOR. (*with a low tender cry as if she were awakening to maternity*) Michael!

CAPE. (*passionately sure of her now—in a low voice*) Nelly! (*Then unable to restrain his triumphant exultance*) You've failed!

ELEANOR. (*smiling dimly at herself*) My acting—didn't convince me.

CAPE. We've failed!

ELEANOR. Are we weak? (*Dreamily*) I'm happy.

CAPE. Strong! We can live again! (*Exultantly—but as if testing her, warningly*) But we'll hate!

ELEANOR. (*in her same tone*) Yes!

CAPE. And we'll torture and tear, and clutch for each other's souls!—fight—fail and hate again—(*he raises his voice in aggressive triumph*) but!—fail *with pride*—with joy!

ELEANOR. (*exalted by his exultation rather than by his words*) Yes!

CAPE. *Our* life is to bear together our burden which is our goal—on and up! Above the world, beyond its vision—our meaning!

ELEANOR. (*her eyes fixed on him—dreamily*) Your dream!

CAPE. (*half-sobbing as the intensity of his passion breaks the spell of his exultation*) Oh, Nelly, Nelly, I want to say so much what I feel but I can only stutter like an idiot! (*He has fallen on his knees before her.*)

ELEANOR. (*intensely moved—passionately*) I know! (*She bends over and kisses him.*)

CAPE. (*straining passionately for expression*) Listen! Often I wake up in the night—in a black world, alone in a hundred million years of darkness. I feel like crying out to God for mercy because life lives! Then instinctively I seek you—my hand touches you! You are there—beside me—alive—with you I become a whole, a truth! Life guides me back through the hundred million years to you. It reveals a beginning in unity that I may have faith in the unity of the end! (*He bows his head and kisses her feet ecstatically*) I love you! Forgive me all I've ever done, all I'll ever do.

ELEANOR. (*brokenly*) No. Forgive me—my child, you! (*She begins to sob softly:*)

CAPE. (*looking at her—gently*) Why do you cry?

ELEANOR. Because I'm happy. (*Then with a sudden tearful gaiety*) You be happy! You ought to be! Isn't our future as hard as you could wish? Haven't we your old dreams back again?

CAPE. Deeper and more beautiful!

ELEANOR. (*smiling*) Deeper and more beautiful! (*She ascends the stairs slowly*) Come! (*She reaches the top of the stairway and stands there looking down at him—then stretches out her arms with a passionate, tender gesture*) Come!

CAPE. (*leaping to his feet—intensely*) My own!

ELEANOR. (*with deep, passionate tenderness*) My lover!

CAPE. My wife! (*His eyes fixed on her he ascends. As he does so her arms move back until they are stretched out straight to right and left, forming a cross.* CAPE *stops two steps below her—in a low, wondering tone*) Why do you stand like that?

ELEANOR. (*her head thrown back, her eyes shut—slowly, dreamily*) Perhaps I'm praying. I don't know. I love.

CAPE. (*deeply moved*) I love you.

ELEANOR. (*as if from a great distance*) We love! (*He moves close to her and his hands reach out for hers. For a moment as their hands touch they form together one cross. Then their arms go about each other and their lips meet.*)

CURTAIN

EUGENE O'NEILL was born on October 16, 1888, in New York City. His father was James O'Neill, the famous dramatic actor; and during his early years O'Neill traveled much with his parents. In 1909 he went on a gold-prospecting expedition to South America; he later shipped as a seaman to Buenos Aires, worked at various occupations in the Argentine and tended mules on a cattle steamer to South Africa. He returned to New York destitute, then worked briefly as a reporter on a newspaper in New London, Connecticut, at which point an attack of tuberculosis sent him for six months to a sanitarium. This event marked the turning point in his career, and shortly after, at the age of twenty-four, he began his first play. His major works include *The Emperor Jones,* 1920; *The Hairy Ape,* 1921; *Desire Under the Elms,* 1924; *The Great God Brown,* 1925; *Strange Interlude,* 1926, 1927; *Mourning Becomes Electra,* 1929, 1931; *Ah, Wilderness,* 1933; *Days Without End,* 1934; *A Moon for the Misbegotten,* 1945; *The Iceman Cometh,* 1946; and several plays produced posthumously, including *Long Day's Journey into Night, A Touch of the Poet* and *Hughie.* Eugene O'Neill died in 1953.